DOORMEN

FIELDWORK ENCOUNTERS AND DISCOVERIES

A series edited by Robert Emerson and Jack Katz

DOORMEN

Peter Bearman

The University of Chicago Press / Chicago and London

Peter Bearman is chair of the Department of
Sociology at Columbia University and director
of the Institute for Social and Economic Research
and Policy.

The University of Chicago Press, Chicago 60637

The University of Chicago Press, Ltd., London

© 2005 by The University of Chicago

All rights reserved. Published 2005

Printed in the United States of America

14 13 12 11 10 09 08 07 06 05

1 2 3 4 5

ISBN: 0-226-03969-2 (cloth)

ISBN: 0-226-03970-6 (paper)

Library of Congress Cataloging-in-Publication Data

Bearman, Peter S., 1956–

Doormen / Peter Bearman.

p. cm. — (Fieldwork encounters and discoveries)

Includes bibliographical references and index.

ISBN 0-226-03969-2 (cloth: alk. paper) —

ISBN 0-226-03970-6 (pbk.: alk. paper)

1. Apartment doorkeepers.   I. Title.   II. Series.

HD8039.B895B42 2005

305.9'6472—dc22   2004028621

⊛ The paper used in this publication meets the
minimum requirements of the American National
Standard for Information Sciences — Permanence
of Paper for Printed Library Materials,

ANSI Z39.48-1992.

For Nora

CONTENTS

Many books are reported by their authors to have a long history. This book is an exception to the general rule. But, as with all things, one can look back to a beginning of sorts and tell a story. Here is a story of this book. In 1987 I came up to Columbia University from Chapel Hill, North Carolina, to give a talk. In the evening, I was to meet the chair of the sociology department, Ron Burt, at his apartment. From there we were going out for dinner. I was late getting to his apartment. I had already arrived at the conclusion that coming to Columbia at that time was a mistake, and I compounded the problem by making a series of bad decisions all evening. Fear of the subway led me to try to take a taxi. But I wasn't very successful. Now I find it somewhat amusing to watch tourists in New York City hail a taxi. They have a certain hesitancy that seems to invite taxi drivers to pass right by them. Back then it wasn't funny, and as hard as I tried, I couldn't seem to get a taxi to stop. Inability to hail a taxi led me to decide I might as well just walk. And I had a long way to go. Burt's apartment was on Riverside Drive. It was a cold and wet night, and the wind off the river made walking up the sidewalk especially painful. A light rain, almost sleet, cast an eerie silence on the street. As I walked up Riverside, I saw few signs of life. The neighborhood was deserted.

I finally arrived at the building, entered through the first set of doors, found Ron's name, and pushed the buzzer. As I was talking to him on the house phone, a shadowy figure appeared at the outer door and started to come in. I don't remember much about what he looked like. I remember thinking then that I should try to get a good look so I could pick him out of a police lineup, but I didn't want to let him see that I was looking at him. He was wearing a dark raincoat. I briefly saw a large hat covering his face. As I reached for the door, waiting to be buzzed in, I positioned myself to block his entry. The door buzzed, I slid to the right, opened it, and tried to slide through. Behind me I could hear him saying something. As I got through the door, his hand reached out and grabbed it. I knew that I needed to stop him from entering the building, and so slashing at his arm, I broke his grip on the door, slammed it shut, and raced for the elevator. Luckily, the elevator was waiting on the first floor. Looking back through the door, I could see that he had his hand back through and that, somehow, he had managed to push the inner door open. The elevator door closed and I went up to the tenth floor. I pushed the buttons for floors 11 to 14. I figured that this way, the elevator would continue to go up before it went back down to the lobby, giving me more time to find and get into the apartment. As it turned out, it was no problem finding the apartment. There were just two to a floor, and my host's name was on the door. He opened right away and I sped in, relieved to be safe but also still extremely worried.

During the first few minutes we were in the apartment, I told Ron about the guy who had broken in and how I had feared that he would follow me up. I was especially worried because I was afraid he might have thought I had seen his face and therefore had motivation to figure out what floor I had gone to. I knew that Ron had little children, and I was worried that I might have also put them at risk. I felt bad that I hadn't made sure that the door was really closed behind me. Ron seemed concerned, too, and asked me to describe the intruder. I did the best I could — but there was not much to say. The coat and the hat obscured most of his personal features, and I really hadn't gotten a good look at his face. But, somehow, I had said enough for Ron. He went to the phone and made a call. When he returned, he said that we needed to get moving since we were late. On the way down the elevator, I thought I saw him fumbling for his wallet. I thought I should follow his lead and so shifted my wallet from my back to my front pocket, for extra safety. The door opened to the lobby. Directly in front of us was the intruder; he hadn't followed me up, but he had waited for me to come down. As I stepped back, Ron stepped forward and (I believe) handed him some money.

> "I'm sorry," he said. "He didn't know who you were. You scared him."
> "That's okay," he said. "I tried to keep him out of the building, but he just pushed me away. It was my fault."

That was the first doorman I ever met.

It would be eleven years before I returned to Columbia. When I came back to New York, I was a little more sophisticated, but not much. The city had changed. No longer did it seem (to me) reasonable to think that every corner was a potential minefield replete with crack-crazed killers. The crime rate was lower; the city was in a renaissance. And this time, instead of criminals everywhere, I saw doormen everywhere. On the street where our temporary apartment was located, there were always at least four doormen out at any one time. In our building we had doorman service from 4:00 p.m. until midnight. Within the first few days, the doormen learned our names. They recognized my kids and started to keep an eye on them. And they were exceptionally polite and respectful. In some ways, I found them obsequious and it bothered me that they were seemingly so oriented to my comfort. More disturbing was the attitude that the other residents — mostly Columbia faculty — seemed to have toward the doormen. It was hard to put my finger on it, but they seemed to adopt (or fall into) a paternalistic frame when talking with the doormen. They would refer to them by their first name; in turn, they were almost always addressed as "Professor." I noticed this and it made me uneasy, but I could not exactly understand what was bothering me — the doormen, the tenants, or their joint performance.

At first, I found my new colleagues difficult and arrogant for no obvious reasons. I spent a lot of my time trying to understand why Columbia professors were so difficult. The real problem that one faces when trying to explain something is to identify the features of the context that are unique. It couldn't be that I found Columbia professors arrogant because they taught at a prestigious Ivy League university — since I had not found other Ivy League professors to be so problematic. Whatever caused their arrogance, it had to be something unique either to Columbia or to the city. There were a number of competing explanations that I considered, but by the end of the first month, I had developed an elegant theory. Their arrogance was the result of the doormen.

The logic was simple. Doormen, as with all people, need to feel good about what they do. Putting myself in their shoes, it seemed obvious that I would feel better about serving really important people than ordinary people. And it seemed obvious to me that the higher the status of their residents, the higher would be their own status. Consequently, my theory went, for inchoate and unarticulated self-interested reasons, each doorman had a personal interest in elevating the status of the people who lived in his building. Columbia professors, under this model, were being bombarded each day with undeserved status "gifts." My idea was that after a while — how long was unclear to me — the faculty actually started to believe that they deserved such status, that they really were important people. I thought I was observing a whole new arena for the Matthew effect.[1] It didn't take long to

---

1. The Matthew effect is the idea that prominent individuals benefit and marginal individuals suffer as contributions of similar quality are evaluated differentially depending on the status of the contributor. Merton, "The Matthew Effect in Science"; Zuckerman and Merton, "Patterns of Evaluation in Science"; Cole and Cole, *Social Stratification in Science*.

generalize this theory to all New Yorkers, most of whom I had also found arrogant and difficult to get along with.

This was a pretty theory, but obviously wrong. First, initial impressions notwithstanding, Columbia professors are no more arrogant than other professors. Second, New Yorkers are nicer than most people, and, in any case, most New Yorkers do not have doormen opening doors for them. And, finally, I misunderstood the nature of the work that doormen do, their experiences, their aspirations and hopes. While it is also true that doormen's status is in some part conditioned by the status of their tenants, the conditioning effect is less strong than I imagined. And over the years, I came to better understand my colleagues, those who are arrogant and those who are not. But my interest in doormen did not leave. One could say that this project is a product of that interest.

While written in the first person for ease of presentation, this book is in many ways a collaborative enterprise. Much of the work was done in the context of an introductory class in sociology — Evaluation of Evidence — at Columbia University. I had been thinking abstractly for some time about the feasibility of a large-scale collective class project that would involve a multi-method, multi-level design. The desire to make use of multiple kinds of data and the desire to design a multi-level study played a large role in the decision to study doormen. There were, as well, independent of intellectual reasons, some pragmatic issues that also had to be confronted in designing a collective study for college students — especially a study that actively involved extended hours in the field, observational data collection, sampling, surveying respondents, and in-depth personal interviews.

Paramount in the pragmatic decision to study doormen — again, not considering the deeper intellectual issues discussed subsequently — was the issue of risk. There is in sociology (and one supposes, as well, in everyday life) a general distaste for the ordinary. Most people would indeed find it more interesting to study heroin addicts, gangsters, petty crooks, denizens of the subways, or prostitutes — the "stuff" of much ethnographic research — but it would not have been prudent. Those on the margins of society live and work (if they do) in places that are dangerous. Sending students with little field experience, and often little urban living experience, out into the underworld was impossible. Instead, I needed to identify a population of "interesting" people who were easy to recognize and safe to talk to, who could be found in safe neighborhoods, and who could complete their interviews in semi-public (i.e., visible) places. Doormen fit the bill perfectly. They typically wear uniforms, so they are often easy to recognize. They work in safe areas of the city (they help make those areas safe), and people who can afford doormen live in safe areas of the city. They could be interviewed in semi-public places, either building lobbies or on the street. And, best of all, as they say themselves: "Most doormen are people people." They like to talk, and they are often extremely voluble. Or perhaps more accurately, in the same way that judges are (expected to be) somber, professors erudite, and funeral home directors empathetic, doormen are (generally) friendly. So for a class project, doormen worked fine.

There were other pragmatic reasons to study doormen as well. The design of a study is by far the most critical element in research and one of the most difficult things to teach students. In my opinion, the most interesting kind of study design is a two-stage design in which one first samples large units and then samples individuals within those units. Two-stage designs of this sort allow one to explicitly consider how the larger social context shapes individual behavior and provide for the possibility of multi-level analysis, what in the ethnographic tradition is discussed as the "negotiated order." In our case, as I describe in more detail subsequently, we first sampled neighborhoods in the city, then enumerated buildings with doormen, and then sampled doormen within those buildings. Attacking the problem this way has an added benefit. One not only gets a representative sample of door-men; one gets a representative sample of the neighborhoods and buildings in which they work.

As TA for the class, Henning Hillmann, now assistant professor of sociology at Stanford, organized all the work, kept all the records, and made sense of the fieldwork component, which quickly became both much more com-plicated than we had ever imagined and impossible to manage effectively on our own. Consequently, we hired two remarkable research assistants — Oliver Sellers-Garcia and Katerina Ratkowski — to keep up with the material, organize the data, and develop the data entry forms. When individual stu-dents failed to complete critical steps on time, Oliver and Kat stepped in and did their work for them. It happened enough so that without their efforts, the project would surely have floundered. I owe a special debt to Kat, who carefully constructed the complex Excel spreadsheets that turned out to be critical for both monitoring the research and organizing the survey data. A number of students got hooked on doormen and continued to help with the project. Three students in particular — Ian Rapoport, Peter Gerkin, and Michael Rotjan — pushed the project along in a subsequent semester. Special mention should go to Peter, who conducted many of the early tenant interviews. Oliver subsequently spent countless hours working on data, organizing a Web page, and studying guidebooks of neighborhoods, and Michael developed sufficient experience in GIS to produce journey-to-work maps. Despite all their help, the project would have failed completely without Henning, who helped me think through the idea, organized the students, helped produce the quantitative census data, and devoted an entire semester to the course and the student field-workers.

The class, by the way, worked pretty well, and students who encountered data on doormen and their lives at work were able to learn firsthand about classical sociological problems, from network effects on job search to the institutional bases of racism, from dynamics of contention to the generation of stable roles. In the appendix I describe the class in more detail for the sociologists reading this book, for I believe that much could be gained from classes that enable students to collectively enter the field and thereby produce a study significantly richer than the sum of the independent parts in terms of orienting students to the nature of our discipline.

I live in a doorman building. Early on I decided that I would not burden the doormen who work in my building with this project. It is one thing to talk with doormen and spend some time with them in the lobby. It is quite another thing to redefine an existing relationship because one of the parties gets the strange idea that they can write a book about the others. The same logic was also extended to my neighbors. It seemed best to me if I kept those relationships, already complicated, from another level of complication. Even if this is what we all do, I wanted to ensure that neither my neighbors nor the staff in my building had the sense that I was observing them all the time. Perhaps a better field-worker would have been able to manage these tensions and gain deeper insight by exploiting the detailed inner knowledge of a specific setting that comes from residing in a building for a long time. It is my failing that I did not, but since I did not, I also have the chance to reassure my neighbors and doormen that they are *not*, and their experiences are *not*, in this book. That said, I did learn much from the staff in my building(s), and so my first acknowledgment goes to them.

A number of friends read the whole manuscript and helped move the project forward. I am especially indebted to Sudhir Venkatesh, who read the whole book early on and made very helpful suggestions that improved the manuscript significantly. Conversations with Mitchell Duneier about ethnographic work helped enormously and provided much-needed confidence at critical moments. Subsequently, his comments on the first three chapters significantly shaped the final revision. Dalton Conley, Robert Faulkner, Herb Gans, Jack Katz, Catharine Silver, Art Stinchcombe, Charles Tilly, Florencia Torche, and Harrison White read the penultimate version of the manuscript and made numerous diverse and important suggestions. This book is much better than it was when they read it because of their help, and I deeply appreciate the time that each of them spent on the manuscript. Before I went public, three of my former students — Hannah Brückner, David Cunningham, and Katherine Stovel — read an early version and helped me to tone down and reorganize the material. Not surprisingly, they were also my toughest critics. Sidney Bearman read the whole manuscript and offered extremely useful editorial advice. The book was completed while I was on leave visiting the Department of Political Science and Sociology at the University of Genova, Italy. I am deeply grateful to Giorgio Sola, chair at Genova, for providing a wonderful environment for work. The Institute for Social and Economic Research and Policy at Columbia has been my physical and intellectual home for some time, and I am pleased to acknowledge the support provided by the Institute, both financial and practical, and, most importantly, intellectual.

I have been extremely fortunate to have had the opportunity to work with Doug Mitchell and his fantastic editorial staff. Erin DeWitt did a spectacular job copyediting the manuscript, for which I am enormously grateful.

It is customary for authors to note how the writing of their book was a shared burden of their family. Perhaps it is a shortcoming of mine, or of this book, that I cannot say the same. Much of the text was written quietly every other weekend at home with my partner, Alessandra Nicifero, and it was just what we wanted to do: work together, have coffee every now and then, and enjoy the thought that we were actually getting something done. So for that incredible gift, I am deeply thankful. Discussions with Ben about his work as a doorman helped immeasurably, as did his ridiculous sense of humor. And just when it seemed impossible to finish, Sophie gave me "James, the Doorman" for Christmas as motivation. I can see him whenever I want, holding a door or just hanging around.

To my eldest daughter, Nora, a great enthusiast for most of my projects, and perhaps even this one, I dedicate this book.

CHAPTER 1

Interpersonal Closeness and Social Distance

What's the strangest thing to happen here, in this building? I don't know. Having you come and interview me. That's pretty strange.

esidential doormen can be found in most major world cities, but like bagels, they are quintessentially New York.[1] While it surprises New Yorkers, for whom doormen are a critical element of their sense of self and place, no one has thought to study them or the larger social ecology of the lobby, where tenants and doormen meet.[2] But for those living elsewhere, such neglect is less surprising, for as noted in the preface — either for reasons of personal biography, prurience, or (generally) accurate perceptions of marketability — sociologists since the 1960s considering field-based projects tend to study heterodox populations: gang members, sidewalk booksellers, prostitutes, junkies, micro-criminals, and so on. There are some exceptions to this general attraction to the unusual, and

---

1. Paris has, by contrast, concierges, who are different from doormen since they reside in their buildings. In Italy the same function is filled by *amministratóre*, typically residents who are assigned their role by building owners. In California, Arizona, and other states where gated communities have blossomed, security guards, rather than doormen, man the gates. In London, as well as other major U.S. cities, some residential units have doormen, but these exceptions aside, one finds a population of doormen only in New York. Hereafter, rather than sing the cumbersome phrase "residential doormen," I talk about doormen. Doormen have been a part of the city for a long time. Consider the following from a *New York Times* article, "New Yorkers Who Idle for Their Living," that appeared March 6, 1927: "New York is full of those who 'stand and wait' — not mere idlers but men for whom standing and waiting is a remunerative job. They are to be seen mostly on the sidewalks, sometimes beneath a gay arched awning and also within the plate-glass doors of Persian carpeted halls; and their brass buttons, gold braid, and gorgeous uniforms add a note of color to the city streets. In these ornamental figures survives the livery which once danced attendance upon grande dames of the carriage era."

2. Note that Jerry Seinfeld (perhaps one of the better active social scientists) devoted a whole show to the subject, "The Doorman" (first aired, February 23, 1995). Other comedians centered in New York City have elaborate doorman routines as well. A Canadian film company has produced a documentary on doormen, following the workdays of four men, in *All Visitors Must Be Announced*.

these are often occupational studies such as this, many of which also focus on workers in the service industry. There are, for example, outstanding studies of airline flight attendants, bill collectors, cooks, holistic health workers, milkmen, Hollywood composers, and even cosmetologists in nail salons.[3] In these studies, sociologists often focus on and reveal the careful management of personality in front-room settings, often in sharp contrast to the tensions, conflicts, and disgusts that make up the more expressive backroom behavior;[4] careful discussions of the negotiated order;[5] and deep insights into the strategies and tricks of the trade that people develop to get by.[6] Likewise, there are a number of excellent ethnographic accounts of complex settings similar to the lobby, for example, the hospital waiting room, the factory floor, public bathrooms, lounges, laboratory life, and street corners.[7] But overall, given their distribution in the population, everyday workers in everyday occupations and everyday contexts command less attention from

---

3. Among numerous other studies, see Hochschild, *The Managed Heart*; Fine, *Kitchens*; Bigus, "The Milkman and His Customer"; Faulkner, *Music on Demand*; Kleinman, *Equals Before God*; Mars and Nicod, *The World of Waiters*; Whyte, "The Social Structure of the Restaurant"; Zerubavel, *Patterns of Time in Hospital Life*; and Kang, "The Managed Hand." There is a much longer tradition in sociology of studying the "ordinary" worlds of people, and this book is closer in spirit to this tradition than much contemporary sociology. Here, for example, one would consider the studies of "Middletown" (Lynd and Lynd, *Middletown*), "Kent" (Moreland, *Millways of Kent*), and "Yankee City" (Warner and Lunt, *The Social Life of a Modern Community*) as the key references.

4. The distinction between the front and back is an analytic convenience introduced by researchers following Goffman as if it were real, rather than simply a shift in standpoint. There is no foundation, in other words, to assume that either the back or the front contains behaviors that are more authentic, revelatory of personality, deep, honest, or natural. Individuals may come to feel that they are more authentic in the back room — that is, they may define their front-room interactions as somehow put-on, in contrast to the back — but both are shows. Goffman, *The Presentation of Self in Everyday Life*.

5. By the "negotiated order" is meant understanding how interaction shapes and is in turn shaped by structure; that is, the process by which micro-interactions become patterned over time, congealing into social structure and cognition thereof. In this context, following the argument developed by Fine in his work on occupational cultures, *Kitchens*, the key issues taken up are, first, how structural constraint shapes possibilities for understandings of both doormen and tenants and, second, how doormen (and tenants) jointly define the production of quality service. The idea of the negotiated order is developed more explicitly in Strauss, *Negotiations*. One can think that the promise of multi-level analysis is to reveal, for multiple sites, the negotiated order(s) operative.

6. By "tricks of the trade," sociologists refer to the cluster of unspoken procedures that allow one to get by, typically those elements of the work process that are sacrificed when workers "work to rule," as in a labor action, but also the social-psychological orientations that individuals bring to bear on the world of work.

7. Zerubavel, *Patterns of Time in Hospital Life*; Burawoy, *Manufacturing Consent*; Humphreys, *Tearoom Trade*; Whyte, "The Social Structure of the Restaurant"; Latour and Woolgar, *Laboratory Life*; Liebow, *Tally's Corner*; Anderson, *Streetwise*; Duneier, *Slim's Table*.

social science than might be warranted.[8] Why this is the case is considered subsequently. But first there is a prior question: Why study doormen?

One answer by analogy might be as follows: Recall the time before there were ice makers and plastic ice-cube trays coated with a miraculous substance that allows ice to just drop out. Instead, ice cubes were released from the grasp of sticky metal containers by wrenching a lever that fractured the ice, breaking its grip on the sides of the tray. As a child, I was always interested in looking at those fractures in the ice, which revealed the structure of the cube in ways hidden under the sheer gloss of uniformity. In order to see new things, one has to shatter the old ways of seeing, and, for this, one needs a lever of some sort; doormen are my levers. By looking closely at one job, one set of relationships, and one setting, the goal is to reveal the patterning of the fractures that make up the larger social structure(s) in which we are embedded. Like all standpoints, the fractures revealed with this lever differ from those revealed by others and remain only partial. But the intent is that they will reveal processes, dynamics, and models useful for understanding other diverse contexts and problems.

TENSIONS

A second answer can be more specific. As implied earlier, doormen can provide a strategic lever for understanding social structure for a number of reasons. First, while many workers in the service industry have sporadic contact with individuals from different social strata, doormen have repeated interactions with the social elite over long stretches of time, typically years. In this context, status signifiers are highly developed and subtle, as doormen and tenants make claims with respect to the nature and meaning of their relationship. Consequently, analysis of the patterning of doormen-tenant interactions at the micro-level yields insight into the expressive nature

---

8. But this is a common problem in sociology, where much energy is devoted to understanding less than .00001% of human experience; at the macro-level, for example, social movements and revolutions. But micro-level studies are in this regard just as problematic, tending to ignore the continuity principle that governs most of our experience — the simple fact that what happened just before is likely to continue to happen, for example, our experience that as we are driving down the highway, the car behind us is likely to be behind us in the second after we last looked, or our experience as we walk down the street, which is that the street is likely to remain below our feet, which will continue to move in the same direction, in a landscape unchanged in the last minutes, and so on. Since nothing can be said about it, there is a similar tendency to avoid the routine in social science.

of distinction, social distance, and social class in contemporary American society. Beyond this, doormen are a paradigmatic example of a new occupational group, best captured as the "professional working class," revealing the complex ways in which social class in the United States is refracted through the lens of professional rhetoric.

Second, doormen have to develop and act on theories about their tenants in order to do their job. In this sense, good doormen are also good sociologists. Yet when doormen act on the basis of these theories, they often inadvertently induce and solidify ethnic and racial cleavages operating at the macro-level. How doormen get and do their jobs; how doormen manage guests, tenants, and time; and how doormen think about their role, career, and the world of the residential building turn out to reveal much about the macro-structure of race and class in the United States. In this regard, doormen are like police, whose theories about crime induce strategies for policing that tend to induce arrest rates that confirm their orienting theories. Third, the study of doormen reveals something about the grammar of everyday life. This book focuses on this grammar — the unspoken rules that organize social interactions, shape decisions, and motivate behavior. One of the arguments of this book is that one can best see social grammar by focusing on tensions and contradictions in interaction that appear when viewed from multiple standpoints, typically across levels.[9] Since this is rather abstract, it might help to focus by considering, by way of example, the following small set of contradictions:

• Getting a job as a doorman is both impossible and too easy. Doormen jobs are so hard to get that most people who apply never get past the door. But doormen never wait for their jobs and perceive that they just stumble into them by chance. Why are jobs both so easy and hard to get?

• Most doormen do not feel that they are racists, and are not racist, but in almost all buildings, blacks and other minorities who come to visit are

---

9. Analysis of classificatory kinship systems may provide an appropriate model. One could, following Lévi-Strauss, consider only the normative rules governing alliance and descent. Alternatively, one could, following Homans (among others), only consider observed exchanges from a single standpoint. Better would be to analyze the full spectrum of relations from all standpoints simultaneously. The value of the latter approach is that asymmetries and contradictions at the micro-level are shown to be resolved at the macro-level, congealed into an enduring structure, which, while not cognitively accessible, is real. Lévi-Strauss, *Elementary Structures of Kinship*; Homans and Schneider, *Marriage, Authority, and Final Causes*; Bearman, "Generalized Exchange."

treated quite differently than whites. Why do doormen block access to their buildings to minorities more than for others? Does this have something to do with how they got their job?

• Most doormen are bored much of the time, and most tenants see doormen doing nothing. Yet when tenants need them, the doormen are more often than not busy. At the same time that doormen say they are bored, they report that their jobs are extremely stressful. How is it that they are both too busy and too idle? How do doormen manage to project to tenants an eagerness to serve, even if they cannot serve them exactly when tenants believe they need service?

• Everyone worries about the "Christmas bonus." Is it a gift, a shakedown, or neither? Why does the bonus generate perverse incentives? Do tenants free ride on their neighbors in order to give *larger, not smaller,* bonuses to doormen? Tenants are worried about their position in a distribution of tenants. While doormen prefer large bonuses to small ones, they do not shift their behavior in response to bonus size, all things being equal. Doormen are constrained in their response to the bonus by commitments they have to an idiosyncratic interpretation of professional behavior. Is this why signaling fails?

• For doormen, the claim to professional status is central to their sense of self. The formal rules for their job imply universalism, yet doormen try to induce tenants to develop idiosyncratic preferences, many of which contradict building policy. Thus, the delivery of professionalized service requires that doormen act differently to different tenants and take an active role in shaping tenant preferences. How do doormen balance on the tightrope of delivering personalized service and maintaining formal commitment to the norm of universal service?

• Doormen say, and many tenants agree, that their main job is security, but few doormen can ever recall doing anything that was security related, except for protecting tenants from the behavior of other tenants. Why is security the central trope for describing their core role, when it plays the most trivial part in both tenant and doorman everyday experience?

• The doorman union was notoriously corrupt, yet wages and benefits for the doormen in the union put them among the elite of the working class. Doormen in residential buildings help tenants prepare for strikes — to replace them — and therefore appear to act as scabs. Likewise, tenants align themselves with doormen against management. How does this strange pattern of alliance develop? Is the history of union corruption, now ended, positively associated with higher wages?

These and other tensions and contradictions provide some of the raw material for this book. From an analytic perspective, such tensions provide the sociologist the seams through which one can enter the world of the other. In the absence of such tensions, one has only a clear gloss of normative prescriptions, as if skating on an ice-skating rink moments before it has been opened to the public was revelatory of the bump and grind of the morning rush to work. To make sense of the world, in the end, requires an eye for and sensitivity to friction, for friction helps reveal the underlying grammars that organize social life.

SOCIAL DISTANCE, OR UPSTAIRS/DOWNSTAIRS

The central problem around which all of the tensions described earlier revolve is how doormen and tenants negotiate interpersonal closeness in the context of vast social distance. Doormen are close to their tenants but socially distant. They know a lot about their tenants: what they eat, what movies they watch, whom they spend time with, whether they drink too much, work too much, play with their children, abuse their partner, have kinky sex, are generous or tight, friendly or sour. They infer much of their knowledge from both direct and indirect observation typically extending over many years. Tenants realize that doormen know a lot about them. In talk about their doormen, they try to neutralize the impact of this knowledge in a number of ways: as an expression of their "dependence," by incorporating doormen into the personal or familial sphere,[10] or as a necessary by-product of ensuring the safety and security of the building. At the same time, tenant knowledge of doormen as persons who live lives outside of work is typically

---

10. Tenants often refer to the doormen in their building as "part of the family," in much the same way that others come to think of their pets as part of the family. Some readers may find this imagery unkind. But the rhetorical device "they are like a part of the family" for both pets and doormen is too common to ignore. Tenants do not see doormen as animals, but the claim that they are part of the family, obviously patronizing, is not different from similar claims they make with regard to pets, their young children's friends, and so on, and is stated in the same way. I believe it performs the same "function," which is to rhetorically draw the doormen into the personal sphere, thereby making "natural," and thus neutralizing, the knowledge that they are perceived to have.

severely truncated, so that the closeness of the relationship is strongly asymmetrical, conditioned by remarkable social distance. Doormen and tenant interactions in the lobby, and the distinct ecology of the residential building, are shaped within the narrow shoals of too much closeness in a context of too much distance. Most of the peculiar tensions described earlier arise from this fundamental sociological element, and most of the everyday grammars that organize social life in the lobby reflect this fundamental contradiction between closeness and distance.

There are other models for and cases in which closeness and distance play a central role in organizing interaction. Historically, and still the case in some contexts, the sociological tension between simultaneous physical closeness and social distance was simply resolved by negating the social identity of the other, through slavery or other physical and psychic forms of inducing social death. The sociological "trick" of such systems is the radical negation of the other as a strategy for neutralizing the intimacy that arises from close physical context — bathing, dressing, scheduling, serving, feeding, and nursing. In such systems, the servant is defined as socially dead — as someone without interests. Therefore their knowledge of the master is of no use in social life; the socially dead exist solely to serve the master. Slaves provide one obvious group; members of the household in patrimonial regimes provide another comparison, as do those whose social death is engineered through physical or psychic intervention, for example, eunuchs in the Chinese civil service or priests in the royal treasury. But these are extreme solutions from systems and cultures largely from the past, and therefore they are not accessible to the middle- and upper-class New Yorkers who live in residential buildings. While the social distance between doormen and tenants may be vast, it is not culturally possible to define it as infinite. Consequently, the closeness that arises from the relationship must be managed more subtly. This book considers such subtle management.

For many, it is natural to think that this book could be considered as a study in upstairs/downstairs dynamics.[11] For younger readers, *Upstairs Downstairs* was a wildly popular English television show that aired on PBS in the 1970s and focused on the interactions between servants and masters in an English upper-class household in the years immediately before and

---

11. *Upstairs Downstairs* aired on TV in the mid-1970s for five seasons in England.

after World War I. *Upstairs Downstairs* was about many things: descriptively it concerned the gradual breakdown of the English class structure after World War I and the emergence of industrial labor. The central narrative elements focused on the ways in which events, internal or external to the household, differentially shaped the parallel worlds of the Bellamy family (upstairs) and their domestic servants (downstairs). The appeal of the show was precisely in its capacity to unveil two simultaneous realities, connected by the accident of place (165 Eaton Place, the principal home of the Bellamys), punctuated by the occasional moments when — as the class structure broke down — the intimacies between the two worlds collided into the sordid world of family secrets, blackmail, and revenge. The comparison is in some regards apt, but in many ways misleading. The nature of the doorman-tenant relationship is different than the master-servant relationship, even if the levels of intimacy are in some ways comparable and equally asymmetric. At the macro-level, the radical separation between classes constitutive of the English class structure at the turn of the century is not relevant today, at least in the residential apartment buildings that provide the focus for this study. The buffer that radical class (or race) segregation provides to insulate the elite from intimacy with their staff (or slaves) is now absent. Consequently, the strategies for negotiating the boundaries between closeness and distance are now much more complex and subtle.

This said, the analogy is apt in one regard: *Upstairs Downstairs* concerns the ways in which working-class individuals learn to interpret, respond to, and in some instances shape the preferences of the elite in a context where in order to do their job, they must develop general theories about those with whom they interact on the basis of only partial knowledge. The need to develop general — everyday — theories about those with whom they work distinguishes doormen from other occupational positions whose members are close to their clients, and so it is important to think about doormen in this broader context. Consider what we could call the "close professions." Lawyers, doctors, psychiatrists, teachers, social workers, and personal advisers are all close to their clients, in the sense that they come to learn much about their clients through the services that they provide. This closeness is buffered by a number of important facts. First, more or less, those in the close professions have the same or higher status as those they serve. In contrast, doormen work closely with people who are socially distant (and of higher social status) from them.

Second, and perhaps more important, those in the close professions learn, more or less, only about those aspects of their clients' lives that they have professional claim to and that the clients agree to reveal as part of their relationship. For example, teachers may observe students and infer something about their family from such observation, but their access to family "data" is restricted. Likewise, bankers may suspect that their clients are one kind of a person or another, but their purview is limited to aspects roughly financial. Psychiatrists may penetrate into the deepest recesses of their clients' minds and behavioral routines, but such penetration occurs in a context in which the client agrees to hand over such information, even if inaccessible to him or her. The boundaries drawn around the kinds and contents of legitimate "professional" data are relatively strict. These boundaries provide a buffer that allows people in contact with those in the close professions to segregate domains if they wish, thereby limiting access to just that which they agree is professionally accessible.

In contrast, doormen are constrained by a normative expectation that they deliver uniform service. Their claim to professional status rests on their ability to respond to, read, and/or induce differences among tenants. But in contrast to those in the close professions, knowledge that shapes the capacity of doormen to deliver professional — that is, personalized — service is not bounded by preexisting social conventions governing the relevant structure of knowledge domains. Knowing what kind of movies tenants watch may (or may not) be more helpful in shaping personal service than knowing much about tenants' financial profile. If close professionals are kept distant through self-segregation of knowledge domains, such segregation is not an available strategy for tenants and doormen.

There are perhaps more familiar examples, though, of occupations whose workers are socially distant from, and yet strikingly close to, those they work for. Doormen, like child-care providers or live-in nurses, believe that they must understand the broad everyday world of their tenants (clients) in order to do their job. This knowledge is not garnered for prurient reasons, but rather to deliver professional — that is, tailored — service. For many door-men, the information that they use to build the theories that help them make decisions is simply local knowledge; that is, arising from observation in the lobby and of use and importance only there. Yet if tenants and doormen come to think about it abstractly, they realize there is much that doormen know, that such knowledge is intimate, and that it often extends well beyond what the tenants' family, friends, and acquaintances know about them. In short, doormen are close and yet distant, and how they deal with this fact, and how tenants deal with this fact, is an essential element of the social ecology of the lobby.

For many tenants, doormen may be uncomfortably close. In contrast to the kinds of limited information that professionals collect on their clients as a necessary foundation for providing professional service, doormen collect a wide range of surface information, which tends to be highly personal because it arises from the home. The stream of information that doormen receive about their tenants is substantial, even if much of the data are discrete and as trivial as movies delivered, food ordered, and visitors arriving.

Tenants would likely not care if sociologists set out to study their garbage, though garbage reveals much about the life lived. They would not care because they would not know the sociologist, would not know others that the sociologist knew, and would not have to come face-to-face every day with the fact that the sociologist knew what he or she knew. People know lots of things about us, and as long as we do not have to confront this knowledge, we can largely ignore it. Most of the information we know about others that is derived from the same kinds of observations that doormen make is essentially useless, though we naturally have curiosity about those physically close to us. But the information is not useless to doormen because this information provides a foundation for their delivery of personal service to tenants. Of course, doormen do not care whether tenants eat Chinese food or pizza — though they attend to this fact. In the same way, doormen do not really care about their tenants' friends; but they do care about the *kinds* of visitors who come their way. Since they must often make snap decisions about visitors who consciously or unconsciously emit signals of their own status, motives, and goals, doormen invest heavily in knowledge about their tenants to give themselves a foundation upon which to read these signals. And finally, while doormen may not care about tenants' wine collections per se, they often do care about estimating wealth from the patterning of expenditures that they can observe, and consequently they attend to the patterns of consumption they see.

Here, distance could be thought to provide a natural buffer. That doormen are distant from their tenants with respect to life chances and social class means in theory and practice that their worlds rarely overlap. It also means that, as with butlers and others, tenants should simply be able to ignore the knowledge that their doormen have about them because, for all practical purposes, the doormen are "socially dead." That is, they do not enter in their world. If doormen were content to be automatons who just held doors and followed rules, this might be fine. But neither tenants nor doormen want this. Tenants want to feel that they are distinct, and doormen want to act professionally. Tenants want to know that their doormen know who to greet and who not to greet. Doormen want to know whom their tenants wish to see and not to see. For tenants to be distinct and doormen to be professionals, doormen have to become "closer" to tenants.

Because the whole experience of coming to know someone is in part built from observation of their trace (in visits, in exits, in deliveries), doormen pay attention to the flow, in order to draft a model of each tenant. This model is then used to develop a relationship that allows the doorman to "confess" to some knowledge — thereby deconstructing the fiction that he is socially dead — in the service of providing tailor-made service. Tenants who see that the door is open to their world agree to the terms of exchange, because it allows them to establish a relationship, thus containing the information that the doorman has within a social envelope. The construction of a relationship is not blackmail. Doormen rarely if ever see their knowledge as potentially damaging to tenants. Rather, they see their knowledge as the vehicle for doing their job well, for acting substantively in pursuit of particularized — that is, professional — service. Tenants see in the relationship a way to simultaneously control knowledge and achieve distinction.

Both sides, doormen and tenants, use the relationship to establish and shore up status claims. And this is quite a different dynamic than one observes with other close "help" who are hired directly by their employers. When doormen and tenants are in sync, they jointly establish, legitimize, and buttress their status aims. Tenants strive for distinction, and doormen strive to be professionals. For doormen to be professionals, they must have distinct tenants. For tenants to have distinction, they must have professional doormen. For the system to work, then, both sides have to bridge the extraordinary gap between too much closeness and too much distance, acknowledging both, but connecting each side through the lens of professional service. In this regard, one can say that the relationship is normalized by the capacity to make legitimate claims to professional status. But this is but one way to manage the simultaneity of closeness and distance, of upstairs and downstairs, field and house. As with all solutions, it gives rise to other, perhaps smaller, problems and tensions, inconsistencies and ambiguities. And as noted earlier, focusing on these traces of the distance/closeness puzzle is an effective way to proceed.

THE SOCIAL SCIENCE LITERATURE (ON DOORMEN)

It is customary for scholarly books to review and discuss the prior literature on the topic under consideration. I already noted that there are no studies of doormen in the social science literature; so narrowly conceived, such a review would be short. But doormen are not completely absent. Rather they are touched on indirectly in two distinct literatures. The first literature is concerned with survey validity, the second with occupational prestige. In the first, one discovers that doormen block sociologists from getting access to interview subjects, thereby bringing into question issues of survey validity. Here, I consider the ways in which the social science literature confronts doormen, focusing first on controlling access and second on the importance of status and prestige. If seemingly indirect, both issues are relevant to the experience of the door, and considering them now will help shape our orientation subsequently.

Studies in Survey Methodology

As noted above, doormen appear in an arcane literature on survey design, survey non-response, and bias in household surveys. Doormen figure in this literature not because any surveys have considered oversampling them, but for the simple reason that they do their jobs well, all things considered. One aspect of their job is to protect residents from unwanted visitors. Few people actually look forward to talking with survey interviewers, and doormen, who block access to residents if requested, prevent survey researchers from reaching the apartments of their intended respondents (or, from the perspective of assiduous doormen, potential victims). In research reports, monographs, and in more than a dozen research articles published in peer-reviewed journals that specialize in political and/or social surveys, one finds reference to what I call the "doorman problem," which is a problem of biased samples.[12] Technically, the problem is not the "doorman problem" — rather it is the tenant problem.

---

12. Cf. Smith, "The Hidden 25 Percent"; Woodward, "Public Opinion Research 1951–1970"; and Reisman and Glazer, "The Meaning of an Opinion."

As we know from the great many surveys we read about, those with a biased sample are of little scientific or predictive value. If we want to know something about political attitudes, for example, it doesn't matter so much how many people we ask, but it does matter whom we ask. Since most surveys start out trying to get enough people to participate, the practical matter that makes the most difference in assessing the reliability of survey findings is whether or not the respondents are representative of the population that one wants to make inference to. Specifically, survey validity is conditional not simply on the number of subjects or the response rate, but on bias. What one hopes in survey design is that respondent non-response is idiosyncratic and not associated with any of the dependent variables (what one seeks to explain by considering their association or causal relationship to the independent variables) of the study.[13] With the "doorman problem," this is an impossible hope, since doormen block access to tenants who are different, with respect to wealth, than others. Consequently, for urban populations, when doormen do their job, the resulting sample consists of too few (and a select group of) wealthy individuals. It does not help matters that the very wealthy are one of the two groups considered most difficult to recruit into a study (the other group is the impoverished, but for quite different reasons). Doormen simply compound the problem.[14]

While the focus of this book is not survey design, the fact that the most frequent mentions of doormen in the social science literature are about sources of bias in social surveys is instructive. When doormen do their job, they stand between the tenant and the demands of the external world. They absorb the pressures of the street in order to insulate their tenants. That they need *not* absorb the pollution (symbolically) of the street in a servile mode distinguishes them from other service providers, like hotel doormen, with whom they share similar task descriptions. But a central aspect of their work experience is to provide such buffer services to tenants. How doormen come

---

13. The idea that characteristics of respondents shaping response are independent of some dependent variables may seem absurd, since all of the things that cause people to not participate in surveys are, in the limit, characteristics that distinguish them from participators, and therefore may be linked in a causal chain to the dependent variable of interest from the standpoint of some theory. For example, non-participants are likely to be busier than participants, out of the house more often, more paranoid about telephone calls, less outgoing, or perhaps sadder, and so on. One can always construct (ex post facto) a theory that links the basis of selection to the observed results.

14. An interesting aside is that more than half of the five million trees in New York City are behind doors. Inspectors who have to check every tree for the beetle that causes Dutch elm disease are reported to have difficulty getting access to apartments with trees because of doormen.

to construct their job, not as servile, but instead as professional service is a central theme of this book.

Studies of Occupational Prestige

Given the centrality of stratification to the organization of human societies, it is reasonable that much of sociology touches on the analysis of stratification regimes and dynamics. Here, I consider one aspect of these regimes — prestige — for it is in this context that one can find some attention to doormen, already implied in our consideration of the role doormen play as a buffer between tenants and the disorder of the street. It is commonly recognized that occupational prestige is associated with ritual purity.[15] Occupations considered to be among the highest in relative prestige are those that involve the least contact with the impurities of everyday life — especially those impurities that are human by-products, from physical human wastes (of all kinds) to mental human wastes, or what we commonly consider to be "human problems." Consequently, service industry work in all societies — whether in Indian caste systems (where the logic of ritual purity is worked out in intricate detail, encoded in the idiom of food) or in modern industrialized societies — tends to be ranked relatively low with respect to prestige.[16]

---

15. Douglas is often cited as the central authority, for example, *Purity and Danger*. The argument is also developed by Weber in *Economy and Society*; and Dumont, *Homo Hierarchicus*. In the United States, the most famous study is Hodge, Siegel, and Rossi, "Occupational Prestige in the United States, 1925–1963." See also Cohn, "Social Status and the Ambivalence Hypothesis," which starts: "We tend to think more highly of doctors than doormen. . . . In this paper, we address ourselves to the problem of why that should be so"!

16. Readers may already believe they can reject the argument, countering that in the United States, in any case, two service sector occupations — doctors and lawyers — have high prestige. But it is interesting that with respect to prestige, as Abbott noted in an important article from 1981, "Status and Status Strain in the Professions," that within the professions there is a pronounced regression away from service. That is, the doctors with the lowest prestige (among doctors) are those who have routine contact with the efflux of human life — the general internist — whereas those with the highest prestige are distant from their clients, and if their practice involves contact with persons, it is bloodless (micro-brain surgery for example) and mediated by instruments that insulate the practitioner from the disorder of the body. Likewise, for lawyers, those with the lowest prestige have the most contact with human waste — generally, divorce lawyers, those practicing family law, ambulance chasers, and the like; whereas those whose practices are nestled in arcane aspects of corporate or constitutional law have the highest prestige. On the logic of caste systems and the idiom of food, Dumont, *Homo Hierarchichus*, and Mariott, *India through Hindu Categories*, provide mainly theoretical and empirical discussions, respectively.

Though ranked higher than bootblacks (shoe shiners), who have the dubious distinction of being the occupation with the lowest prestige,[17] door-men are below clerks in stores, policemen (who must confront the disorder and impurity of criminal activity), and many industrial workers. This is the case, despite the fact that their jobs are clean (though certainly more blue than white collar), better compensated, and involve less production of waste (sweat, for example) than many jobs ranked higher on the prestige scale. Doormen also often wear uniforms, elements of which (like the white collar signifying that the wearer does not sweat at work) symbolically represent purity — for example, white gloves. While the uniform strives to project purity, the simple fact of the uniform is indicative of low status in the U.S. context. It is just hard to get away from the negative connotation of the uniform. As Isaac, a doorman on the Upper East Side, says:[18]

---

17. Oddly, bootblacks are ranked even lower than shoe salesclerks, who adopt the same submissive posture in serving clients, and who could be argued to have even more personal contact with their clients, whose shoes are taken off, thus exposing clerks to waste in the form of odor, sweat, and so on. But in contrast to the bootblack, the clerks' contact with disorder is significantly lower, since the clients remove their own shoes (potentially polluted by contact with the street) and the clerk handles only the symbolically sanitized foot (covered, in any case, by a sock) and the new (and therefore ritually unpolluted) shoe. In contrast, the bootblack comes into contact with and absorbs the disorder from the street, marked on the shoe. In one sense, this is the same distinction that can be made between doormen in residential buildings and hotel doormen.

18. Throughout, the names of the doormen have been changed, and location of their building is provided by broad neighborhood designation if relevant. I have mixed feelings about the benefits of changing names. On the one hand, I agree with Duneier, *Sidewalk*, who argues that changing names often protects no one but the author. That is probably true. But human subjects' concerns are not only about what is; they are about what could be. And aside from people (like sidewalk book vendors) who are not embedded in a formal institutional world, human subjects' concerns necessitate the guarantee of anonymity to participants, and thus one must be especially sensitive to the possibility of deductive disclosure of respondent identity, because we can never know what specific kinds of comments, analyses, descriptions, or accounts are or will in some future turn out to be potentially harmful. Problematic as well are the potential impacts of a "full-disclosure" regime on science. It seems to me that only the most callous ethnographers could — if they did not protect their respondents by changing their names — blithely report unattractive things about them. If these unattractive aspects were crucial for understanding, under a full-disclosure regime, either science becomes a restricted realm for the hard and unsympathetic or we suffer a collective loss in richness and accuracy of description. Thus, as with most things, the practical demands of the context ought to shape the approach one takes to ethnographic research. Here, in order to reduce the chance of deductive disclosure of identity, individuals' names have been assigned randomly with respect to ethnicity. One cannot assume, therefore, that "Fernando" is Hispanic or that "Serban" is Eastern European. Second, language has been "cleaned up" somewhat. "Ems," "ums," "uh-uhs," and excessive "likes" have been eliminated. Likewise, colloquial speech has been somewhat "normalized," thus, for example, "gonna" is often translated into "going to," and so on. This is especially true where ethnic identity could be deduced from the colloquial language used.

You aren't going to see many Americans wearing a uniform. I have an American coworker; he doesn't put his hat on because he thinks it's demeaning. He doesn't put it on. He takes it off. He thinks it's demeaning. You know, you can be a good-looking man, but if you are wearing this uniform, all the good-looking women look right through you. They'll be polite to you, nice, smile, but you can't start a relationship because you are at zero. But that's Manhattan for you. And we talk about that . . . he said when he met his girlfriend, American girl, when she found out he was a doorman, working a building, she didn't want to start a relationship with him. She didn't even meet him on the job; she just heard that. I think it happened on the phone. Not for immigrants, Eastern Europeans, Polish, or Spanishes, but for Americans, I'm talking about white American girls, who lives in this place, here, something is wrong with you if you are wearing this uniform, there is something wrong with you. It's like, "That's all you are capable of, that's all you can hold?" That is the harsh reality, man, I'm telling you from experience, but if you had money, you can be bald, you can be fat, and you can have the best girls. That's the reality, man, that's the reality.

The ranking of doormen below clerks and many others in the service industry is relatively stable. Nor is their ranking a function of their income. Doormen may earn significantly more than clerks. Doormen have lower prestige than others because their job is defined as one that absorbs impurities by mediating the relationship between the street and the tenant. That is, the job seems to involve ritual pollution. There are degrees of pollution. Bootblacks get the worst of the street — what gets stuck on shoes. And residential doormen are not as bad off — with respect to social pollution — as hotel doormen. This is because hotel doormen manage a specific form of impurity that arises from the absence of clear boundaries between them and the street. Anyone who comes into the building requires service. It is different for residential doormen, who orient to tenants, their guests, and those who service them. The service relationship in the residential building is thus somewhat removed from the impurity of the street. This does not mean that the doormen do not have to manage the street. They do.

What should we learn from the social science literature? A few simple ideas will suffice. First, doormen do their jobs well. Part of their job is to manage the street, and part of street management is blocking access to tenants. Second, because doormen manage the street, they manage uncertainty and absorb impurity. They provide a buffer to tenants. Consequently, being a doorman is often seen as a low-prestige job. Third, doormen wear uniforms (mostly). The uniforms communicate something to others about their job, distinguish them from the tenants (in their own uniforms, of course) whom they serve, and symbolically represent their unusual position, marked off in the boundary between the street and the inside of the apartment building, close to yet distant from their tenants.

NEIGHBORHOODS, LOBBIES, AND DOORMEN

This is a book about doormen[19] *at work*, in the context of the lobby. It is about what doormen talk to tenants about, what doormen know about their tenants, and what doormen think about their tenants. It is about their work lives, specifically about the ways in which doormen handle being close to, and distant from, tenants. It is about the daily experiences of doormen, and also the city and the places in the city where they live and work. It is also about what tenants think of doormen, how they try to "manage" them, their fears and concerns; in brief, the reproduction of role structures and the grammar of everyday life that takes place in the field settings — the neighborhoods and lobbies — where doormen and tenants are found. Here, I consider some aspects of each that are especially salient, for while the lobbies and neighborhoods with doormen vary significantly, underneath the surface heterogeneity are important generic constants.

For the founding fathers of sociology and those who followed in the Chicago school tradition, the city posed special problems for the generation of social order. In contrast to the thick, multivalent, and sustained interactive world of the country, urban interactions were seen as thin, episodic, instrumental, and univalent. Bombarded by stimuli, urban denizens, it was feared, would turn inward, insulating themselves from the chaotic intrusions of the

---

19. There are one or two female doormen. None were selected in our sample. The occupation is disproportionately male, perhaps more so than almost any other occupation in the country. Thus, throughout, doormen are discussed as if they were male. The first female doorman in New York City, Sadie Sutton, was hired in 1971 and was the subject of a long feature article in the *New York Times*: Thomas, "The Doorman Who Is a She." Here, the building manager at 315 East Sixty-fifth Street decided to hire a woman. Not surprisingly, as we will discover in chapter 2, Sutton heard about the possibility from a "weak tie," a postman who used to have lunch with her had heard about the vacancy and passed on the news.

street, ceasing to be "world-open," and therefore ceasing to contribute to the collective good.[20] The intensity of urban life, the city itself, was seen as an agent, transforming citizens and residents into mere denizens and inhabitants. Against this background, sociologists have long puzzled over the problem of how the fleeting, instrumental, and often aversive encounters of the urban world could sustain the social fabric.

The answers have taken many forms. One best answer is that both the city and the country as represented in sociological theory are imaginary; that the city is really a collection of small urban villages that sustain local identity through kinship, shared ethnicity, shopkeepers, and in more recent incarnations (at least in some settings) the denizens of the sidewalks selling wares, either legally or illegally; and that the country is really much more aversive and unfriendly than the idealized communities populating the classics. The city is really an accretion of small communities, and the country has its dark sides — not the dark side of social capital now so popular to consider, but the dark side of social isolation and instrumentality. So while the social fabric may be stretched a bit, urban life is not so different than country life. And the solution to the problem of order — to the problem of generating moral community — is the same. People in cities, like plants in hothouses or people in small towns, become intertwined in complex webs of relationality that provide the bedrock for social and moral solidarity. In short, there is not an "urban interaction" problem — people carve out of the everyday spaces for social interaction and social solidarity as effectively in urban as in rural settings.[21] You just have to know where to look. Here, we look at one interactive setting — the residential doorman building.

---

20. Turning inward, on casual observation, does seem to have increased. To counter this complexity, urbanites often appear heavily insulated, especially in contrast to their country and suburban brethren. They seem world-closed. Today, the visible armor of the urban world shuts out all sound except those brought from the home onto the street — whether voices from others on cell phones or music imported through iPods or Walkmans. In this wired world, interactions on the street are increasingly fleeting and episodic, but shutting out the world may provide little lasting comfort.

21. Still, one has to say that completely denying the sense that the city is different goes too far and in the end lacks face validity. The city *is* different interactively. Only nuts say "hi" to everyone they meet, the eyes of city dwellers are more often than not downcast, and interactions, stripped of their veneer of civility, appear more nakedly instrumental than in the smaller towns beyond the urban pale. Furthermore, urban interactions are quicker; they are interactions on the move, and they are interactions with often unknown others. These facts makes their meaning harder to assess, their triviality and speed allowing each to carry multiple possibilities for interpretation; their ambiguity heightens risk of rapid descent into disorder and threat. So that while one may carefully carve out a space for the familiar and reassuring, outside of one's small urban village — beyond the world of the familiar sidewalk booksellers, the comfort of the usual (i.e., domesticated) street people, the

Indoors/Outdoors, or Differences in Neighborhoods

At the start of *their* working day, whether for the morning, swing, or night shift, each doorman is at home So, one reasonable place for us to start is at home as well. The average residential doorman lives in an area quite different from the one he works in. First, in terms of sheer distance, the typical Manhattan doorman lives a long way from his job, although a few live in the same building or neighborhood (5% in the same building, 10% in the same neighborhood). The vast majority of doormen live in the outer boroughs, the Bronx (especially those who work on the Upper West Side) and Brooklyn (especially those on the East Side), with a handful traveling to Staten Island (off the map) or northern New Jersey. One doorman lives as far off as Pennsylvania, but he does not commute every day. Sixty percent of the doormen in our sample spend between thirty minutes and one hour traveling to and from work (with the median at one hour). Most doormen (slightly over two-thirds) use mass transportation (the subway or bus), fewer than 10% walk to work, and the balance drive. In this regard, they are typical New Yorkers, who rely on public transportation to get around and who put in long hours commuting to and from work. In an average week, doormen spend roughly ten hours on the subway or bus, just getting to and from work.

The neighborhoods that they leave from and return to differ remarkably from those they work in. The residential neighborhoods with doormen in Manhattan are and feel wealthy. Sidewalk flower gardens are cared for (often by the doormen); the streets are clean and well policed. The larger avenues are tree-lined; garbage is discreetly tucked away in the backs of buildings. The parks are well lit. Stores are airier and brighter. After hours, one can see into the windows; missing are the metal grates in store windows ubiquitous in the outer boroughs and the poorer areas of Manhattan that block views of the merchandise on sale. The dominant language on store signs and overheard on the street is English. Aside from workers, the vast majority of people one sees are white. One can notice even more subtle differences, for example, the presence of pets, the absence of graffiti on mailboxes, and the presence of benches on the edge of green zones or in the median strips of the major avenues. Where doormen work, the boundary between inside

---

regular coffee shop, newsstand, and fruit store — reside uncertainty and disorder — the threat of the largely unknown.

and outside is demarcated more strongly than in the neighborhoods where doormen live. In wealthy neighborhoods, the street is demarcated as "other." Residents rarely sit outside their buildings. These aesthetic "feeling tone" differences reflect substantial class differences between neighborhoods, and because class and race are strongly consolidated in New York (though perhaps less so than in other areas of the country), these differences in neighborhood also reflect ethnic cleavages that organize settlement patterns in the city. So when doormen come to work, they enter a different environment, one that signifies stability, money, and what tour operators regard as "urban grace and charm."

These aesthetic differences between neighborhoods might seem unimportant. After all, most people live and work in environments that are quite different without seemingly affecting the nature of their work experience.[22] Yet these neighborhood differences are important; minimally, they register quite different definitions and uses of public space. These shifting norms over the public uses of sidewalks, entrances, flower gardens, flowerpots, trees, and the management of trash are salient in the lives of doormen at work. In neighborhoods with doormen, the interior of the building is projected onto the street. This projection domesticates the area immediately in front of the building, insulating it from uncertainty. Doormen are a critical element in this projection. First, by standing at the door (whether inside or outside), they project the interior onto the street. Second, doormen clean the area in front of their building. While it is obvious that neighborhoods with doormen are cleaner than those in other areas of the city — one can assess this simply by looking — it is the management of trash by doormen (and also the city) that makes these neighborhoods cleaner. Likewise, flowers in flowerpots in front of buildings may magically flourish by themselves, but in doorman neighborhoods they routinely flourish because doormen water them. Where present, doormen often manage the small garden patches in front of buildings.

Thus, the doormen in part produce the aesthetic differences that one notices, and it is this *production of difference*, the tenant and doorman understandings of the role doormen play in producing neighborhood, that I explore further in this book. The production of aesthetic difference is not

---

22. To be clear, the work environment shapes work experience, but the difference between the work and home environment is not generally thought to be particularly important. For most occupations, it is not.

simply about making neighborhoods nice. Doormen domesticate the exterior of the building in order to induce a border region between inside and outside. As borders are not lines drawn in the sand, neither are they doors to buildings. Rather, they are liminal spaces heavily occupied by contradictory signifiers. The projection of the building onto the street (with awnings, flowerpots, and small border fences) creates the border region between inside and outside as a space neither exactly inside nor exactly outside. The ambiguous nature of the border has implications for its use. Wealthy tenants may sit in lobbies, for example, but they never sit in front of their building. One encounters the wealthy outdoors in formal "outdoor" settings, not border regions.

Many doormen directly and actively contribute to the "quality" of the neighborhoods where they work, through gardening, cleaning, and planting. Likewise, supers and doormen play an active role in ensuring that adequate city services are provided for the management of trash and recycling, removing graffiti, and pruning trees (for example). In this regard, doormen directly contribute to expanding the boundary zone between indoors and outdoors. In the tenant world, one passes from the privacy of an apartment through the liminal space of the lobby before entering the outdoors — itself domesticated by projection of wealth in the form of awnings, flowerpots, benches, and, of course, the doorman.[23] In the neighborhoods where doormen live, this carefully constructed and nurtured boundary between inside and outside is largely absent. Residents talk on the street. They

---

23. As Jack Katz has suggested, the carefully cultivated front lawns of suburbia demarcate the inside from the outside; that is, they are projections of inside to outside, through domestication and definition of public space. But the suburban boundary is elongated temporally and spatially. It is much more than the front yard. Returning from work, the typical suburbanite passes through the social to the private long before entering his or her home. From the train, bus, or car to the threshold of their community, and beyond to their driveway and garage, the experience of the city recedes, surrounded by the comforting constancy of familiar totems, the neighborhood, their neighbors' yards, their own driveway, the garage door opening at the precise moment of arrival, the reassuring bark of their dog, announcing all is just the same as it was this morning. This progressive insulation from chaos is both material and symbolic. The suburban home is marked off from the world of work by the process of reaching it, by the fact of transit through progressively more private symbols of home. In contrast, the urban dweller moves through spaces not solely occupied by familiar totems. The unknown is always present, and progressive insulation, at least without doormen, is absent — at the threshold of one's home, a single door is simply the difference between outside and inside. For some, then, into this world stands the doorman, whose presence acts as a totem of security marking private from public, and whose activities extend the boundary between inside and outside. This extension of the boundary between inside and out, between private and public, domesticates for those who live in doorman buildings the urban world. And thus returning home, seeing one's doorman signifies that the order one left in the morning remains just as it was in the evening.

may sit on the stoop. The experience of community is consequently more direct.

Many tenants are surprised to learn that most doormen, not only those who own their home, would prefer to live where they do, rather than, for example, in a doorman building like the one where they work. In our every-day lives, we often fail to see the ways in which the reality we live in is the product of others' active construction. The insulation of the elite residential building made possible by the doorman's domestication of exterior space and the cordoning off of the lobby as a liminal space seems somehow normal to those who live there. But doormen, whose activities in part produce this effect, recognize that the boundary is not exactly natural.

Lobbies (for Buildings, Doormen, and Tenants)

While obvious, it makes sense to remember that apartment seekers in New York have preferences for certain kinds of apartments, location in the city, and costs, either in terms of rent to be paid or purchase price and mainte-nance fee. Some people will only live on the East Side, others in the Village, and so on. Net of these preferences, there are those who prefer, assuming that trade-offs have to be made, views to size, open spaces to separate rooms, modern designs to traditional floor plans, wood to tile, and so on. In addition, most people have preferences for the style of the building that they would like to live in, with some preferring (one imagines) modern skyscrapers over the older buildings constructed for the rising middle class at the turn of the century. These preferences for buildings and apartments have an aesthetic element, and as with most preferences arrayed across a diverse set of aesthetic considerations, they may not be well ordered, or ordered in a sense immediately perceptible to even those who hold them. But still, given the possibility of choice, New Yorkers (as with other people searching for homes in the suburbs or the country) have preferences that they often summarize broadly as a "feel," in the sense that one has feelings about specific places, by virtue of what they signify about the residents and those around them. Thus, in New York there live people who strongly prefer the feel of the West Side to that of the East, and vice versa, and who could not really imagine living elsewhere.

The feel of places is simultaneously aesthetic and social, since buildings in cities, like houses in suburbs, articulate specific social feelings, by virtue of their design first and by virtue of the persons who inhabit them who have preferences for design or the residents' style or comportment.[24] But more narrowly, building design exerts a quite profound influence on the feel of each neighborhood, helping to select and shape the people who live there. Just as particular suburban street plans induce characteristic forms of sociability — suburban layouts with cul-de-sacs have strikingly different patterns of sociability than those with parallel streets, for example — so do different building designs shape the social world of those who reside in them, or their immediate environs. Such shaping is not complete, for even the most social individuals can find that by virtue of their (poor) housing choice, they are socially isolated, independent of their own preferences to the contrary.[25] Likewise, those seeking the privacy of the suburbs may find themselves, despite all efforts, embedded in deep neighborhood networks, simply by virtue of the location of their house. In the city, compared to the suburbs, building design tends to exert stronger influence, and this may be simply because variation in design and what design signifies are more easily perceived at first glance. There are buildings that seek to signify through design a sense of community, and buildings that seek to signify through design a specific form of urban anonymity. And the lobby plays a key role in defining the feel of a building.

For this reason there is no single lobby, for just as buildings vary, so do their lobbies. Yet despite these differences, one can immediately recognize (as one would recognize, for example, when reading a fairy tale that one is indeed reading a fairy tale) that one has entered a lobby. That is, in the same way that we recognize a fairy tale by its structure (technically a series of operators working on an heterogeneous but limited set of cultural goods, a frog here, a prince there, and so on),[26] we recognize a lobby, even if the "goods" it is working with — a sofa here, a desk there — are also quite heterogeneous. Nor can one say that the lobby requires a certain spatial

---

24. The difference across New York neighborhoods in the types of people living in them is quite marked. For example, in one of our unsuccessful recruitments at Columbia, the candidate found the idea of living on the Upper West Side problematic after his wife, wearing a fur coat, was called an "animal killer" as she walked down the street. He correctly noted that this would not happen on the Upper East Side of the city, where fur is more commonly displayed.

25. One of the more interesting studies of suburban living is Whyte's *The Organization Man*. Fascinating in this context is the discovery that people who live in specific houses tend to be isolated within the suburban community, even if the same people living in other houses were the center of social life. In the suburban setting, where selection dynamics are oriented toward sociability, spatial effects are quite strong.

26. Propp, *The Morphology of Fairy Tales*.

form, for one can enter lobbies that consist of nothing more than a hallway with a podium (placed at an angle to minimize occupied space) and a thin bench or two along the walls, while one can also enter lobbies with grand vistas, a fountain, lounge chairs, and, perhaps against a far wall, a bank of counters, behind which are the back rooms of the building, for storing packages and dry cleaning, telephones, and so on. In some lobbies, one can find antique furniture, carpets, spectacular chandeliers, even medieval suits of arms standing guard by the doors. In others, linoleum floors, fluorescent ceiling lights, and empty walls (aside from the ubiquitous signs informing visitors that all of them must be announced and that menus are not allowed) greet the tenant and visitor upon their arrival. In these desolate lobbies, there are no signs that announce that "you have entered the lobby," and yet one knows that one has, not simply because there is a doorman present — for the lobby can work as a lobby without a doorman, though not as well — but because, instead, one reads a certain kind of generic domestication from even the most fragile signifiers; for a lobby is exactly that space that is neither an undomesticated hallway nor a living room, within which by one's choice of furnishings and decoration one strives to present a specific personal feeling, that is, personality. Because lobbies are designed — however full of furnishings — to be liminal spaces, they are rich with interactive possibilities. In this sense, the form of the lobby, by virtue of its generic nature, makes possible a wide range of contents.

This is not to say that the generic nature of the lobby space prohibits its signifying content. In fact, the opposite is more accurate; the generic nature of the lobby affords a wide range of contents. The lobby serves to signify specific values, its decor indicates something about the status of the residents — or their status aims, more accurately — and the nature of the building and the people who live there. These signifiers, however fragile, provide material for those to experience the feel of the building, and in this way, one can see that the lobby (as with other aesthetic elements) "selects" residents of the building. This is necessarily the case if all other things are equal — the choice of an apartment will involve the nature of the lobby and the feel of the building that the lobby seeks to express.[27]

---

27. Tenants I have discussed this idea with tend to reject it out of hand, stating that in New York City the constraint over apartments is so great that people never have the luxury of thinking about the lobby when they decide to rent or purchase an apartment. The marketing of apartments suggests

With respect to sociability, the building and lobby that promise through design the possibility for sociability therefore attract different kinds of people than the building and lobby that offer through design the guarantee of anonymity. In this indirect way at first, and often more directly subsequently, there is a matching of persons to the personality of the building, a matching that is strengthened over time through practice. With respect to status or status aims, the lobby and the doormen serve as the key signifiers, defining a specific form of lifestyle as gracious living. This is a central insight of the Trump real estate group, who signify that their properties are something truly unique and special by figuring the lobby and their doormen (or the concierge desk) prominently in their advertising. In fact, all of the Trump on-line virtual tours start with the lobby sitting area, and many extend to the sub-lobbies, the elevator lobby, and the main entrance areas. What Trump recognizes explicitly is what other real estate agents know intuitively: The first impression is the most critical. And the first impression takes place in the lobby.

Considering sociability first, even if it seems somewhat "Pollyannaish," the lobby with gracious design and attractive furnishings, flowers, plants, and comfortable areas for sitting while sorting through mail or waiting for guests to arrive will feel warm and welcoming to those who care about the possibility of such activities. Consequently, at the margins of the choice for apartments, the lobby (and the building more generally) will attract different kinds of people, who will subsequently use the spaces available to them differently. While some social people will end up in anonymous complexes and some asocial people will end up in buildings oriented toward inducing community sentiment, the slight tilt toward sociability or not provided by design is sufficient to give different buildings different feels. These "feels," in turn, act on residents, so that one really does encounter buildings with remarkably different personalities, not completely reducible to design.

Less abstractly, if people prefer an open and luxurious lobby because it is a better place to sit and wait for their guests than in their apartment, or

---

that they may be wrong. New buildings on the market routinely advertise both the floor plans of units for sale and visualizations of the public space, most prominently the lobby. At the same time, when people first look at apartments, they collect feelings about the possibility of living there, starting from the neighborhood, then to the building, the lobby, and only then the apartment they enter. Tenants may not think about the lobby per se. But they do surely register the feel of the building, and the lobby plays the critical role in organizing this feel.

perhaps a better place in which to display one's status, the open airy lobby will attract more sitters, in turn making it more attractive to sit in and identifying it (for prospective apartment hunters) as a feature of the building. While it is true that all things being equal, the aesthetic and social interests of tenants will be matched with the physical appearance of the lobby — since those who value the social possibilities inherent in larger lobbies will disproportionately select apartments in buildings so designed over comparable apartments in buildings with desolate public spaces — residents' preferences will also be shaped by the lobby. Naturally, then, the lobby and the lobby decor are expressive of the residents — indirectly, through selection dynamics, and directly, through influence.

At the risk of redundancy, one can also say that in the same way that the waiting room of a clinic differs in feel and intent from the waiting room of a private physician, the lobby is experienced differently by those who spend time and pass through it on their way to their apartment. In sparsely furnished lobbies with little more than a bench locked to the floor (to prevent it from wandering), the outsider cannot help but feel upon arrival that the building is at best a shell for the persons who inhabit the interior spaces, and at worst that the kinds of people living there would not hesitate to steal, if the opportunity was present, the frugal furniture that was there. Such buildings announce a specific form of pragmatism, one appropriate for an urban setting, where sociability is both commodified and privatized. The residents appear to scurry past the doorman to the elevator. In contrast, one enters lobbies so grand and imposing that one can sense a collective hush, as if one had slipped into a spectacular cathedral just seconds after the sermon had begun. In the winter, fur-coated ladies exchange pleasantries with one another and the doorman. And between these extremes, one finds those comfortable lobbies that carve out a small public space, neither imposing in their grandeur nor expressive of a peculiar urban desolation.

While not determinant, the physical appearance of the lobby thus shapes the structure of interactions between tenants and between tenants and doormen. There may be in this regard an irony. In smaller buildings, those with fewer than thirty units, the space allocated to the lobby is generally small, and one can enter through the exterior doors and traverse the distance to the elevator(s) in just a few steps. In these smaller lobbies, one finds only a seat or two, to hold visitors temporarily detained on their way up to apartments or waiting for the imminent descent of their host. Here, tenants tend to pass through the open space quickly, pausing only at the elevators or by the mail.

The doorman is likely behind a small podium or desk. At night, when the traffic flow is less intense, they may sit behind the podium or at the desk, whereas during the day shift, one typically finds the doorman standing by the doors or just in front of the building, with the interior doors propped open. Here, there is little opportunity for discussion between tenants, aside from short conversations that occur while waiting for the elevator or for the doorman to retrieve laundry, packages, or videos from the back room. In contrast, in somewhat larger buildings, with two to three times the number of units, the correspondingly larger lobbies facilitate conversations between tenants, who tend to pause on their way through, interacting with those around them.[28] There is thus an irony that does not go unnoticed by those new to the city: the smaller buildings that appear to facilitate community are often experienced as the most alien and alienating. It is in these varied spaces that doormen, if not outside the door or in the back rooms, meet and interact with their tenants. Necessarily, the lobby, directly and indirectly, plays some role in defining the nature of these interactions — the way doormen think about tenants and tenants think about doormen. In some buildings, with two or three doormen on shift at any one time, doormen are less able to develop and nurture the kinds of personal relationships that they would like to have with their tenants. In turn, tenants spend less time thinking about their doormen (except during the Christmas bonus season, considered in chapter 6).

These differences aside, there remains a generic nature to lobbies, and their form induces — except for those periods where tenants and their doormen may be alone for long stretches of conversation — generic conversation. In only a few hours of sitting in the lobby, one can get a sense of the sheer triviality of most interactions between doormen and tenants. One hears over and over conversations or fragments of conversations about the weather, sports, traffic, "life" (in its most abstract formulations, such as "I can't complain, no one will listen anyway" or "Whatever, you do what you have to do," etc.), so that one wonders how any actual knowledge about the other could be communicated. On more exciting days, one might catch a snippet about a new lobby desk, a new posting on the bulletin board, progress in the construction in the apartment on the nth floor, activity in the garden, new

---

28. From observation, the actual relationship is curvilinear. In the very large lobbies, one rarely observes social interaction between tenants and between tenants and their doorman.

plants in the planter, the problem of dog poop on the streets, new families in the building, "kids these days," or when the scaffolds will go up (and then, when they might come down), and so on.

Note that in general, the goods to think with share the same generic nature as the lobby, which neither revelatory of the individual nor empty of meaning provides a shell for trivial conversation, in the same way that the mixer, designed to introduce persons who do not know each other, is characterized by trivial conversations not revelatory of individuality, on such topics easily at hand as the food, furnishings, crowd, design, lighting, and so on. People, in short, make use of the goods at hand in their social relationships. So while lobbies are different, they are also similar enough to treat as a unitary space, and to consider the kinds of interactions that occur within them, without conditioning all the time on their nature as grand or small, fancy or plain, and so on.

DOORMEN

While most doormen prefer to not live in a doorman building, their preferences for their children are different. For their children, doormen hope that they can live like the persons who live in their buildings; that is, live like persons who do not experience their neighborhood as foreign, as constructed. In this regard, doormen believe that they are part of the larger process of intergenerational upward mobility that provides a salient ideal in many ethnic and immigrant communities. This ideal is shaped in part from their own experiences. Most doormen arrived in the United States with few prospects and the wrong skill sets — either too sophisticated (e.g., training as radiologists, physician assistants, engineers, and musicians) for use in the entry-level jobs that were available to them or inappropriate for urban employment.

When they go home, one-quarter return to homes that they own, the balance to homes that they rent, at an average cost of $700 per month, well below the rents paid by the tenants whom they work for. One-quarter of the doormen in our sample live alone. Of those who live with someone else, forty-two different languages are spoken at home by the 25% who do not speak English at home. Three-quarters are married, and almost all have children. Many live with their parents as well. Those who have relatives in other countries routinely send back monthly checks, to support parents, cousins, or in some instances their children. Thus, there is widespread participation in the global economy, linking the outer boroughs of New York with the barrios of Central and Latin America. If doormen remit funds to relatives in other countries, their tenants tend to know about it, and this element of the doorman's life is often one of the things that tenants like to talk about when they describe their doorman.[29] Many doormen have been able to bring their relatives over to the United States, and thus doormen often live in three-generation households, a not uncommon feature of urban immigrant life. The contrast between the households of doormen and those of their tenants is often revealed in sharp relief in terms as simple as household size, number of bedrooms, or square feet per capita.

Labor Force Experience

Most doormen are mature workers who have been in the labor force for a number of years. The median age of the doormen in our sample was forty, though roughly 25% were under thirty when we interviewed them. Most had worked elsewhere before becoming a doorman. Because they have had diverse work experiences, they are also able to recognize that they have, all things considered, a good job. Consequently, job satisfaction is remarkably high, across most of the usual dimensions. Over 70% of all the doormen we talked to were satisfied or very satisfied with their base salary, and 78% were satisfied or very satisfied with their benefits. Eighty-seven percent report being satisfied or very satisfied with the people they work with, and more than three-quarters report high levels of satisfaction with their schedule. Not surprisingly, as discussed subsequently, tenure rates are very high. Since doorman jobs are good jobs and since doormen are satisfied, on the whole, with their jobs, it is not surprising that they stay in them a long time.[30]

While they believe that the benefits and salary are good, some doormen cannot make ends meet without additional work. One in four holds another

---

29. There are a number of reasons for this. I believe that most tenants use wage differentials between the United States and foreign countries as an indirect way of not having to think very hard about how much money their doormen make. If by sending small amounts of money to the old country doormen can elevate their parents' (or other relatives') status and life situation, then tenants can think that their doormen must in some sense be doing okay in this country.

30. Of course, one expects the current job to be thought of as better than the previous job, on average, but for doormen, such evaluations are marked. Whereas only 3% of all doormen with a previous job thought it much better than their current job, almost 50% thought their current job was much better or better than their previous job. These positive sentiments may also reflect the slight bias toward long-tenure doormen in our sample; though the strong positive sentiment (much higher for other similarly positioned occupations) cannot be an artifact of the sample.

full- or part-time job in the formal economy. A few report side jobs in the informal economy. Of the former, those holding a second job in the formal economy, half work in another building, as a doorman, handyman, super, or porter. The rest work in a range of positions — as a banquet porter, on a UPS truck, as a painter, and as a Web salesman. Of those who pick up extra cash in the informal economy, many parlay their skills in maintenance to work as painters, handymen, or small machinery repairmen. Just over 50% of the doormen we interviewed report having recently taken classes or being in school part-time. Most of these are in some form of a credential-granting program or vocational education. These courses may be offered by the union (32 BJ) but are more commonly taken in one of the many community colleges in the city. Not surprisingly, older workers are much less likely to be involved in educational activities than younger workers, either skill enhancing or degree granting.

Thirty percent of the doormen we talked with had other doormen in their immediate family.[31] Needless to say, this is extremely unusual. Most of the doormen we interviewed liked their jobs and were satisfied with their pay, schedules, benefits, and the work environment. Still, few would like to see their children as doormen. For the older generation, being a doorman has meant that they could achieve stable lower-middle-class status and have had the opportunity to launch their children into higher-prestige professions. Commitment to an achievement ideology of upward mobility is very strong among the older generation of workers, displaced one generation on to their children. This commitment is less strong for those under thirty, who often view their job as a way station on the path toward achievement of their own occupational dreams — which tend toward the romantic, as motorcycle racer, musician, actor, commercial pilot. In describing the tenants, this generational difference emerges in accounts that doormen provide for the source of their tenants' wealth. The younger generation is much more willing to see tenants as beneficiaries of inherited wealth or opportunity, whereas the older generation are more willing to ascribe hard work and effort to their tenants' successes.[32] Ironically, the older generation hopes to pass on

---

31. In an earlier time, it was customary for sons to inherit, under certain circumstances, their father's occupation; consequently, the rate for intergenerational occupational inheritance observed here (30%), while high, would not be out of line. But at the turn of the twenty-first century, the level of familial co-involvement in the residential trades is strikingly high.

32. There is another process going on that complicates interpretation. Older doormen have worked as doormen longer than younger doormen. Younger doormen who develop oppositional

opportunity to their children (what they deny occurs for their tenants) and the younger generation would like to be successful on their own — in their chosen, if romantic, occupations (what they deny occurs for the tenants). Either way, despite the fact that many have other family members as doormen and that almost all think they have a good job, most don't want their children to be doormen.

Social Activity

Doormen spend much of their time watching their tenants go in and out, especially those on the swing shift. Consider a building with a hundred units, in which the occupant from each unit does something — goes out to dinner, a sports event, the theater; meets a friend at a coffee shop; takes a walk by the park; attends a dance or a party — only two or three times a week. If each unit has only a few social events at their apartment per year (a dinner party, cocktail party, discussion group, poker game, etc.), on any evening something is going on in the building that means guests are arriving. As a consequence, with even light or very moderate activity per unit, the doorman is likely to see, on any given day, many exits and entrances for events. Even quiet buildings may seem to be a hubbub of activity.

In contrast to the collective sense of activity they experience, doormen *perceive* that they live a quiet and relatively inactive life. In describing and enumerating their activities, doormen as a rule report going out very little. They travel rarely. They belong to few organizations. Most of their time is spent reading, watching TV, or engaged in household activities with their family. Almost three-quarters of all doormen belong to no organizations or clubs, not counting the union that represents them. Of those interviewed who do belong to an organization, thirty-seven (or roughly 20%) belong to just one. Only 6% of the doormen we talked with belong to two or more organizations or clubs. Many of these memberships do not involve collective activity — for example, memberships in local gyms. Nor are doormen likely to participate in other organized activities. Sixty percent do not participate in any religious activities. Almost 90% participate in no community-based activities. Sixty-nine percent report no outdoor activities, such as sports,

---

relationships with their tenants — one expression of which is the perception that they are all silver spoon and spoiled — tend to have short tenures in the position. Either they get fired or they move on. Consequently, the comparison between older and younger doormen needs to take into account the selectivity of the older doormen.

hiking, walking, or running. Just under half of the doormen (44%) report no hobbies, only 40% attended a movie in the past six months, roughly one-third went to a bar, and 30% attended a sporting event. In contrast to Robert Putnam, who finds that Americans are increasingly "bowling alone," doormen, as a rule, appear to not even go bowling.[33]

The contrast to their *observation* of most tenants' behavior is worth noting. Doormen see tenants coming in and out from social events, shows, and weekend retreats. Their tenants may in fact be no more active than they are: but the collective experience of activity is significant; and doormen sense that there is a gap between the lives they lead and the lives that their tenants lead. They want the former for themselves and the latter for their children. Likewise, if doormen watch tenants head out for social events, they also often see tenants who ask for assistance in routine household management, fixing leaks in the sink, jammed toilets, and chipped paint. Tenants consider it reasonable that they involve the doorman and the handyman in scheduling such repairs since they are typically part of the rental or cooperative contract. Still, doormen spend much of their free time fixing just those kinds of things. The combination of watching tenants "live it up socially" and "have no time" for household repairs serves as a crisp — if exaggerated — reminder of the differences in lifestyle and trajectory that they have with their tenants.

Careers and Generational Difference

Again one is able to pick out and isolate generational differences. Many younger doormen have outside interests in music, acting, or performance of some sort. Like the proverbial taxicab driver with a PhD, many of these men see working the door as an opportunity to focus on their real occupational interest — racing cars or motorcycles, playing in a band, performing as an actor, and so on. In this regard, many see the door as an opportunity to meet people who can help them in their own careers. Thus, they may hope that lawyers in the building can advise them on contracts they might need to sign, agents will help them meet producers, and actors and actresses will help them meet agents. In general, they are disappointed that this does not seem to turn out to be the case, either because "the wrong people live in the building" or because "they don't really take the time to help out." While many doormen will report that tenants helped them when they got into a personal

---

33. Cf. Putnam, *Bowling Alone*.

jam — a car accident, conflicts with management, and so on — few can report that their tenants assisted them in pursuing their off-work career goals.[34]

These generational differences cannot be stressed too strongly, however, and more likely reflect differences in the life course. Younger doormen with children are much less likely to be thinking of alternative careers. Instead, they think about their job as a career. But here, it is important to understand that the idea of the career is quite different than a succession of positions with increasing authority, skill, and responsibility. Rather, the career is conceived of as a stable job extending over the life course that rewards the occupant with a livable pension at the conclusion of a long period of service. This orientation cannot be stressed too strongly, for doormen's orientation to career has a powerful influence on their relations to tenants, the union, their super, and all others with whom they interact in their everyday ecology.

One of the key elements of the job is that it does not change with tenure. Because the formal skill set for a doorman is limited, all doormen receive the same union-negotiated salary (not counting those on probation) and come under the same supervisory controls. The doorman in his first year is consequently under the same general regime as the doorman who has worked for twenty years. Thus, the only tangible benefit to tenure is schedule, with older doormen able to choose the shift they would like to work. Consequently, younger doormen can look forward to very little change in their working conditions, year after year, and may face, depending on the demography of their building, ten- to twenty-year waits for a change of schedule, allowing them, for example, to shift from swing to day work. When doormen are frustrated with their career, it is because the probabilities of promotion are very few and because they perceive that the educational opportunities provided by the union are irrelevant with respect to promotion probabilities.

The only thing that changes with tenure is the relationships with tenants. But this is critical, for it is through interaction with tenants that doormen generate their claims to professional status and create opportunities for exercise of responsibility and judgment. Thus, while careers are not rewarded formally through higher pay, they are rewarded informally, most practically in the size of the bonus they receive at Christmas, but perhaps

---

34. Again, at the risk of being redundant, the problem is selectivity. We only interviewed doormen working on the door, so those who left because their tenants did find them an agent, et cetera, were no longer available for interviews.

most importantly in shifts in self-concept and identity. And it is in this latter regard, where the work they do is more than a job they go to each day, that the most interest lies, for the professional doorman is engaged in a career that is quite unlike others, by virtue of their simultaneous closeness to and distance from those whom they serve in small and often intimate ways, day in and day out, over long stretches of time.

BOOK STRATEGY

There is a seemingly enormous gulf in the sociological literature between those whose work focuses on models and those whose work focuses on description. This mismatch has to do with the necessary duality of views that organize any real setting. That is, settings are the interfaces for multiple views conceived here in simple terms as the "underside," where views of lived experience and cognition percolate up to discourse and are related to self and others (as in interviews), and the "upper side," wherein lie systematic processes, dynamics, and flows that give rise to structures not necessarily observed or theorized by those who live and work in the setting. In general, ethnographers, interviewers, and field-workers (however much they might object to being lumped together) are interested primarily in describing the underside view of the complex worlds in which they find themselves. The central idea of those who focus on the underside is that through description, deployed as a lever, new insights arise. In general, social science modelers are interested in formalizing processes that appear to operate across settings — that is, in upper-side views. In this instance, the model is the lever that allows one to see what participants may not, or cannot, see, or may see but have no words for.

The gulf between modeling and fieldwork is akin to the gulf between history and sociology, where the aim of history is description and the aim of sociology is abstraction. Abstraction without empirical referent, without attention to context, is of little value sociologically. Likewise, sociology has little to gain from sheer description, even presuming such an activity could exist. And just as with social science history, there are good reasons to think that explicit linkage between models and thick description is desirable and beneficial to both perspectives. As such, this book experiments with such linkage, sometimes explicitly and sometimes implicitly. Where relevant, I consider how the under- and upper-side views are organized in such a way as to make each "right." Some may well wonder why in a discussion of getting a job, there is an apparent detour into the markets for friends and organs. And others will certainly wonder why no real formal models are presented. Likewise, while the collective-action problem of the bonus may seem too abstract for some, others will see that the system bears resemblance to the order-effects problem in contexts with heterogeneous interests and wonder why this is not more fully developed. The idea is to get some balance. Hopefully, this book will lie between (perhaps uncomfortably) these different communities of thought; opening up some vistas for each, while closing none for either, providing an integrated whole.

(Narrative) Structure

At one level, the book has a narrative structure. I start with getting a job (chapter 2) and end with the wage strike (chapter 7). This seems to encompass the beginning and one of the possible ends. In between, I discuss the sheer experience of time (chapter 3); interactions and struggles with tenants around security, sex, and relationships (chapter 4); short and long conversations in the lobby (chapter 5); and the annual Christmas bonus (chapter 6). While one can see a narrative, it is also the case that the structure may be read as a series of detailed explorations of specific problems that arise from the distance/closeness tension and that, taken together, provide an integrated view of the doorman's world. From this perspective, this is what the reader should expect.

Chapter 2 considers how doormen got their jobs, what kind of jobs they are, and why and how they get their jobs matters for tenants' and others' experiences. The first claim is that doorman jobs are good jobs. The main message is that informal network dynamics govern the market for doorman jobs. Reasons why such a matching system evolved are considered, from doormen, super, and tenant points of view, and these are contrasted to other kinds of markets, fair and unfair. Here, the central consequences are that doormen jobs are inaccessible to some people by virtue of their race and/or ethnicity; that once hired, doormen experience low mobility in and out of the occupation; that, consequently, doormen tenures are extremely long, shaping their relationships with tenants; and that as a by-product of their background and their understanding of tenants' preferences, doormen engage in relatively systematic discrimination against some ethnic and many black visitors to buildings, even if they are not racist or do not intend to be discriminatory.

Chapter 3 considers what happens when doormen do work — that is, after they have gotten their job. The phenomenological experience of being a doorman is that they are bored and stressed out at the same time. They have both too much and too little to do. Chapter 3 considers why this is the case, through comparison to server-client systems. I also consider how doormen deal with the fact that most tenants see them doing nothing, except when they need them. I consider how doormen work on tenants in order to handle the conflicting demands that they are subject to. Part of this work involves training tenants into having preferences, so that doormen can then direct personalized service to them. The capacity to direct personalized service buttresses many of the status aims of tenants and allows doormen to articulate their work as professional versus as service.

Chapters 4 and 5 narrow the focus from the more model-driven observations of the previous chapter on the temporal experience of work to the central problem of closeness and distance, seen through interactions around three substantive issues that color the experiences of doormen and tenants, crime (security), sex (relationships), and honor (respect) in the context of lobby interactions. Chapter 4 focuses on crime and sex, chapter 5 on respect. The central ideas develop at a micro-level the themes considered more formally in the preceding chapters. The analytic themes I consider in more detail are doorman claims to professional service, status struggles, and conflicts over coveted roles; the main descriptive problem is concerned with how doormen and tenants negotiate boundaries, sustain relationships, and understand (or misunderstand) signs and signals that are class specific. Throughout, we consider how doormen and tenants come to see and define their work and relationships, hence focusing on cognition and interpretation.

Chapter 6 shifts focus to a specific moment in the year — the holidays and the Christmas bonus — and considers how tenants interpret the bonus, how doormen come to think about the bonus, and how neither doormen nor tenants can interpret the signals they give through the bonus. The bonus is deployed as a vehicle for encoding the relationship between tenants and doormen, for neutralizing dependence or knowledge, and for inducing distance. But does it work? How bonuses work differently than tips and how doormen and tenants try to shape each other's understanding of the bonus are the central themes. In chapter 7, I consider how the larger labor movement and the union impact doormen's work experience and doormen-tenant relationships. The focus turns on the 1991 strike and the threat of strike in other years. I consider how doormen help tenants prepare for a strike, and how tenants help doormen while they are out on the picket line.

In the end, we consider the broader themes of structural power in the labor movement, against a backdrop of remarkable union corruption.

The final chapter comprises a theoretical reprise of the central arguments. The focus returns to the problem of building a social structure in a context of both great closeness and distance. I consider the changes that the new security regime since 9/11 has brought to the residential apartment, and the ways in which these changes, by legitimizing above other rhetorical claims the importance of security, threaten to transform the relationship between doormen and tenants by stripping away the foundation for delivery of personalized, professional service.

CHAPTER 2

A Foot in the Door

I was getting very tired working at the job I had and, without knowing that, a person who was a friend to me was the president of the board in the building who was very kind to me. So one day I told him I was very tired of this, I [was going to] look somewhere else. A couple of days later he said, "Do you want to be a doorman in my building?" I said, "Yes," and that is how I got here. I just came here.

You know what is peculiar, years ago when I was a little boy, my brother-in-law, my sister's husband, was a superintendent of a building something like this. I don't really recall exactly where it was, but I used to go out and talk to the doorman because I used to get bored, and I would go out and talk to him, never knowing that someday, I'm going to become one of you. You know what I mean? This was years ago. I was maybe eight years old. Never realizing that someday you might be doing this, and here I am in the same shoes that he was in. My brother-in-law was the super, so I used to go out and chat with the doorman, thirty years ago, and here I am now one of them. I guess that's strange; you could put that down as being a little peculiar.

Just after 5:30 in the morning, Allan shuts his front door and walks to the subway station. He will take three trains this morning from Carroll Gardens in Brooklyn to his apartment building on West End Avenue. His shift starts at 7:00, and he needs to arrive by 6:45 in order to be changed and ready to go, even if nothing really happens for an hour or so, when people start leaving for school or work. He has been making this same commute for more than thirteen years, though only the past few years in the morning. In those thirteen years, he has managed to get two of his kids through high school and one into college. He saved enough to buy a three-bedroom apartment in a duplex. He has a good and stable job. Most of the time he doesn't think about it at all, but every once in a while he remembers that he got his job by chance one night waiting for the #1 train at Fifty-ninth Street. On that night he bumped into Clive, the father of an old classmate of his. Clive was a super in a large apartment building near Seventy-second and Broadway.

Clive's friend was the super in his building where his son worked now, and he had a vacancy. The next day, Allan went over with Clive and nailed the job. It was that easy, and he was that lucky.

But for most people, doorman jobs are hard, almost impossible, to get. At one level, this is simply because of the law of supply and demand. There are a lot of people who could become a doorman. From the outside, the job doesn't seem to require much skill, although we will see later that this is *not exactly* the case. There are no special educational requirements that people need to have to become a doorman. While most doormen need to be able to understand simple things in English, they can get by without complete fluency. Physical strength is not a prerequisite for the position, although the ability to stand for long periods of time is often required. Since most people have sufficient English skills and are able to stand, there are relatively few people who could not be doormen. And the pay is good. The typical doorman earns over $17 an hour. Overtime opportunities are common, and when unionized doormen work overtime, they earn $26 an hour. Work on holidays pays time and a half, and all doormen work on some holidays.[1] So the typical doorman can expect to make roughly $38,000 a year, not counting tips and end-of-year bonuses. As we see later, although the range of tips and bonuses varies significantly across buildings, many doormen report that they receive up to $10,000 a year in tips. Since income from bonuses and tips is not typically reported to the IRS, doormen will take home wages comparable to someone earning $55,000 to $60,000 taxable income per year.

By comparison, doormen earn roughly what an assistant professor of sociology can expect to make in his or her first year of work. They earn more than tenured public school teachers in New York City and roughly 70% more than teachers in their first year of employment. New York City police can expect to make $35,000 in their first year, not counting opportunities for additional earnings. A quick glance at the vacant jobs advertised in the newspaper indicates that doormen can expect to earn more in an average year

---

1. Most doormen work some overtime each week as well, which pays time and a half. There are a number of reasons for this. First, in buildings with twenty-four-hour doorman service, four doormen can work forty-hour weeks and leave just eight hours per week uncovered. Rather than hiring an additional doorman or part-time worker, most buildings simply pay overtime. In the short run, this appears logical, but under normal tenure distributions, amortized across a year, buildings would be wiser to simply hire a fifth man. One reason they may not is that supers have an interest in awarding overtime to doormen, since it is a tangible benefit that they can distribute as they wish, thus garnering doorman loyalty to them, rather than to tenants.

than most clerks, technologists, computer specialists, service managers, and nurses. And relative to the U.S. population as a whole, doormen earnings place them in the top 30% of the income distribution. Another way of saying this is that 70% of Americans earn salaries below those made by doormen. Since entry requirements are few and compensation is high, demand for doorman jobs is greater than supply.

There are more doormen in New York City than taxi drivers, yet it is much harder to get a job as a doorman than a taxi driver, with even fewer explicit job requirements. Just the sheer number of positions does not define a job as hard to get, of course. It is hard to get a job as a professor, on the one hand, because there are not so many professor positions around. So absolute numbers play some role. But something else is going on as well. And the something else is that good jobs are harder to get than bad jobs. Once people get good jobs, they tend to stay in those jobs. This is true for doormen. In our sample, the average doorman had worked in his building for almost ten years. More than a quarter of all the doormen we interviewed had worked in their building for more than ten years. And many of these had worked in another building earlier, also as a doorman. Getting in the door is the hard part. Once in, doormen tend to stay.[2] When asked how long they expect to continue working, most doormen we talked to said they planned on staying in the same building for at least five more years, and many reported that they expected to retire as doormen. Assuming a conservative retirement age of sixty-five, the average doorman in our sample plans to work as a doorman in the same building for at least fifteen years, and many for a quarter of a century or longer.

Comparatively long tenures mean that doorman vacancies are few and far between. Imagine if there were only five times as many people who wanted to be doormen than positions. If, when they finished high school, people got in a queue for the next doorman vacancy, the average wait time to employment would be enormously long. In fact, under the current tenure distribution,

---

2. Readers will perhaps get tired from having to think about selectivity, but here, as elsewhere, it raises its head. As noted above, doormen see their career in terms of a stable job building toward an increasing pension. This vision contributes to their long tenures, on average. But there are many other things going on. First, people who for some reason are predisposed to see careers as a set job extending over a lifetime are more likely to find such jobs attractive. Thus, there will be selectivity on entrance. Second, doormen who enter with different views on the career are more likely to exit; therefore, one observes in the cross section the association between tenure and career association, but it could as easily be produced by either a stable trait of people who become doormen or selectivity pressures once in.

most people in the queue would not ever get a job. And some others would be too old to stand when they were hired and would have to retire immediately. This cannot be going on, since most doormen are typically in their late twenties or early thirties when they get hired. If there were some sort of employment queue, with jobs going to individuals based on how long they waited in the queue, this could not happen — the typical doorman would be hired in his late fifties or early sixties. Most people don't get jobs by waiting in long employment queues, and doormen are no exception. So how do they get into the door? The simple answer is that they have their foot in it already. The doorman market is not a perfectly fair market. To see the process more clearly, we should look at other markets, most of which are also imperfect in some way or another.

MARKETS FOR ORGANS, APARTMENTS, AUTOMOBILES, FRIENDS, AND JOBS

Markets are solutions to matching problems. For job markets, the problem is matching a set of job vacancies with a population of persons with characteristics appropriate for the vacancy. What a fair market would look like would depend on the goals one was trying to maximize. If we tried to maximize equality of opportunity, then job seekers would be selected on the basis of time in the job queue. So long as the characteristics of individuals matched the specified description of the characteristics required for the vacancy, a first come, first served model would suffice to provide equal opportunity. This model is, after all, the kind of model most familiar to us in our everyday life. We expect to buy tickets for shows after the person who has arrived in the queue immediately before us; we line up for ice cream with the expectation that orders will be filled on the basis of time of arrival. When waiting for service at a restaurant, we get upset if a new entrant to the queue gets more attention than us. And so on.

First come, first served works well for undifferentiated products or where matching dynamics are simple. If we queue up to wait in the bus line, we all know that when we get on we will get the same ride (although we may not all get a seat). Likewise, the ice cream we are served just after the previous customer is essentially the same as the ice cream we would have received had we been in line ahead of her. So most often, where products are undifferentiated, we are content enough with first come, first served as a principle of fairness, since it expresses most clearly the ideal of equality of opportunity. Since doorman jobs appear to require little skill (that is, require little differentiation of persons) and since buildings are relatively homogeneous (with respect to the demands of the position), one could imagine that the market could operate formally as a first come, first served market. But it does not, and the reasons are instructive.

Most simply, first come, first served models fail to achieve the substantive ends they are designed to achieve (fairness) for more complex kinds of products, for example, most job matching or the market for human organs. In job matching, though fair with respect to access, first come, first served for good jobs could lead to the true absurdity already noted above; young people would always be in bad jobs, that is, until they aged into (and likely immediately out of) good jobs, and the characteristics of people could not be used to allocate them to positions. It would be a fair system — everyone would have the same chance — but substantively irrational. No one would be happy — neither managers, nor tenants, nor doormen.

Collective unhappiness in first come, first served markets is evident in the even simpler case of the market for human organs. The organ market tends to be organized as a first come, first served market because it is hard to set differential value on persons, and organs are undifferentiated, once type and match compatibility are established. But it is not the case that the people in the organ market are equal with respect to need. In most markets for organs, individuals at different stages of risk enter the queue at the same time. Those with poor prior medical care may be identified as a potential organ recipient late in the course of their illness. Their life expectancy without an organ replacement may be very short, compared to those under the close supervision of a doctor. Likewise, the course of the illness could vary across persons, independent of the quality of prior medical care. Some people may face an aggressive disease, whereas for others, the course of the illness could be significantly slower.

A solution would be to rank individuals with respect to life expectancy, but this would create incentives for doctors to misrepresent the life chances of their patients. Physician honesty would not be rewarded, therefore leading to a tragedy of the commons, since the pressure to define all cases as "severe" would eliminate the real differences between them. Thus, attempts to distinguish individual recipients with respect to need, thereby providing a competing fairness norm to first come, first served, quickly degrades into a first come, first served model, which in turn reproduces the inequalities of the health care system. The process would be fair — people would get organs depending solely on time in the queue — but, as with doorman jobs, it would be irrational.

As complicated as figuring out a fair and rational system for the distribution of donor organs is, the organ market is even simpler than the job market for two reasons. First, the matching problem is really only difficult from the recipient side. That is, equality of opportunity (access) is the only obvious goal to maximize. Within each blood-type set, organs are thought to be homogeneous. This is not the case, of course. Some organs are not as good as others. Some have been handled more poorly after death than others, and some are just less attractive than others because of the way the donor lived. Some are older than others, and all organs certainly vary on unobserved characteristics that only reveal themselves in the future. Organs, in this sense, are like people. They have histories and unlived futures that make them more or less attractive as partners. But it is convenient to think of organs as homogeneous, in part because they are so rare that with respect to the millions of organs that never arrive in the system, they are similar. So the "human capital" distinctions that organs exhibit can be safely ignored. In the world of organs, you take what you can get. This is not really the case for people and jobs. The characteristics of both matter a lot for the market to work substantively.

Organ markets are also simpler than job markets because they are one-shot high-stakes markets. The stakes are high in organ markets because once used in a transplant, organs cannot be reused, that is, sent out on the market again. If they stick — that is, if the transplant works — the vacancy is always filled. If organs could be reused — like jobs, automobiles, friends, and the other kinds of things around which markets emerge — a much more difficult problem would crop up: the problem of lemons. Imagine if this happened with organs. Organs that failed upon transplant would be reentered into the market. Assuming that some proportion of the failures were because the organ was no good, good organs would stay with the new recipient and bad organs would cycle through multiple users (presumably failing at an increased rate as they decayed). More people would get organs, but their common experience would be that they were lemons.[3] From both sides of the matching problem, matching persons to jobs and matching jobs to persons,

---

3. A somewhat different dynamic takes place for limited-engagement shows. Because the "good" in question is a fixed quantity, like an organ — a specific performance where the star is present for only one night — one cannot observe the self-fulfilling dynamic associated with "lemon markets."

lemon markets are easily induced, especially when first come, first served is the ideal.

Lemon markets are common for goods that can cycle through multiple owners. The most obvious examples are markets for apartments, automobiles, and friends. It has long been known in New York City that looking through classified advertisements for apartments is not going to help you find a good apartment. Many apartments that are vacant simply never come on to the market at all. They are passed on from friend to friend or relative to relative, often for generations. This is especially true of the good apartments. So, in general, the apartments that circulate tend to be bad apartments, or at least not great ones. Consequently, a market for lemons emerges. From the employers' perspective, the problem is not hiring "lemon workers." If people have equal access to jobs and lemon workers last less long in positions than "good workers," the typical unemployed job searcher could be a lemon. At least this is the fear.

The market for apartments in New York City is instructive. The typical apartment that one sees without inside information is likely to be a lemon in the same way that the market for used cars tends to be saturated with lemons or a market of organs would tend to be saturated with organs that don't work if organs could circulate. First, the basic mechanism is the same: people will try to move out of bad apartments just as they try to sell bad cars. In contrast, if they get a good organ, apartment, or car, they tend to keep it. So, on average, the quality of used apartments and cars on the open market is lower than the overall distribution of cars and apartments in the population. Second, the worse the car (or the apartment) is, the shorter its tenure with a particular owner. Thus, real lemons tend to circulate even more rapidly than marginal lemons. The lesson for searchers is that when searching for cars or apartments, the best strategy is to try to exploit inside information to avoid getting a lemon. Typically, this inside information comes from social networks. And the best kind of information is a recommendation from a friend. Not because friends are good judges, necessarily, but because friends have an incentive to make sure that you don't get a bad shake because of them. If employers are searching for workers, the substantively rational

---

But fixed quantities provide the reason that people say you have to "be someone" in New York to get to see concerts, because if you are not "someone" and have to wait for the advertisement in the paper to hear about the show, it will be sold out. To "be someone" really means to know someone, which is to be in a position to get information about a scarce good, like hard-to-find tickets or scarce organs.

thing for them to do is ask friends. And for people looking for jobs or supers looking to hire doormen, the same is also true.

The market for new friends also tends to produce contact with "lemons," and consequently the common experience is that the first friendships one makes in a new community tend to be short-lived. The mechanism is the same. Think about the people who have time to meet new people. The less interesting and nice they are, the less likely they are to have friends. Since they have few friends, they have more spare time. Ipso facto, they are more likely to be around with free time to meet newcomers. In this sense, just like cars and apartments, these "lemon" friends tend to circulate rapidly, relying on the social needs of newcomers, who have not yet had time to establish the kinds of friendships they want.[4]

Friend markets are actually closer to job markets, mainly because both sides of the matching process are actively involved in the construction of the match. One of the ironies of friend markets is that while the "lemon" friends could find each other and become friends, their characteristics (the fact that they are more likely to be boring and intolerant, for example) are especially unappealing to other boring and intolerant people. So while they meet, they avoid each other. In the same way, bad jobs don't easily find matches with bad workers. In fact, there are good reasons to expect that bad workers last less long in bad jobs than good workers. This means that both bad jobs and bad workers tend to circulate more, one of the reasons why one can observe vacancies and unemployment at the same time.[5] Because there tend to be more bad jobs and bad workers floating around, good jobs and good workers must distinguish themselves in order to make the right match.

This is the case for doorman positions, which are good jobs looking for good workers. When matching on both sides is an issue — as it is for doorman positions, where employers have preferences for good workers and employees have preferences for good jobs, for example — both sides will actively

---

4. This was likely the experience of people who used dating services to meet partners before such services became more legitimized. If only losers participate in these kinds of markets, and losers are as discriminating as "winners," they will never find anyone who fits the bill, but instead cycle through new people in short-duration relationships, thereby defining themselves as losers — that is, people who have not been able to sustain a relationship.

5. The imagery above suggests a static world in which nothing changes, that is, a world in which actors are insensitive to their environment. Bad friends can become good friends by virtue of the friendship. Likewise, since an element of the definition of a good worker is tenure, individuals who in some environments appear as bad workers may, in another, become "good," that is, stay. This will in turn enhance their opportunities for other jobs, at least in the medium term.

engage in search strategies that exploit inside information. This means that they will forgo simple formal systems that enhance equality of opportunity, like first come, first served. Instead, the market is made through shortcuts — through social ties. In labor markets, the benefit from exploiting inside information gives them a peculiar characteristic, which is that most jobs are impossible to get for most applicants and ridiculously easy to get for some. They are easy for those who have their foot a bit in the door. This is the nature of the doorman job market, and the key elements to understand are the dynamics associated with information networks on each side of the matching equation.

INFORMATION NETWORKS AND SEARCH PROCESSES

There is a large sociological literature on information networks and job search processes that we can draw from. From the side of employees searching for positions, Mark Granovetter conducted a foundational study in 1973. In a famous article called "The Strength of Weak Ties" and in his book *Getting a Job*, Granovetter shows that "weak ties," network relationships that people have with acquaintances and friends, play a large role in the job acquisition process. Over the past quarter of a century, hundreds of other articles and studies have supported his early findings across a diverse set of occupations and social contexts. There are really two independent mechanisms going on that help us understand why ties make a difference for job seekers and employers alike. The first mechanism operates on the information side and is principally relevant to job seekers. The second mechanism involves trust and is more salient for employers.

First, consider information. The easiest framework is where information is relevant in only one direction, for example, the problem of people searching for apartments in sellers' markets, without the complication of apartments simultaneously searching for people to occupy them. But most jobs, and especially most good jobs, are not like apartments. That is, jobs are not simply positions that "hold" persons. Jobs, unlike apartments, have preferences for specific people.[6] Thus, job markets are more complex

---

6. Apartments can also have preferences for specific kinds of people, especially cooperatives, which set specific income and "stability" standards for potential owners. These standards often operate to block access to buildings by minorities or other persons considered undesirable. Even Madonna, for example, was turned down by one cooperative.

than apartment markets because employers want to make good matches. If searchers benefit from networks, employers have good reasons as well to prefer informal networks as a source for potential employees. The simple reason is that they can trust the information they receive from someone they know (a current worker). If a current worker in the firm recommends some-one, the employer can be fairly certain that the recommendation is solid. First, because people who care about their job are not likely to recommend people that they do not themselves have faith in and, second, because people tend to know people who have similar values and orientations as they do. Just as "slack" people are likely to have slack friends, hard workers are likely to have hardworking friends.

Next, consider trust. We do not trust complete strangers, and we do trust people whom we know extremely well and whose values we share. The interesting aspect of weak ties is that they rest between these two extreme poles. Consider a simple example involving three people whose small worlds slightly overlap. All three are friends and associate with people like themselves. On the borders of each small world, they overlap with individuals in the adjacent "world," but the ties that connect them are few and far between. The sparseness of the overlap is what makes information known in one world (say, A) meaningful for individuals in an adjacent world (B or C). But the fact that the worlds are decoupled indicates that there is a possibility for each to be characterized by different sets of norms, values, and orientations. The individuals in world C, while somewhat similar to those in B, have no overlap with those in A. Consequently, if C hears about a job in A from B (and is therefore a "friend of a friend," or perhaps a "friend of a friend of a friend"), the basis for trust is weakened. Weak ties may provide information, but out on the margins of extended networks, the quality of information (about the job and about the person) is likely to be lower.

The twin dynamics of trust and information are in tension with each other. Information diffuses rapidly across great social distances. The further information flows, the lower the trust one can place in it and, consequently, the less valuable it is. Nowhere is this tension between information and trust more evident than in the search strategies that individuals engage in to obtain illegal services. In her book *Search for an Abortionist*,[7] written

---

7. Women's networks tend to be more locally dense than men's because women tend to have historically limited access to professional occupations whose associations often served as effective

just before Granovetter's *Getting a Job*, Nancy Howell Lee shows that when abortion was illegal, women searching for an abortionist who searched down long paths (spanning many small worlds) received information of lower quality than those who searched within closer networks. Jobs are not like abortionists. Vacancies in firms remain vacancies until they are filled, no matter how many people know about them. Abortionists, when abortion was illegal, did not have the same luxury. If too many people knew about them, they were likely to be arrested or to have moved elsewhere. Consequently, the more distant the source of information about an abortionist, the more likely it was that many other people had access to the same information and the less useful it was.

Equally critical in determining outcomes was the quality of information received. Women whose informants came from worlds quite distant from theirs had a harder time evaluating the quality of the information they did get. For women concerned about safety and medical support, quality of information was absolutely critical. Lee shows that as path length grew — as women used referrals from friends of friends of friends, for example — the disparity between their own expectations and the care that they received increased. This follows logically from the fact that such information arose in distant small worlds, characterized by less overlap in values and attitudes. As source distance increases, comparability in values and orientations decreases.[8]

Only bad cars and bad apartments need to look for people to fill them. The same is true for jobs. If the job is good, employers can be choosy about whom they hire. The best applicants come to them already tied to someone they know (or someone whom they know knows), consequently employers can utilize the information from referrals to make their choice. For this reason, the hypothesis that people find good jobs when they have

---

bridges between distant (geographically) individuals, and in part because they lose distant ties at marriage following adoption of their husband's name.

8. Similar dynamics can be observed in other searches for illegal goods. In the absence of informal networks, men seeking prostitutes, or people seeking drugs, run an increased risk of arrest from police posing as prostitutes or suppliers. Consequently, the vast majority of arrests resulting from sting operations capture the naive users. Such stings only infrequently trap those who have greater contacts in the shadowy underground economy — those with greater experience and deeper inside connections. They look good in the news, but because only the naive get caught, have little impact on the traffic they are trying to interdict.

access to inside information because the information is useful to both sides of the matching process fits for our context — getting a job as a doorman. But the reliance on inside information has unfortunate consequences at the macro-level, even if employers and employees are happy about the match.

THE TWO SIDES OF THE INSIDER'S MARKET: CHANCE AND SHORT QUEUES

A quick glance at the employment section of any weekly newspaper provides evidence that doorman positions are only rarely posted in open searches. Even jobs that are advertised are filled long before they hit the newsstand. Less than a handful of the doormen in our sample heard about their job from an advertisement. Almost no one who fills in an application or drops a résumé off gets hired as a doorman. For everyone who is not already a doorman, these jobs are extremely hard to get. But for doormen, the typical experience is that getting hired was simple, involving a little bit of luck and nothing else. How can this be?

If only a few got their jobs by applying, the vast majority of doormen in our sample got their jobs through relatives or friends. At first glance more surprising, most of them didn't even set out to be doormen, and, consequently, many of them report not having to search at all for their job. In fact, when asked to describe how they got their job, chance plays a crucial role in their stories. Chance as a rhetoric is the underside of "the strength of weak ties" scenario, and it is quite commonly deployed. Here I provide just a few examples. For instance, Alex, who has been working only six months in his current building, describes how he got his job:

> I got the job through a friend of mine. He's the residential manager of the building, so he's a friend of mine for a long time, so that's how I got the job. I really didn't go out looking for the job. He offered me the job, so I just took it. I didn't have a job before that, so I really had no choice but to take the job.

Not looking for a job, Alex, who is known to be unemployed by his friend, just happens to be offered a job as a doorman. Tartan, a doorman working in the Village for the past two months, describes the way he got his job. The same element of chance appears as central; in the background lies the fact that Tartan's cousin Nab was a super. As with Alex, Tartan wasn't looking for a job, but the opportunity seemed too good to pass up.

> My cousin Nab is the super, and I was getting out of work for UPS and it was about twelve in the afternoon and I was on the West Side Highway and I saw my cousin drive by. I told my brother to follow the car, because he was probably going to Staten Island. So I jumped in his car — we had seen him, so I said, "Where are you going?" and he was like, "I am going to Staten Island." So I jumped in his car and he said, "Hey, cousin, do you want a job?" I was like, "Where?" He said, "Doorman in my building, four to twelve in the evening." I was like, "All right," since I work UPS in the morning, eight to twelve, I had time. I wanted to do it since I had nothing else to do. So I got the job. I went home and he was like, "Let's go, you got to get to work." It was just spur of the moment that I got this job.

The same seemingly chance element is reflected by Emilio, a doorman working in Midtown for the past three years:

> Well, basically it was through a friend. He and I had been working together for a couple of years. I was working at a restaurant, and I wasn't making much money and working my butt off, and he said, "Why don't you apply for a summer position over here?" He goes, "I know you and I know you'd do well here, so why don't you come on over and take the interview?" And I did. Pretty simple. It was a matter of ten minutes before they said, "When can you start?"

Sam tells a similar story:

> It was a fluke. . . . [S]o anyway, I was out of work and a friend of mine was a super over at Fifth Avenue — he's at [building address] — and he knew the super that I work for now. So he said, "Listen, I've [got] a friend that is looking for a job, do you have any openings in your building?" So [he] must have said, "Yeah, send him over," or whatever, so I went there and interview[ed], and that same day the guy was like, "Get some work clothes," and put me to work that evening. I literally had to have my wife come down and give me a change of clothes 'cause I was in a business suit, you know, it was really crazy.

The same process, reliance on information passing through informal weak ties, seems to have been going on for a long time. Reflecting on how he got his job in 1983, Seymour says:

> I had, used to have, a business, a restaurant. And one time there was a superintendent who I know personally . . . and he asked me if I would help him out . . . because many times the people he is supervising don't show up or they are like drunk or they used money on whatever and it was very hard on him. And of course, I said, "I would help you with that," and I was just ending that and did things, and didn't know what happened . . . and, so I helped out and within that week he needed me four times and in the next, second week, five times, so it was like nearly every day, like, "Oh, could you come in?" One time he has another supervisor working for the same company who somebody is going to retire and for some time he needs help, so what happened was the guy never came back and it turned into a full-time job. I didn't know, I thought I was going to go over, but he never came back, so I, seventeen years later, closed my business and now. . . .

Only in some rare cases did doormen in our sample describe waiting to get a job. Tyler did have to wait, for what seems like a long time. He knew some supers casually; eventually one of them had a vacancy he could fill.

> I have a friend who I've actually known for about five years. It took me about three years to get the job 'cause there were no openings at the time.

As in most instances, Tyler got his job through social relations. Perhaps oddly, since it seems so clear in the aggregate, most doormen don't focus on their exploitation of information networks in accounting for how they got their job. Here, and elsewhere, we observe a strange duality. As noted above, chance provides the main rhetorical device through which doormen describe how they got their job. Should we believe these accounts? When people tell stories of how they became something, chance often figures as a primary narrative element of the account. In Tyler's case, for example, left out of the story, since it is a story of how he became a doorman, are all the searches and conversations with others about other kinds of jobs that he might have gotten but did not, the false leads and failed applications. Instead, we hear the story of just what happened, the unique set of events and circumstances that led to his job as a doorman. These just-so stories are necessarily idiosyncratic. Left out of the account are the larger social processes at work that make "chance" systematically possible.

As indicated above, one of these larger social processes is "the strength of weak ties" model, operating beyond the level of individuals and structuring individual experience in such a way as to induce narratives of chance. In this instance, the relevant mechanism is the information/trust network of social relations. Whereas each individual narrates only the chance encounter with a friend or the lucky break that brought him news about a vacancy, what we observe is systematic utilization of weak ties. But there is more. Critically important is the social structuring of social relationships along the fault lines of race and ethnicity. The fact of social structure acts as a channel for information and trust, making opportunities available for some while blocking opportunities for others. The network referral process rests itself within a larger context defined by macro-level patterning in the structure of social relations. Class and ethnicity largely shape this structure, and so the macro-level structuring of social relations produces in this and other contexts the labor-market segregation by race and ethnicity we often observe. If friends are co-ethnics and referrals from friends and relatives are critical for getting a job, hiring within co-ethnic networks will result. At the macro-level, such dynamics induce systematic bias.

Recall that earlier I suggested that dynamics are revealed at the intersection of two views — here provided by models and accounts, or upper-side and underside views. If we think about the model view, the dynamic operating in the doorman market is similar to that observed for other occupational sectors. By focusing on the job acquisition process, we can see that both sides of the matching process — doormen and employers — benefit from exploitation of social ties. Employers benefit because they can make better decisions. Employees benefit when they get jobs because their network opens doors otherwise closed. For occupations like doormen where there is a vast gulf between the formal requirements of the job (capacity to stand, speak English, open doors, etc.) and the actual requirements (discretion, good theorizing, capacity to absorb stress and manage priorities, etc.), network referrals that maximize on trust and quality of information are critically important.

While the mechanics of getting a job reveal network processes, doormen's stories are stories of chance. The underside view is thus of chance. The simple reason that chance accounts predominate is because network dynamics appear and are experienced as chance. Recall that a weak tie connects an individual to some other social world. Chance is the underside of weak ties, because a weak tie is a random network tie that crosses small worlds. There are always ties and there are always opportunities. Sometimes ties activate opportunities of little interest. I may through a weak tie learn about a job as a waiter, but since the job is of no interest (now), I ignore the activation. Likewise, news about vacancies for specific kinds of jobs filters through a wide array of ties. Only the chance matching of ties and opportunities and persons capable of acting on the opportunity induce an actual job.[9]

As indicated above, the recruitment via network mechanism, while solving matching problems in markets for jobs, induces other patterned regularities, some of them not normatively attractive, for example, systematic inequalities in job access along the fault lines of race, ethnicity, and gender. Hence there is a natural duality of understanding, the understanding that arises from individual experience (which is the element of chance) and the understanding that arises from systematic playing out of structuring mechanisms. The latter is meaningful sociologically only if it makes sense of the former.

CO-ETHNIC NETWORKS AND THE JOB ALLOCATION PROCESS

How does chance at the individual level induce bias at the macro-level? Why does it matter *how* doormen are hired for the job that they do? First, consider what rules structure hiring in principle, since all job matches work through or around these rules. The most basic rule is that individuals cannot be denied employment for reasons unrelated to the position, for example, their gender, age, race, weight, or ethnicity. This rule is encoded in affirmative action and equal opportunity legislation.

---

9. One way to integrate upper-side and underside views is the garbage can model, first described for the matching of problems and solutions and personnel in complex organizations. The point is that while both views, upstream and downstream, model and account, look different, one can see how both reveal, Rashomon-like, elements of the whole not otherwise seen. Cf. Cohen, March, and Olsen, "A Garbage Can Model of Organizational Choice." In simple terms, the model considers how when problems and solutions are generated independently by personnel, they "find" each other by mixing in a garbage can. The key insight is that organizations generate solutions to problems that do not yet exist and problems for solutions that have yet to be found. Personnel are problem or solution "mobilizers," and all three need to be connected for a solution to work on a problem. Mixing in the garbage can is the chance element. In the same way, here we have vacancies (problems) looking for persons (solutions) through the mobilization of personnel (networks referrals).

Equal opportunity guidelines govern the posting of vacancies so that all people, of whatever race and ethnicity, have a putatively equal opportunity to apply for and be considered for a position. Despite these formal rules, circumvention of fair employment practices is common, and such circumvention takes a number of distinct forms. In most job markets, equal opportunity guidelines are formally followed scrupulously. Most large firms have human relations departments that concentrate, among other tasks, on assuring compliance to hiring guidelines established by the state and federal government. While slavishly adhering to formal standards for comparison of candidates, most hiring decisions are justified ex post facto using litigation-proof phrasing that allows employers to make a positive selection of the candidate they prefer the most.[10]

Formal applications provide employers with material from which to ex post facto justify hiring decisions that may be otherwise difficult to account for. Consequently, most vacancies for positions are associated with formal applications, and doorman positions are not an exception to this general rule. But even the doormen see the applications as window dressing. For the most part, they see through the *formal* nature of the hiring process. As Abram notes:

> Yeah, people apply for a certain position, but usually people come in through, you know, [a] connection. Like, you know this guy and this guy, and then the boss will ask somebody, you know, I called this other super up and he had somebody. It's all connected. It all has to do with connections. They don't even get people no more that apply. It's like people know the other super in the building and he's like, "Do you have anybody there who could come over here and . . . can work for us?" or "Do you know anybody . . . ?" That's how it is now. You could go to the managing office and apply and get interviewed and stuff like that, but you know somebody, you're in, so that's how it is.

---

10. For example, employers are instructed to use such phrases as "The selected candidate demonstrated better verbal skills" over a more honest, but not so litigation-resistant phrase such as "The candidate did not speak proper English" in completing required human relations forms for potential audit. Likewise, rejecting a candidate because they interviewed in sloppy attire — "The candidate looked messy during the interview" — is less desirable than the statement "The selected candidate demonstrated experience working in a professional setting," and so on. But beyond this, as Peterson, Saporta, and Seidel, "Offering a Job," have shown, even non-discriminatory hiring practices can appear to be discriminatory at the aggregate level if ethnicity is consolidated with fit for position. This can occur when, for example, one ethnic group follows a narrower set of opportunities than another.

Still, there is often some confusion. Whereas Abram was pretty sure that his application was an unnecessary element of the process, other doormen are less clear about how they got hired. Carl, for example, initially suggests that he got the job because he filled out an application. But with very little probing, a different account quickly emerges.

Q. How did you get a job as a doorman?

A. How? Well, actually you have to apply. You can go to the main office or you can speak to the super, and if there's any positions available, then I guess, you know, you're hired. They'll hire you. They'll test you for like ninety days. And if they feel that you're good for the job, then they'll keep you.

Q. Did you have any family connections — for becoming a doorman?

A. Not really, but there are friends. Close friends that I knew for a long time.

Q. Who were doormen?

A. Yeah, doorman and actually the super I knew for a long time and stuff so . . . that helped. That helped a lot.[11]

Eric describes the process of getting a job roughly six years ago. Recommended by a friend, he filled out an application (knowing there was a vacancy) and was hired immediately afterward.

Originally, I was recommended by a friend; by a friend that works here. I came. I had an interview. I came and I put in an application. I filled out an application, and then they called me back, and then I came to work. I started.

As noted above, employers have good reasons to prefer to hire individuals they know or who are recommended by current employees or others whose opinion they have good reason to trust. People who come with personal recommendations are, on average, likely to be better employees than individuals who show up in response to a posted job listing. In fact, there are good reasons to imagine that individuals referred to positions without personal ties may be black sheep. So, all things being equal, superintendents

---

11. Here the question was about how Carl got his job, but it is initially answered in terms of how one might get a job, generically, even though he got the job through weak ties.

will strongly prefer to hire doormen through interpersonal networks. This is also the case for men who are recommended for new postings by the union. While the union does at times try to post individuals to positions, they also prefer it if new positions are filled by people close to current union members. As Jordan says:

> But in actuality, I think in the job field, it's pretty much become now that people get in by word of mouth. I mean, now in my case, I happen to know the board of directors from the people who are managing the building, so it was a personal friend sort of thing. So, and usually, that's how it works . . . or relatives. In fact, I think that the union fairly encourages that because they feel that if you're recommending someone you know, that's, that might be a designation for being a better person rather than just taking a stranger from the general union hall, and then you don't know what you're getting. And I think, in an unspoken way, I think there's [a] general tendency by union members to think that if you're being called from that union hall, it's just like "Mmm, there's the loser." And that's generally who they are; they're generally the ones that end up in trouble with the tenants and get into litigation, and always are between jobs and they're waiting for pending legalities, and so now they're open again, you know.

The union shares many of the same motivations as employers. The union seeks workers who are likely to be predisposed to join and, perhaps more critically, to support them in job actions associated with contract renegotiations. But the union, while interested in placing its members, does not want independent thinkers or troublemakers who might end up either challenging union policy, in litigation with tenants or in arbitration hearings with building management. Thus, the union is happy to support those friends of members in good standing who get recommendations. Consequently, if union members refer friends and family to vacant positions, they can be more confident that if hired, these individuals will, as their friends have, join the union.

ETHNIC AND RACIAL INEQUALITIES

Neither the union nor the superintendents who hire doormen need to set out to systematically discriminate against ethnic and racial minorities in order to generate inequalities in access to positions. There is no reason to believe that building superintendents are any less racist than ordinary citizens living in an ethnically diverse city. But whether they are prejudiced or not, hiring through interpersonal networks will generate inequalities in the racial and ethnic composition of doormen if there are inequalities in the ethnic and racial composition of superintendents.

Almost by definition, hiring relatives means hiring co-ethnics. Because friendships tend to be structured along lines of race and ethnicity, hiring friends has the same effect. Serban, a doorman who has worked on Park Avenue for the past quarter of a century, describes the process:

> Years ago there was a lot of Irish and it's an immigrant job, you know. I'm not saying all of them are, but a large majority are immigrant jobs. Years ago it used to be all Irish, and now it's all South American. You see a lot of South Americans. Mostly you see South Americans. Well, it all depends. When I first came here, they had a Romanian super and most of the people that worked here were Romanian. And now we have a Spanish super and most of the people, almost all of the people working here are Spanish. And that's the way it goes. And that building across the street there, that's an Irish super and all the guys working there are Irish. [Pointing to another building near his] This building over here, this guy, the super over here might be born in this country because that building seems to be very mixed. There's no, you know, [. . . it's a] very mixed group. There's no one particular race.

There is some evidence that Eastern Europeans increasingly control the building service industry. Isaac, who emigrated from Hungary in 1990 and who has worked as a doorman on the Upper East Side for the past nine years, describes the ethnic sorting process that got him a job, in response to a general question about his employment history.

> The very first one [job], a moving company . . . in Harlem. And the second one was a beauty salon. I worked as a handyman, and then I was unemployed, because they laid me off. Then I got this job through the Hungarian Mafia. . . . When I say Hungarian Mafia, I mean other Hungarians. You know, it's interesting, how each ethnic group finds its own place. Koreans end up in fruit stands in grocery stores. Pakistanis and Indians end up in newsstands. Eastern Europeans end up in buildings. Like Albanians, Polish people, Hungarians end up working in service. . . . Those are traditional jobs. So I got into contact

with a Hungarian friend who I met in a refugee camp in Austria. . . .
[He told him about a Hungarian who worked as a super.] That's how
I got this job, the superintendent in that building [across the street],
he's Hungarian, and I didn't know him. So I went to him and talked
to him. I asked him if he had an opening and he didn't, but he did
know this place, and it had an opening. That's what I meant by the
Hungarian Mafia. It's legal, but they give you advice. It's the same thing
with Albanians.

Although Isaac's building is disproportionately Hungarian (as is the
building across the street), there are some buildings where the ethnic
composition of doormen is more varied, as Serban suggests. The variance,
though, may be limited to a specific region. Sebastian, a doorman who has
worked in Midtown on the East Side for seven years, describes his coworkers
as "a little bit of everything. Jamaican, Trinidad, Peru." This is a little bit of
everything within the scope of the Monroe Doctrine. Similarly, one building
in the Upper West Side has two Pakistani and one Indian doorman. The
building next door to it has an Hispanic super. Three of the four doormen
are Hispanic. The world is much larger, though, then these regional clusters
would suggest.

It is possible, of course, that building homogeneity with respect to ethnicity is not associated with inequalities in overall access. If hiring decisions,
operating through informal friendship and co-ethnic networks, spanned the
entire distribution of the New York City population, every building could be
populated with just one ethnic group, yet the whole population of doormen
would be unbiased. This is not the case, however. Whole sections of the
ethnic New York City community are left out of doorman positions entirely.
The most notable absences are from the East, followed by the large Islamic
community.

When asked if he knew any Chinese doormen, Sebastian said:

No. Not any Chinese doormen. No. To be honest, I don't know. Maybe,
it's not. I don't know. Maybe they were not introduced to that field, or
something. I don't really know really.

It is reasonable for him to not know any. Out of the 250 or so doormen
we talked to, only one identified himself as Chinese, Korean, or Japanese.
In contrast, just to select a few countries of origin, 7 each were born in
Colombia, Guyana, and the Dominican Republic; 5 each in Ireland, Kosovo,

Albania, Hungary, and Poland; and 14 in Puerto Rico. While there are sub-stantial Dominican, Puerto Rican, and Colombian ethnic communities in New York City, there are also significant numbers of Chinese and Koreans. In recent years, the ethnic Muslim community has expanded rapidly in New York City, but there are few Muslim doormen. They do not become doormen because they are not "introduced to the field." Instead, one often finds them in the taxi business, both yellow and gypsy. But what does it mean to be "introduced to the field"? And why do we observe such strong ethnic-based structuring of opportunity? The answer lies in large part with the supers.[12]

SUPERS

As Clinton Scott, super for an Upper West Side building, said when hiring the first black doorman at his building, "I figured, I'm black, we're here, so why not hire blacks, but when I got rid of a Spanish guy I hired another Spanish guy in his place. I didn't want anyone to think I was prejudiced."[13]

The critical players in the introduction game are the supers, who wield almost dictatorial authority over their buildings, employees, and — if some tenants are to be believed — the tenants as well. The simple answer to the ethnic-based opportunity structure is that supers, who make most hir-ing decisions, were at one time doormen. It follows that the distribution of doormen with respect to race and ethnicity twenty years ago provides a relatively accurate picture of the distribution of supers today; likewise, the distribution of doormen today *may* provide an accurate forecast of the distribution of supers in the next generation.[14] Consequently, shifts in the

---

12. There is a large literature on co-ethnic occupational enclaves, of which this is a partial example. Since this is an instantiation of a more general process, the goal here is not to account for the general process by focusing on the structure of social relations at the macro-level, but rather on the micro-dynamics of the hiring process. For the former, cf. Waldinger, *Still the Promised City?*

13. Roberts, "In Manhattan, Black Doormen Are Rare Breed."

14. While the pathway to becoming a super has typically involved some time as a doorman, this avenue of upward mobility may be breaking down as the super's job becomes increasingly administrative. It is also the case that predicting ethnic composition of supers in the future from current ethnic composition (presuming ethnic-blind promotion rates to super from the current generation) may not be a good strategy. Black doormen may not become supers at a comparable rate to those from East Europe, in much the same way that black ball players are not as likely to become coaches as their white counterparts.

ethnic composition of doormen will be glacial — a product of long-term demographic shifts in the distribution of new immigrant groups to the city and shifting opportunities for those in more established immigrant groups. Since the interpersonal networks of supers tend to be dominated by members of their own ethnic group, most hiring tends to be within group, rather than across. This inward-looking view is accentuated by the fact that supers disproportionately live in the buildings they supervise. Consequently, they are largely insulated from larger demographic pressures that lead to long-term transformations of ethnic communities. Thus, supers may have narrower frames of reference than other co-ethnics of similar status.[15]

Supers may strongly prefer in-group hiring, but they are savvy enough to avoid the appearance of pure preferential hiring on the basis of ethnicity; so every doorman is formally hired through an application process. But it is a process with a known outcome. From each doorman's perspective, some lucky combination of chance encounters led to their getting a job. From a systemic view, a strong preference for hiring within interpersonal networks induces striking ethnic segregation. This segregation produces not just two employment classes — a distinction between those who are in and those who are out — but numerous micro-markets, one for each small ethnic segment. Within each micro-segment, small friendship networks determine which doormen get jobs. And all those individuals in the wrong segment who carefully fill out applications are unlikely to be hired for the simple reason that they have weaker recommendations. As Vartan says, those who make decisions are not really paying much attention to the formal hiring process:

> Well, the only job that I worked before this one, I got it because of my friend, the residential manager. I got connections, the management office told him they need someone over here and they got me, so I didn't even apply. Well, actually I did apply for the job, but it's not like I got interviewed or anything. They sent me there, that's it. It's like, people who do apply they really don't care about, if you go apply actually and you don't know anybody and you go apply for a job, it's like they take your application, but they're not going to really care about it because all these guys have people already. It's like all right, my

---

15. The idea is that because supers live in predominantly white neighborhoods, they have less contact with new immigrant groups, who through processes of neighborhood succession expose the older immigrants to new cultures, viz., the expansion of Dominicans into Harlem, and so on.

boss, he needs somebody, he'll call one of his friends, like super guys in other buildings, and be like, "Hey, I need somebody, do you know anybody that's out?" . . . That's how people get in.

This process, in a nutshell, accounts for one of the facts we started with. Most people who would like to become a doorman don't have a chance, whereas those who do become doormen tend to get their jobs easily because their feet were already in the door when they came to apply. Since most hiring is done within co-ethnic networks, some people are shut out of the system entirely, while others have breezy access. With respect to access, network dynamics induce a formally unfair market, since the basic principles of first come, first served are replaced with insider information. While formally unfair, it leads to substantively rational outcomes, in contrast, for example, to the market for organs, which leads to substantively irrational macro-level outcomes. Supers can't take chances with doormen, for if they do, they are likely to have a revolving door. Where tenure is key to job performance, the only substantively rational basis for decisions are those with more information. The problem lies not with the operation of the information system per se, but with the biased access to information that supers have.

OVERVIEW

It is very difficult to get a job like this. You have to know someone that knows someone, connections. A lot of people ask me how can I get a job like this? It is not easy, you have to know someone who is in the building or know someone.

Doormen jobs are good jobs to get, and doormen stay in them for a long time. Most doormen get their jobs without looking for them, and seemingly quickly. They fall into them, apparently by chance, or so it seems to them as they narrate their accounts of becoming a doorman. But this narration is somewhat naive. Individuals experience chance events, but chance is the product of social structure. In this case, the structuring element is the search process used by employees and employers to make a match in the market. These search processes operate within informal networks of kinship, friendship, and co-ethnicity. These informal networks give rise to systematic opportunities for some individuals and blocked access to others. Those positioned to exploit their personal networks do so seamlessly and with apparent ease. Those on the outside, looking to get their foot into the door, get a chilly reception. They may complete applications, wear nice suits when they show up for interviews, demonstrate great understanding of the requirements of the job, and so on. But they are unlikely to get hired. Does that mean that the market for doormen is not fair? Does the structure of the market subsequently influence what doormen do? And is the market structure irrational and if so, for whom?

One kind of formally fair market for doormen would be one in which vacancies across all positions were posted on arrival and matched to persons whose applications are ordered by date of arrival. Here, all individuals would have equal opportunity to become doormen. Formally fair restrictions could still be introduced. For example, only persons meeting some set of predetermined qualifications could be allowed to occupy positions in the queue for jobs. People who could not stand, people who could not speak English, and people who could not be friendly (for example) could be removed from the list. Even with such caveats, such a market would be fair, but it would be irrational. The only doormen who would be hired would be old. Their average tenure in each building would be correspondingly short. Consequently, their attachment to the building would be low, since they would be almost out the door when they got in it. And a separate market for supers would have to develop, with different skills, since too few doormen could age into positions as supers.

Just as bad, supers would have to hire individuals on the basis of their paper qualifications, in a context where the paper qualifications are only weakly associated with fit for the job. Most people can open doors; but few people can do so consistently for twenty years in good spirits. Most people can remember the names of their friends. But few people can remember the names and faces of people who are friends of people that they serve. Most people can keep a secret every now and then, but few people can store secrets of possibly hundreds of people with whom they are, at some level, only tenuously tied. So, it turns out that the actual characteristics of the doorman job — here considered only as the mismatch between formal qualifications and substantive activities — must play some role in the hiring process. And if this is the case, the critical elements must be those that are unobservable on paper. Such qualities are best ascertained through personal recommendations, which are only useful if they are trustworthy. Trust, in turn, requires commonality of experience and expectation — and such commonality is the product of close-knit networks, which are invariably ethnically and racially segregated. So supers are rational to hire within ethnic networks, where possible, or so they see it. But their rationality gives rise to significant inequalities in opportunity and the strange fact that the doorman job is absurdly easy to get for some people and completely impossible for others. Granovetter showed that weak ties matter in the job acquisition process, and it is hard to not notice the macro-level biases in occupational attainment that characterize American society. Here, by focusing on a single case, we can see how the micro-process is tightly linked to and responsible for the macro-structure we observe. Equally interesting, though, is that those who experience the benefits of such linkage (by getting a job) or the costs of such linkage (by being shut out of the labor market) tend to theorize their outcome in terms of chance.

Why does how doormen get jobs matter? Does the job acquisition process and its macro- and micro-outcomes matter for what doormen do? The answer is yes, and this is the topic we consider next. Once in the door, what do doormen do? Why is it important that they stay so long in the same building? What kind of problems do they confront? Does their job turn out to be complicated and stressful, requiring sensitivity and often deep insight into navigating complex social waters uniquely shaped by the contradictory demands of personal closeness and vast social distance? Or is it something that just about anyone can do? These are three issues I consider in the subsequent chapters.

CHAPTER 3

Serving Time

What do I like the least? The stress, it's very stressful. I have been here quite awhile, it's a stressful, stressful job, and it can get really very stressful. If you don't know what you are doing on the door, you could really screw up.

[This is] basically a job for a lazy person. . . . Well, you'd be surprised. Basically, you could dress a monkey up in this outfit and as long as he could open up that door and open up the other door, they're set, you know? That is the fact. Because, I mean, it really doesn't take any intelligence to do this. All it takes is repetition.

U p on the Upper West Side, it is four in the afternoon on a beautiful early spring day. Doormen are standing in front of their buildings. Across the street, kids play in the park, their parents or nannies sitting on benches talking, one supposes, about this and that. Joggers and dog walkers and bicyclists pass by. Back in front of the buildings, nothing appears to be happening. A couple of doormen have left their posts and traversed the seventy-five feet or so that separates them, meeting in the middle. They converse, often looking back at their door. One or two smoke a cigarette. There is a constant awareness of danger. But the danger comes not from potential criminals, but from supervisors who may appear at any moment from one of the buildings where they live. So conversations tend to be short, just a minute or two. And then the doormen return to their posts. Every five minutes or so, at one of the buildings, someone comes in. As they approach the building, they adjust their tempo subtly to allow the doorman to open the door for them. Always the doorman will greet them, and sometimes one can observe a short conversation. "It's beautiful out today, huh?" is the typical starter for these conversations. If it were cold, a friendly "Bundle up" could be heard. Whatever the weather, there is always something (generic) to say.

Sometimes tenants can be seen leaving the buildings. When the doormen are outside, most tenants manage to open the door by themselves, but every so often, one will wait for service. Suddenly at one building, there is a flurry of activity. An old couple arrives into the lobby from the elevator, waiting to exit. A cab shows up. The mailman arrives; the dry cleaner's truck appears. For a few seconds, everyone is jammed up by the door. Abram (the doorman) lets the old couple exit, and the mailman enters and heads for the mailboxes in the rear. Abram takes the dry cleaning and brings it inside. The cab has to wait since the lobby is active. He barely glances at it.

The cab has discharged a family with shopping bags. Quickly shift focus and consider their experience. They struggle to bring the bags to the door, now shut behind them as Abram logs the dry cleaning in the back room. By the time he returns, they have used their key, entered the building, and called the elevator. When they left two hours earlier, he had been sitting quietly in the lobby reading the *Post*. It's odd, they think: whenever we need him, he is unavailable. Later, after putting the groceries away, they leave the building to take a walk in the park. It is 4:30, and the doorman is preparing to leave. He is talking with his neighbor from down the street who clocked out a few minutes early. Left behind in the lobby is Rickie, who works the swing shift. Having just changed, he is now foraging through the drawer to see what he can read. The elevator lands on the first floor, and the family walks toward the door. Rickie starts to get up, but the kids are faster and already at the door. He greets the family and talks about the weather. They all agree it is a beautiful day, which it is.

For Rickie, the swing shift runs until 1:00 a.m. It has been a quiet night; most of the tenants have stayed at home. A few take-out orders from a Chinese restaurant have arrived and some videos have been delivered. Rickie sent one video delivery directly to one apartment, but held on to the videos for another, instead calling the tenants on the house phone to tell them that their videos had arrived. Shortly after, a small man came down to collect them. The casual observer would have been puzzled by Rickie's behavior — why does he block direct deliveries from one company but allow the other to go right up? One tenant is having a small party. Rickie recognizes some of the guests. They have come before and he sends them up without calling. Other visitors arrive and Rickie asks them where they are going. Without asking the tenants, he sends one young man up to the thirteenth floor and then quickly calls the apartment he is heading to, warning them. The couple heading to 2G is asked to wait until he confirms that there is someone expecting them. As they go up, he moves toward the stairs to confirm that they have stopped on the second floor.

Around 9:30, the elevator comes down to the first floor and Amanda gets out. She looks like she is going out for a run. Rickie greets her and asks how she is doing. He notes that it is late for a run and advises her to "be careful out there." She meanders over to the bench by the window and plops down. She asks about his day. They talk about the weather and the neighborhood. She tells him that the tenant in 6F is planning to move out. Amanda helps pass the time; every now and then, someone comes in or leaves. These exiting and entering tenants almost always say hi, although a few walk by in silence. And for the most part, Amanda talks to them as well. Just before 11:00, Amanda looks at her watch and apparently realizes that she lost the chance to go out. She gets back on the elevator and returns to her apartment. Later Rickie says that this happens at least once a week with her. And there are others who talk too much as well. Listening is part of the job, but most people don't think Rickie is working when he talks. So far that evening, more than a handful of tenants saw him seemingly doing nothing all night. And that is their usual experience. Yet once again, at the same time, when they most need him, he is often busy. The tenants find this puzzling. We can observe something else, perhaps equally puzzling: Rickie treats similar problems differently throughout the evening. Some guests are forced to wait, while others are allowed immediate access. In some cases, he calls tenants so that they can come pick up their videos, whereas others have them delivered directly to their door. There appears to be no rhyme or reason to his selective provision of service. How can we explain these different patterns of behavior? And why do they matter?

This chapter is concerned with the daily experience of tenants and doormen as they negotiate the seemingly minor interactions they have during the course of a day, interactions that occur in the context of the course of a year, and typically over the course of many years. Most tenants in most buildings know their doorman by name. Many have watched him grow older. They typically know a little about his family. But they generally know little else. They do not know what kind of food he eats, the last movie he saw at home, his drinking habits, his friends, or his relatives. In contrast, Rickie — and the other doormen — have watched their tenants for years. He knows their names. If they have kids, he has watched them grow. He knows when they come home, what they do at night, the movies they watch, and what kinds of foods they eat. He knows if they drink. He knows when one of them is having an affair, is in trouble, and when one of their friends is in town. He likely knows their relatives by sight. And he knows their preferences (in large part because he has helped develop them). Do they want to be called when a friend comes? Do they want to have their movies left downstairs and if so, why? He knows which ones have movies left downstairs because they want to avoid having to tip the kid who brought the movies and which have the movies left downstairs because they are renting porno and don't want to take the chance that the kid who delivers the movies will know that and embarrass them. Do they want to be greeted each time they see him, or just the first few times? If asked, any doorman will tell you that it is their job to know all this stuff, though few doormen will tell you anything at all that they do know about specific tenants in their buildings.

Doormen bridge and sustain the border between the inside and outside of a building. They work in the same buildings for years on end, serving the same tenants in the same small ways. It is the constancy of their relationship with the same people, the "smallness" of the services that they repeatedly provide, and the irregularity of the comings and goings that define their day and generate the specific phenomenological condition that structures and gives rise to their experience. In relationships that reproduce themselves daily and traverse years, there is a constant dance where tenants and doormen jointly manage the affairs of the lobby. In this chapter, I focus on one aspect of this management process, the management of activity and time. I consider one of the most visible contradictions of the lobby, the tension between inactivity and boredom and intense activity and stress, seen from both the perspective of doormen and tenants.

When considering the management of time, a central feature of the work experience is the fact that doormen describe their jobs as both boring and stressful. Not a single doorman escapes this seemingly strange problem. I discuss the sources of this contradiction and show that it is a generic problem for server-client systems. While all server-client systems give rise to periods of congestion (and stress) and idleness (and boredom), the peculiar relationship between doormen as servers and tenants as clients leads to a unique set of issues and problems that provides a skein for the daily construction of the lobby as an interactive environment. Before focusing on the deep problem, let's clear away the simple quantitative material, the nuts and bolts of the job, in terms of tasks done.

WHAT TASKS DO DOORMEN ACTUALLY DO?

One idea is that doormen are personal butlers who serve their tenants whatever their requests may be at the moment the requests are made. Typically, this view is held by people, if at all, who have not encountered doormen. But in describing their jobs, some doormen provide this as the essential model. As Isaac says, for example:

> Well, more or less, our job is to make the tenants' lives easier so that they don't have to lift a finger. And that's really our job. So more or less, whatever they need, that's what we do. We accommodate them.

More strongly, many doormen think that their tenants are completely useless and unable to help themselves. In responding to a question about why he thinks people live in doorman buildings, Bob says:

> Why do they need us, because they can't do it themselves. That's the only thing I know. The things we do here, I can do them myself, know what I mean? Opening the door for someone I can do myself. Carry a bag, what the hell, take a package. They can't do it, they got the money, they can afford it.

Even if they do lots of things, there are many things that doormen do not do for their tenants. Likewise, some things that tenants would like their doormen to do for them create problems for other tenants, so doormen cannot easily satisfy all of their clients at the same time. This aside, doormen have many tasks and it is possible to describe the nuts and bolts of the job with reference to a generic task list.

Here, then, are the nuts and bolts. The typical observation of a doorman finds him just standing at the door or sitting at a desk in the front lobby. At any given minute, this is in fact what doormen are doing. While most of their time is spent at the door or in the lobby, and most of that time is seemingly idle time, doormen typically do much more each day than hold the door for tenants and their visitors. In this section, I consider what work tasks doormen have, and how these tasks vary by shift and neighborhood. The goal is simple description in quantitative terms, as background. As the bottom row of table 3.1 shows, virtually all doormen greet visitors (92.6%), sign for packages (88.7%), announce visitors (89.7%), and provide security (90.2%). More than half of all doormen report that they call taxis (69.6%), keep public areas of the building clean (63.2%), shovel snow (56.9%), and deliver packages to their tenants (52.9%). Roughly one-third of all doormen are responsible for delivering mail (35.8%), maintaining outdoor areas in front of their building (39.7%), delivering newspapers (32.4%), operating elevators (33.3%), and helping with minor maintenance duties in their

TABLE 3.1. Shifts by Tasks

Shifts	Greet visitors	Call taxis	Deliver news-papers	Deliver mail	Park cars	Sign for packages	Shovel snow	Keep public areas clean	Remove tenants' trash	Maintain outdoor public areas	Announce visitors	Provide security	Minor main-tenance duties	Operate elevator	Deliver packages to tenants
Day N = 57	51 89.5%	43 75.4%	19 33.3%	23 40.4%	4 7.0%	50 87.7%	32 56.1%	31 54.4%	11 19.3%	21 36.8%	50 87.7%	50 87.7%	17 29.8%	18 31.6%	31 54.4%
Swing N = 95	92 96.8%	63 66.3%	30 31.6%	28 29.5%	9 9.5%	86 90.5%	51 53.7%	56 58.9%	18 18.9%	36 37.9%	87 91.6%	84 88.4%	31 32.6%	32 33.7%	48 50.5%
Night N = 10	10 100%	7 70.0%	4 40.0%	2 20.0%	3 30.0%	7 70.0%	7 70.0%	8 80.0%	3 30.0%	2 20.0%	9 90.0%	10 100%	4 40.0%	2 20.0%	4 40.0%
Multiple N = 42	36 85.7%	29 69.0%	13 31.0%	20 47.6%	4 9.5%	39 92.9%	26 61.9%	34 81.0%	9 21.4%	22 52.4%	37 88.1%	40 95.2%	16 38.1%	16 38.1%	25 59.5%
Total N = 204	189 92.6%	142 69.6%	66 32.4%	73 35.8%	20 9.8%	181 88.7%	116 56.9%	129 63.2%	41 20.1%	81 39.7%	183 89.7%	184 90.2%	68 33.3%	68 33.3%	108 52.9%

tenants' apartments (33.3%). Significantly fewer doormen are responsible for parking tenants' cars (9.8%), removing trash (20.1%), or other activities (not shown), such as gardening (6.7%) and checking IDs (6.7%).

The balance of table 3.1 reports the distribution of these activities by shift. While any twenty-four-hour day has potentially only three non-overlapping eight-hour shifts, some doormen regularly work different shifts (half-swing or half-night, for example). Only 5% of the doormen we interviewed solely worked a night shift (12–7 a.m.); of those who did works nights, most alternated between the swing and night shifts. So typically, when doormen consider their jobs, they tend to summarize across the multiple shifts that they may work. Against this background, which could lead to a blurring of distinctions between shifts, I consider how shift structures tasks in relation to the overall distribution of work tasks. With this possible caveat in mind, one can see from table 3.1 that the shifts are remarkably similar in terms of the tasks that doormen do. Whatever it is that doormen do, their official tasks do not seem to vary by shift. As Peter, a doorman who alternatively works the day and swing shifts on the East Side, says:

> What would be an average day? We come in; we do the book. Log in; get rid of what we don't need. Receive packages, dry cleaning, sort mail, and food deliveries. We coordinate food deliveries; we coordinate workmen, handymen. We direct the handyman and the superintendent to problem areas in the building. We receive complaints and we direct it to the handyman. We have to announce everybody and be aware of everybody who comes in the building. And we have to be aware of danger — we're responsible for the lobby and the inside area. That's basically our duty. That's a basic day. Everything else in between is the usual stuff. That'd be the basic coming in, logging in. Logging packages, deliveries, dry cleaning, sorting the mail, greeting tenants, getting taxis, coordinating, making sure everything's functioning. That's basically our job.

In response to the same question, "What about shifts? Do they matter in terms of what you do?" Nicolai says:

> No, not really. Swing I read more after 8:00. I got more deliveries for food — pizza and Chinese food — I got the trash to collect from downstairs and sort, nights I take the trash out to the street, but swing shift

you just get it ready. I got the dry cleaning and packages to log out when people come back from work. Nights get pretty boring sometimes, that's all. After 2:00 I sit back with my feet in the air; then early the papers come, I got the *Post*, the *Times*, the *Journal*, all to mark apt. 14C and 13A, like that. I clean the lobby and get ready for the next day.

Which suggests that if the tasks do not officially vary — the door has to be attentive, log in when logging is required, keep track of things, and so on — the feeling of each shift varies quite a bit when broken down by the flow of time. Swing frees up after 8:00 p.m., relative to the crush of activity at the start of the shift, whereas the night gets slow after 2:00 a.m., with only sporadic activity, such as when the morning papers are delivered. And with flow variation, relationships to others and satisfaction with one's schedule and opportunities for promotion also vary. Those on the day shift are more likely to be very satisfied with their schedule, their relationships, and the promotion possibilities; those who work on the swing and night shift less so. These relationships are observed in tables 3.2, 3.3, and 3.4, where I consider shift worked and satisfaction with people, work schedule, and promotion opportunities.

TABLE 3.2. Shifts by Satisfaction with Contact with Other People

Shift	Very satisfied	Satisfied	Less satisfied	Not satisfied	Total
Day	24 (41.4%)	25 (43.1%)	6 (10.3%)	3 (5.2%)	58 (100%)
Swing	30 (31.6%)	54 (56.8%)	5 (5.3%)	6 (6.3%)	95 (100%)
Night	2 (18.2%)	8 (72.7%)	1 (9.1%)	0	11 (100%)
Multiple	11 (26.2%)	26 (61.9%)	3 (7.1%)	2 (4.8%)	42 (100%)
Total	67 (32.5%)	113 (54.9%)	15 (7.3%)	11 (5.3%)	206 (100%)

TABLE 3.3. Shifts by Satisfaction with Work Schedule

Shift	Very satisfied	Satisfied	Less satisfied	Not satisfied	Total
Day	26 (45.6%)	19 (33.3%)	6 (10.5%)	6 (10.5%)	57 (100%)
Swing	18 (18.4%)	49 (50.0%)	17 (17.3%)	14 (14.3%)	98 (100%)
Night	1 (10.0%)	4 (40.0%)	3 (30.0%)	2 (20.0%)	10 (100%)
Multiple	6 (15.0%)	19 (47.5%)	9 (22.5%)	6 (15.0%)	40 (100%)
Total	51 (24.9%)	91 (44.4%)	35 (17.1%)	28 (13.7%)	205 (100%)

TABLE 3.4. Shifts by Satisfaction with Opportunity for Promotion

Shift	Very satisfied	Satisfied	Less satisfied	Not satisfied	Total
Day	7 (14.9%)	11 (23.4%)	6 (12.8%)	23 (48.9%)	47 (100%)
Swing	5 (5.8%)	26 (30.2%)	22 (25.6%)	33 (38.4%)	86 (100%)
Night	0	3 (33.3%)	3 (33.3%)	3 (33.3%)	9 (100%)
Multiple	3 (8.1%)	16 (43.2%)	8 (21.6%)	10 (27.0%)	37 (100%)
Total	15 (8.4%)	56 (31.3%)	39 (21.8%)	69 (38.5%)	179 (100%)

NEIGHBORHOOD EFFECTS?

Tasks do vary somewhat by neighborhood, however, although rarely significantly. Here I just focus on the Upper East Side, East Side, West Side, Midtown, and downtown, which are the simple socio-spatial regions of the city. Table 3.5 reports how tasks vary across these neighborhoods. As expected, the differences across neighborhoods appear most clearly for less frequent tasks. Still, even across all of the more common activities, doormen on the Upper East Side do more than other doormen. Likewise, across all of the less frequent activities, doormen working in Midtown do less, in some instances significantly less than all other doormen. And in general, keeping with New York City stereotypes and their experience, Upper East Side doormen always do more and Midtown doormen always do less. But across all of the possible comparisons, most of the differences are not statistically significant — doormen pretty much do the same kinds of things (formally at any rate) wherever they work.

This does not mean that there are no neighborhood effects, or at least discussion about neighborhood effects. In comparing experiences working as a doorman on the East Side to the West Side, one doorman remarks:

> It's better over here [West Side]. The people in this building are real people. They have jobs, so they know what it's like to be a worker. So they treat you better. When I am busy, they understand and wait. On the East Side, everybody thinks they have something special.

Canseco echoes this sentiment as well:

> Well, personally, I say it's harder to work on the East Side. Because they, the tenants on the East Side, are more demanding and I mean this is a strictly straight A of a class A building. And it's hard. I mean you really got to pay attention. You got to be alert. There is no playing around. You know what I mean. You have to be serious.

TABLE 3.5. Neighborhoods (Workplace Zip Codes) by Tasks

Neighborhood	Greet visitors	Call taxis	Deliver newspapers	Deliver mail	Park cars	Sign for packages	Shovel snow	Keep public areas clean	Remove tenants' trash	Maintain outdoor public areas	Announce visitors	Provide security	Minor maintenance duties	Operate elevator	Deliver packages to tenants
Downtown N = 17	14 82.4%	7 41.2%	4 23.5%	4 23.5%	2 11.8%	13 76.5%	8 47.1%	7 41.2%	3 17.6%	4 23.5%	14 82.4%	17 100%	5 29.4%	3 17.6%	4 23.5%
Midtown N = 11	8 72.7%	5 45.5%	2 18.2%	3 27.3%	0	9 81.8%	3 27.3%	6 54.5%	1 9.1%	2 18.2%	8 72.7%	9 81.8%	2 18.2%	1 9.1%	2 18.2%
East Side N = 39	39 100%	32 82.1%	3 7.7%	8 20.5%	3 7.7%	38 97.4%	20 51.3%	28 71.8%	5 12.8%	14 35.9%	38 97.4%	35 89.7%	13 33.3%	4 10.3%	19 48.7%
Upper East Side N = 80	78 97.5%	70 87.5%	41 51.3%	37 46.3%	9 11.3%	72 90.0%	54 67.5%	52 65.0%	22 27.5%	34 42.5%	75 93.8%	75 93.8%	28 35.0%	37 46.3%	48 60.0%
Upper West Side N = 60	53 88.3%	28 46.7%	17 28.3%	21 35.0%	7 11.7%	52 86.7%	31 51.7%	37 61.7%	10 16.7%	27 45.0%	51 8.05%	51 85.0%	20 33.3%	23 38.3%	37 61.7%
Total N = 207	192 92.8%	142 68.6%	67 32.4%	73 35.3%	21 10.1%	184 88.9%	116 56.0%	130 62.8%	41 19.8%	81 39.1%	186 89.9%	187 90.3%	68 32.9%	68 32.9%	110 53.1%

But, as with many other things, this seems just as likely a simple stereo-type, since other doormen with similar experiences (working in different buildings) report exactly the opposite; for example, Carmen, now on the East Side — having moved up from a large building in Midtown — says about his new clients:

> They're a better sort of people in this building. Some of my friends say that people here [on the East Side] are snobby, but that is not accurate. They are proper. And that means that they treat you right. The better, the higher-quality people don't look down on doormen, and the lower-quality generally have hang-ups about them, their personal inferiority complexes, so they try to make up by putting somebody else down.[1]

In short, sides of town make less difference in tenants-doorman interaction than social class distance — approximated by city side, but only partially.

BOREDOM

Still, all things considered, neither shift nor neighborhood plays as much of a role in structuring activities as one might have expected. While doormen certainly have many more tasks as part of their daily job description on the Upper East Side, they are just as likely to report boredom and inactivity as those in other neighborhoods are. Nor are they more likely to report stress. All doormen, wherever they work and across all shifts, describe their jobs as alternating between periods of sheer boredom and intense activity. Consider, for example, John, a doorman working on the West Side, who in describing his routine day says:

> Something like this, busy then quiet, then busy, see like now I'm able to interview, other times I couldn't even say hello to you because I'm so busy. I got people coming in with groceries, delivery boys as you can see, it gets hectic and then like now, look, dies out.

In a similar vein, Eric describes the same alternation of activity and bore-dom, although here he distinguishes between busy (Saturday) and deadly (Sunday) days.

---

1. This sentiment could arise, though, because as Bob (a doorman on the West Side) says, "When you wait on rich people, you start to become a snob yourself."

Well, it depends on what shift you work on. I work the relief man. I got two shifts: four to twelve and midnight to eight. And usually four to twelve is pretty busy because people go in and out. Going out to movies, dinner, and all that. People don't cook for nothing here. So they go out to dinner and everything, and I get busy, back and forth. . . . Sundays are the worst days. Every hour it feels like three [from lack of anything to do].

For long periods of the day, doormen often have absolutely nothing to do. And they are often bored. As Eamon says, in response to a question asking him to describe a routine day:[2]

Boring, very boring. Between one person coming in to the next person coming in is quite long. Sometimes it could be a half hour, fifteen minutes, and they want you to be standing at attention or something when they do come.

Mario expands on the theme:

I come here, I smoke a cigarette about every twenty minutes, I read the newspaper every day, I read whatever is under the counter. At 8 p.m., I take my dinner break. Sometimes my friends come by and we talk and hang out. I have to buzz the deliverymen in and ask the tenants if they want to come down or want them to come up. That is about it.

And Felix describes his job in similar terms:

Well, this shift here is really boring. And it's just four to twelve, so most of the people are just coming home. So what I usually do is help them with packages or take the groceries in. The hardest part of this job is just trying to stay awake. That'll be the hardest part. You'll see. You could be here twenty minutes and not have one person come in. So it kind of drags at night. I just got to watch the door and not try to do anything extracurricular. No reading or telephone, they kind

---

2. Midway through five quotes, the reader may be feeling bored by the repetition of sentiment. Books are, as Sudhir Venkatesh tells me, not like movies, where directors can shape audience mood, since readers, unlike filmgoers, can just skip sections when the going gets slow. I take the chance here because the experience of boredom is so pronounced that it is difficult to convey without, in some sense, boring the reader.

of want you standing like a statue at the door. The job doesn't take too much.

But boredom is only half of the story doormen tell. The other half is about stress. The same doormen who in one part of the interview describe their job as deadly simultaneously report high levels of stress and responsibility. Consider Pedro, who in answer to a question about his least favorite part of the job, says:

> What do I like the least? The stress, it's very stressful. I have been here quite awhile, it's a stressful, stressful job, and it can get really very stressful. If you don't know what you are doing on the door, you could really screw up.

Similarly, Laran describes his routine day as stressful and busy:

> The routine during the day is a lot of work . . . and it is taxable. Sometimes the busiest hours can be when the mail comes in, packages come in, and the laundry comes in. Chinese guys are trying to sneak into the building putting menus up, which is a constant problem. There are people, businesses in the buildings, they have messengers who come and go, tenants give you things for somebody to pick up. They give you messages, everything they talk about, and also this kind of stuff can be very simple, but all this may come out and you have maybe five to seven to twelve things all at once, and they all think they are number one.

The "Chinese guys" problem, which sounds absurd, is a frequent lament. All the buildings have posted signs saying "No Menus," but this doesn't really seem to derail the serious. As Tom, a doorman for the past twenty-one years on the East Side, says (note how he finds himself at risk when he is getting a car!):

> Twenty-one years . . . I don't know how the Chinese man, the Chinese people, the Chinese guys from the restaurant, how they sneak into this place and put menus under each door. That's what beats me. They'll watch you, you know, I think. They sneak up, when you go to get a car from somebody, the guys run in. But he's hiding somewhere in the bushes. It's the strangest thing I ever think about happening.

Radzac, working on the Upper East Side in a cooperative building with a lot of turnover in tenants, describes his day:

> You've really got to make sure that no one goes up unannounced or who's not welcome there. And we've got security cameras on the back door, so you've got to sort of keep your eye on that door. You've got people coming in as someone's leaving; you have to worry about logging in packages. UPS will come with fifty boxes and you have to keep logging them in while you're dispatching a handyman to go to an apartment or taking service orders over the phone, like, "Oh, my bathtub leaks," so you've got to sit here entering it into the book. Then you've got to log and enter all of the stuff, for all the repairmen, the workers, who come in here. And so on and so forth. You've got to put stickers out on boxes so tenants come home and know they have a package. You know, it's a lot of responsibility; it's not an easy thing to do. You're answering phones, you've got walkie-talkies, the intercom is ringing at the same time, you've got fifteen people lined up for packages, you've got delivery people there. I mean, sometimes it's like, "Leave me alone!"

The problem that needs to be explained is how it is possible for the same job to be experienced as both boring and stressful. Can other jobs be similarly described and if so, which ones and why? One obvious comparison is to other jobs in the service industry, flight attendants on transatlantic flights, bartenders and wait staff, wedding planners, security personnel at airports, and hot dog sellers in the park all come to mind as people whose jobs are experienced in bursts of idleness and intensity. Making sense of this experience — from the upper-side model view — is the focus of the next section.

QUEUES AND CONGESTION

Why are doormen bored from lack of activity and stressed out about too much to do at the same time? The answer comes from a strange source — people working on problems of traffic flow at airports, on switching networks for telephone and electric service, and on organizing optimal server networks for high-demand, high-sensitivity computer systems that cannot afford breakdowns — operations research, in short. There is a long and distinguished tradition of scholarship arising from operations research that is concerned with congestion, queuing, and waiting. While there has been considerable recent progress in modeling dynamic serving systems (mainly through complex simulation, a direction first seriously attacked by Leonard Klienrock), for our purposes the early classical work is the most germane. Here, the introductory text by D. R. Cox and Walter Smith (1961) provides an easily accessible starting point.[3]

Within reasonable bounds, servers are designed to efficiently handle mean client flow over some period of time. In the grocery store, one does not expect to have only one checkout lane operating between 4 and 7 p.m., and, likewise, one does not expect to see eight cashiers working between 2 and 4 a.m. If firms have too many servers to handle routine mean flow, they are wasting money. On the other hand, if there are too few servers, they are unable to process normal client demand. So firms try to find the right number of servers for the typical flow, defined technically as "mean client flow over some period of time, T." But while the "mean client flow over some period of time, T" will be closest to the observed number, on average, for any given period of time, T, the actual observed flow will vary. Some periods will be characterized by light client flow, others by heavy flow. Systems designed for mean flow will at some points be naturally swamped, while at other times, naturally idle.

If this was the only problem, client-flow variation around the mean, server systems would be impossible to calibrate perfectly but the complications would be relatively few, certainly not sufficient to give rise to a subfield of mathematical theory — the theory of queues. The real problem, well known in operations research, is that given any degree of irregularity in the arrival of clients and variability in the time taken to serve a client, server-client systems (where servers could be anything from clerks at counters to runways for airplanes) will induce congestion.

First, consider just the problem posed by variability in arrival time. Define arrival time as the moment a client (customer, plane, message, etc.) enters the system. This could be a phone number dialed, a tenant coming downstairs to take a taxi, a Chinese food delivery, someone arriving at the door, and so on. What kind of model best predicts the arrival time of the next client? Unless there are pre-allocated schedules for arrivals (appointments

---

3. Klienrock et al., *Communication Nets*; Klienrock et al., *Queuing Systems*; Cox and Smith et al., *Queues*.

every fifteen minutes, as with the doctor, or takeoffs every four minutes for runways, for example), the simplest, and also most likely to be accurate, model would simply predict that the probability of an element arriving is random across time. More complicated models exist, of course. But they tend to exacerbate the situation produced by a random arrival model, as we will see.

Arrivals

Assume that on average there are N events in a specific period of time, T — which could be a minute, an hour, or a day, whatever is a socially defined interval for the system in question. In our case, we would think in terms of eight-hour shifts. If event arrivals are random with respect to time, then the probability of an event arrival is simply T/N. Imagine a simple case of N = 100 events, arriving over a single shift broken up into 100 little time periods (for an eight-hour shift, this would be 8×60 minutes $= 480$ minutes / 100 or an event roughly every 5 minutes). Life would be simple if events took less than five minutes to complete and each event arrived evenly spaced out every five minutes or so. A single server could handle them day after day, if human, without stress or boredom.

But life is not so simple. Ignoring the second deep problem of variability of time taken to complete an event, just consider the timing of the events across the 100 five-minute sections of the day. Some periods of the day are empty, and others are dense with events. This pattern of sparseness and density is natural. It comes from the fact that the probability of a client arrival is independent of the arrival of other clients. The chance that an event will arrive is the same across all remaining moments in time. And naturally if arrivals "don't care" about time (which is the meaning of independence), they will come as they please. And this means that, probabilistically, they will tend to bunch up in some periods. If they bunch up in some periods, other periods will not have any events in them. When arrivals bunch up, congestion occurs. When congestion takes place, doormen are stressed out. When clients don't arrive, servers are idle and doormen feel bored. It is as simple as that.

Independent, then, of the time it takes to service a request, the simple distribution of client arrivals will generate congestion at some periods and idleness at others. If all clients are the same, they can be pretty much scheduled at will; thereby organizing server systems to avoid congestion. This is the case, for example, with mailbox collection. The postal service treats each location as similar and sets up a collection schedule that maximizes the number of boxes that can be serviced (emptied) once or twice in a single day. Most assembly processes work in the same way. For example, similar jars (as clients) travel down an assembly line at fixed intervals awaiting tops (as servers) to be placed on them. But these simple cases for operations research specialists involve instances where events are scheduled, when clients are homogeneous, and where there is no variability in the time taken to serve a customer. They are rare.

The first problem is that in social contexts, like the lobby, clients come with different needs. Some take seconds to satisfy, others much longer. The sources of variability in time taken to serve a customer are countless. Just to pick a familiar example, consider what occurs at the grocery store. Everybody comes to the store to buy groceries, so at one level it seems that service time ought to be pretty fixed. But obviously it is not. One source of variability in service time (here, checking through the cashier) is the number of items in the grocery cart — which has motivated stores to create express lines for shoppers with just a handful of items. But even ignoring item volume, the possibilities for delay are seemingly limitless. Most of us have had the unfortunate experience of standing behind a customer who painfully counts pennies to be "helpful" and give exact change. Likewise, the shopper whose cart contains canned items with scannable prices will be faster than the shopper whose cart contains exotic fresh vegetables and herbs that the cashier has to look up and enter a code number.

There is no reason to believe that variability in service time can be completely anticipated. In the grocery store, people whose shopping carts contain only cans arrive at the stores at the same time as people who only buy exotic vegetables. In the lobby, difficult deliveries or difficult guests don't arrive only when the staff is free. Because people arrive in the lobby (or the store) with different needs, there is enormous variability in service time; and this means that some clients will have to wait in queues some of the time.

Coupled with variability in arrival time, the consequence of this kind of variability is that servers will be extremely busy at some times, and that clients will have to wait in lines. Even short unanticipated delays can cause congestion for some period down the queue. If congestion is systematically too severe, additional servers can be added (more clerks, another doorman, an additional dentist for the practice, a new runway for small planes, etc.). But unless enormous redundancy is built into the server system, at some moment more than one customer will arrive at the point of service at the same time or when the server is busy, and all but one of them will need to queue up and wait their turn. Waiting is the first consequence of dynamic service systems. If people are forced to wait too long, or if their experience is that they routinely have to wait, deep client dissatisfaction is an obvious second-level consequence.[4] From the client perspective — that is, for those who are routinely forced to queue up — it may be the only important one. But that is not exactly true. There are multiple views that need to be considered, and these views bring to light a set of other consequences that are equally important.

Priority of Service

For those whose serve, congestion generates dilemmas and decisions. The dilemmas center on priority of service, what is known in operations research as the "queue discipline" — or the method by which a customer is selected for service out of those who are in waiting. Who, or what kinds of demands, should be acted on first? How should priority be allocated? At what point, if ever, do individuals fall out of queue? Decisions have to be made in order to enact priority schemes. Nor do priority schemes really provide solutions to congestion problems. As we shall see, even with priority systems, ranking allocation of server time to activities or individuals, there will always be, unless enormous redundancy is built in, instances in which clients with the same priority compete for the same limited attention of servers. Even more complicated are cases in which competing legitimate demands to priority are built into a single server system. Both of these situations induce congestion dilemmas and heighten employee perception of stress.

Consider, for example, the typical airline response to plane cancellations. Imagine a system in which three plans are flying from city A to city B on a single day, and where airlines are competing for runway server space that is completely allocated. If the first flight of the day is delayed, the runway remains idle during the time it could otherwise be used. Flights next in line cannot leave early, since they have to wait until their scheduled departure — so as to ensure that ticket holders get on board. Delayed flights need to be

---

4. In many systems where congestion dynamics are common, clients may have multiple strategies at their disposal. To use Hirschman's terms, in *Exit, Voice, Loyalty*, they can exit, express voice, or remain loyal. Passengers on airplanes are not allowed the exit option while the flight is in the air, but they can select another airline for their next flight. Drinkers can always find a bar less busy if the place gets too crowded. But tenants have few realistic exit options. Consequently, they either complain (voice) or express loyalty. For reasons considered subsequently, the typical tenant response is loyalty.

scheduled, but when? There are two simple rules. They pick up the next free slot, resulting in what could be a long delay if the runways are completely booked, or they hold their place in queue once they are ready to fly and delay subsequent planes.

For delays in this scenario, all things being equal, airports follow the second alternative and adhere to the first come, first served queue discipline. Strangely, if the flight is canceled, the airlines behave differently with respect to clients. They could follow the simple first come, first served discipline by placing seat holders on the first flight onto the second, bumping the latter to the third, and delaying those on the third flight until a new plane is brought in. This seems the most natural thing to do. This is, after all, the same discipline that the airports follow with delays. And it is what we expect from dentists and doctors. If the 9:30 appointment runs late at the dentist office and the dentist is not free until 10:30 (thereby missing the 10:00 a.m. appointment), s/he would never consider first seeing the 10:30 patient and skipping the 10:00 until some other free time at the end of the day. The burden of the lengthy first appointment is passed on as delay all down the line.

Obviously, some competing principles are in play. And equally obvious, there are industry norms that govern client expectation of treatment from servers. Airlines cannot easily bump individuals from seats on scheduled flights. But they can pass on delay. They don't because by localizing delay for one group of travelers (those unfortunate few who have their flight canceled), they minimize widespread client annoyance. Of course, this also helps them score better marks on the statistic that they jointly agree to adhere to in advertising their service: proportion of flights delayed. But why don't doctors and dentists do the same thing, that is, "burn" some clients, keeping the rest on schedule? Why is it that they don't make a similar claim: Ninety percent of our patients are seen on time!

Airport controllers know something else about their clients, and this helps them make decisions about enforcement of the first come, first served queue discipline. They know the size of the plane, the number of passengers it is carrying, the congestion status of the receiving airport, the number of passengers on the plane who have subsequent connections to make, and the airline it is "employed by." If the airline has a hub at the airport, if the plane is large, if capacity is full, if most passengers will miss connections, and if the receiving airport is congested, the first come, first served queue discipline is easily sacrificed for getting a higher-priority plane off the ground. Some planes are clearly more important than others. But when they are equal, the airport adheres to the first come, first served discipline. This is because airports jointly agree to advertise their service with respect to volume of landings and takeoffs per hour. Volume is insensitive to specific planes. Passing on the delay does not detract from volume, so airports are happy to do it.

Dentists don't have such a luxury. They have no foundation from which they can prioritize clients, except for emergencies, since all clients are equal. The homophily principal operates here as well: dentists get patients mainly through referral. People refer people who are similar to them; consequently, most patients at most practices share the same social status. Dentists cannot, therefore, make strategic decisions about which patients to burn very easily.[5] Nor do cashiers at grocery stores have the luxury of deciding whom to serve first. All clients arrive equal, whatever they are buying. On the other hand, sales clerks at fancy department stores can make guesses about expected purchase volume and allocate attention to customers who seem likely to make substantial contributions to their monthly sales record.

QUEUE DISCIPLINE IN THE LOBBY

Doormen are stuck in the middle, somewhere between clerks in high-status retail shops and dentists. For doormen, one line of argument insists that all clients are equal, or at least that all tenants are equal. This is the dental model, net of emergencies. Another line of argument insists that delivery people, who have schedules to keep, FedEx carriers who need a signature, and Chinese food deliverers with food quickly getting cold deserve quick attention. This is the high-end clerk model — some clients have queue priority. Certainly, delivery people are not happy about waiting for service, and they have the capacity to exert some structural power over residents and doormen.[6] Serving delivery people first carries some risk since waiting for

---

5. They can, of course, make decisions on the basis of treatment need, sacrificing routine care for emergency treatment. And they can differentially see patients whose treatment regime involves a long process that is temporally sensitive. But these are changes to the priority service rule that operate on the margins. Readers with dentist phobia who may feel that they are doing others a favor by making appointments and then canceling them at the last moment, with excuses that make undergraduates whose grandmothers die at an impossible rate just around exam period look creative, should continue to feel bad, since dentists, like airplanes, typically assume cancellations (the rate varies by practice) and so overbook.

6. Doormen cannot easily justify serving delivery people before clients without recourse to the rhetoric of security. If they do not justify priority service to delivery people on the basis of security,

service is not a skill that the people for whom the doorman works — the building tenants — have either. Typically, they are people who in other walks of life make others wait for service. So a final line of argument is that not all tenants are equal. And the reality is that some tenants appear to the doormen to be either more demanding or more important than other tenants. This is in fact the case. But it is not advertised.

Against this confusing background, if everyone arrives at the same time, the doorman has to respond in crisis mode. Decisions have to be made about priority. Some clients cannot be immediately served. If four events arrive at the same time, three have to wait. It is a simple reality. And throughout, congestion is likely to become worse. This is because arrivals arrive without respect to queues. So they are as likely to arrive when the doorman is busy as when he is free. This experience of managing the competing demands of clients induces stress. The experience of stress is heightened because unlike our relationship with cashiers at stores or even our dentist, tenants and doormen are stuck together in long iterative sequences of service, often stretching out for years. The repetition of small tasks for tenants, who are both socially distant and close at the same time, creates additional problems for doormen. They cannot prioritize their tenants' demands by ignoring a food or dry-cleaning delivery, since the materials brought to the building are going to another tenant. Consequently, while they have to enforce queue discipline, they cannot easily commit to the specific priority scheme they adopt. The schemes are constantly changing in relation to the specific tenants who need service.

Doormen face problems of enforcing queue discipline since clients with different priority are likely to arrive at the same time. While Peter was being interviewed, for example, a Chinese food delivery arrived at the door. Many doormen allocate food deliveries high priority in the queue, since delays result in cold food and unhappy tenants. Delays also keep outsiders in the lobby, and this is something doormen do not want, since they have to attend to the outsider during his or her sojourn. In this case, though, the food was brought to the wrong address. After the mistake was taken care of, Peter said:

---

they have to try to claim that serving delivery people first is a contribution to the collective good. After all, one could argue, each tenant would prefer that the other tenants waited so that their Chinese food would arrive hot. But, as with all collective goods, each tenant cares little about the temperature of their neighbor's food and would prefer to be served first, all things being equal.

She [the individual who ordered the food] is not in this building and telephoned someone somewhere outside. It was 9530 instead of 5530 [phone numbers], so this lady is telling me, "What are you talking about? I didn't order any Chinese food." That is another thing that always happens. They will screw up in a restaurant, so when you come here, you call the wrong person. They get angry with you because you called them and it is not for them. I didn't screw up — they screwed up. You see it gets so crazy, and one thing in this job is you can't panic. You could when it gets busy have five guys standing here with all deliveries, the phone will be ringing, you will have a cab pull up, you know it will get really hectic. Most buildings have two doormen. Now I do the job of like two or three guys. I handle the street and whatever deliveries come in; I'm constantly running around, unless it's slow like this.

Continuing, he describes how he enforces queue discipline when clients pile up on one another at the same time. First come, first served rules are quickly violated; the inside of the building is managed first, then the outside, unless . . . the client is an old lady!

I have the experience; another guy will be like, "What do I do?" The phone will be ringing, a cab will pull up, groceries coming in, Chinese food, and you['re] like, "Well, what do I do first?" But I got it down; I know what to do first. The cab will have to wait because I have no business in the street, anyway, my objective is right here. It can get so hectic, believe me, you wouldn't be able to handle it. You don't have the experience. It can get so crazy, but I'm used to it already; I mean, it's a piece of cake. You know what I mean? In other words, I'll concentrate on the most important thing first, if I see an old lady pull up in a cab, actually I'm going to help her first before I help the kid.

Eamon describes his attempts at enforcing queue discipline with clients who are often difficult to control. Here the situation is radically different from airplanes queuing on runways or patients in a dental clinic. Instead of passive clients waiting to be served, doormen often contend with active clients content to serve themselves, if they think it is needed.

You try to line up things, and sometimes some people just want to jump out of the line and do it on their own. So then they complicate it for you because you have to slow that person down or you have to stop that person running into the building because he can't just run into the building. First you are going to have to find out that he is running and then you have to find out why. So in the meantime, he slows you down because there are other people also, and they may come before him, and until you get them answered to their situation, you can get involved in four or five other things. So you try and keep it in order, what I want, keep it fair.

It is not always possible to line things up neatly and keep them ordered, especially when the things lined up are people with their own programs and expectations. In all of these cases, doormen try to solve problems posed by congestion that are exacerbated by simultaneous arrivals of clients, who from competing first principles demand to be served first. In some cases, the demands are illegitimate. In others, the problem of competing legitimate demands is quite common. Whether they are illegitimate or legitimate does not really change the experience for the doormen, since they still have to manage the stress of trying to accomplish too many things at once. Nor does their self-understanding of the job always provide great assistance in making decisions about how to proceed, although it helps eliminate one class of events as competing for priority — visitors and guests.

THE GUEST PROBLEM

As we saw earlier, most doormen report that the first priority is to provide security. Fundamentally, this involves managing the relationship between the inside and the outside of the building. Strangers who arrive with a clear function — delivering food, laundry — can be screened quickly. Most doormen see the same delivery people day in and day out, so the screen can be as quick as a glance. On the other hand, those strangers who arrive without a clear function need to be screened more carefully. The screening takes time, but it is critically important, for a primary risk that doormen face is that someone they allow into the building breaches security. While exceptionally rare, if such an event were to occur, the doorman could easily lose his job. Doormen have strong reasons, then, to be naturally suspicious. As a general rule, if a stranger claims to need to visit a tenant, the tenant has to be contacted and the legitimacy of the visit confirmed. Some tenants prefer such contact. Others find it intrusive and want their guests to be allowed to visit them without having to be screened and then announced at the door. Doormen have to know which tenants have which preference, and consequently, for some, they need to make decisions about who to let in without screening on the spot, a decision based on the appearance and demeanor of the visitor.

Ironically, the tenants most concerned about their safety and most likely, therefore, to insist that their visitors are screened are the least likely to have visitors whose appearance (to the doormen or other tenants) might generate suspicion. Such ironies are common in many settings. For example, those most concerned about contracting AIDS are those who are at the least risk (since their concern translates into behaviors that would protect them from HIV acquisition). Likewise, those most concerned about being mugged are the least likely to put themselves in situations (dark lonely streets late at night, the subway after 2:00 a.m., and so on) where mugging is most likely. Since the least traditional tenants are the most likely to prefer less intrusion and the most likely to have less traditional visitors who don't "look so good," doormen have to rely on instinct as they confront the decision whether or not to call the tenant, and the decision has to be a snap decision. They need to read the signals that the visitor emits very quickly, in terms of the specific person he or she is claiming to visit.

It is widely reputed that doormen are less likely to admit blacks to a building than they are to admit whites. The real test of this hypothesis would be an audit study, but the sense is widespread enough to try to understand how such a situation could arise. Because doormen are recruited from within ethnic networks, they are less likely to be black than expected by chance. While not necessarily overtly racist, the fact that doormen tend to be white creates the possibility that they systematically make access to their buildings harder for blacks than for whites. This is the simplest explanation. It is also the least likely. More likely is the idea that others perceive this to be the case, simply because doormen are exercising the preferences that their tenants have as well as making snap decisions where tenant preferences do not provide sufficient guidance. That the former exercise (doing what tenants want) is purely innocent is not the case, however, since doormen work to shape their tenants' preferences when they can. Jacob describes one such situation in detail:

You also adjust your work to the personal requirement of the client. I'll give you an example, one tenant, a couple of them — it's not one — a couple of them [are] extremely strict. They want exactly that you call up; if they say "yes," they can go up [based on] who that person is, then you can let that person enter. But then there are other tenants who are very upset if you [call them; they say,] "Don't bother me — just let them up!" Now you notice, let's say two different people come and you stop one, ask where he is going, to find out if he can go to the strict person . . . so he has to stay there. In the meantime, [here] comes another person who's going to a different apartment where they don't want you to wait and they don't want you to bother — "Just let him in." . . . I would just let him up. Think about the guys who come five times a day to the same apartment: you don't have to ask; you have to send him up. Now, when you send this guy up . . . the first person [says,] "How come you didn't . . . How come you stopped me?"

I had a situation where one asshole thought because her color — her skin color is . . . that was a black person — that's why I let the other person in and it has nothing to do [with it], and I told her, "Because the other person is going to a different apartment and the tenant in that apartment [has] different ways, different requirements for the doorman." He wants me to work with him in a particular way and the person knew I couldn't force him to work, that's why. [So, the second person said,] "NO, I'M GOING IN." "No, you are not going in, even if I have to stop you, take you from the building, you are not going to go up." You know, you go through this kind of stuff, sometimes you have to be hard-core, maybe any visitor, there are people, no, they are going to here and maybe you are going to there. They are not going to go into the building, so I will stop the elevator, I will put my hand into the door. . . . [T]he point is that you have the rules, and you also know how tenants want it. So you find the rights within the rules [that] you will adjust to that client, to the person.

Here, the consolidation of race and tenant preferences (and perhaps the doorman's preferences as well) serves to block access to minorities, while appearing to provide unfettered access to white visitors. The collective cognitive experience — intended by none — will be one of inequality. In this case, Jacob follows his tenant's preference. It so happens that the tenant with the strict call policy invited a black friend over who happened to arrive at the same time that a tenant with an open-access policy had a white friend arrive. The opposite outcome is equally likely, but the racial context within which guests interpret actions ensures that this alternative scenario will not be imbued with the same meaning or even recounted later in an equivalent way. Queuing dynamics make such congestion events likely. The black guest was not discriminated against, but it appears as if she was. If these events happen repeatedly, the collective experience is one of discrimination, even if each micro-event has a non-discriminatory foundation.

Because the risks to other tenants and to their job are considered high should a criminal enter the building, one would think that doormen would simply always call tenants to check on visitors. But the real risk of malfeasance is low, and the one guaranteed thing that doormen confront is the constancy of contact with tenants. Doormen have to see their tenants every day — and they have to be attentive to their needs and wishes. It is this attentiveness that allows them to construe their jobs as professional — that is, as involving the capacity to make substantive distinctions. Of course, it is not easy to stick to a formal system, for example, constantly screening visitors, when one knows that this is not what their tenant wants. Nor is it professional. Only when doormen work to rule, that is, come to define their relationship with tenants as an employee-employer relationship (as versus a client-server relationship), do they stick to formal systems. An irony is that working to rule, by sacrificing their claim to professional status, generates formally fair treatment but yields substantively irrational outcomes.

Tenants are always the clients, no matter how old, cranky, or experienced in the role (e.g., with fixed preferences) they are. So doormen cannot easily burn one tenant for another. This means that some priority systems will not work. At the same time, doormen cannot afford to burn other service providers, since most service providers, from the local restaurant to national postal services (UPS, FedEx, U.S. mail, etc.), preserve route integrity by sending the same people out on the same route day after day. Consequently, doormen develop long-term relationships with their servers, and they cannot afford to alienate them. Against this constraint, the first clients to get the cold shoulder when work gets stressful are visitors. As Rajah says:

> The other doormen . . . they earn a lot, but they [have] a double standard. When they are not tenants, they are not nice to them. Why, because they do not live here. The tenants . . . excuse my words . . . they [the other doormen] kiss [the tenants'] ass. I am not like that. . . . I am like that the whole year round. I am nice, to everyone.

Because they are more likely to burn tenants' visitors (even the more regular guests) than tenants or delivery people, it is not surprising to discover that of all the people they come into contact with in an average day, visitors are

TABLE 3.6. Shifts by How Many of Tenants' Visitors Do You Like

Shift	All	Most	Some	Few	None	Total
Day	16 (28.6%)	20 (35.7%)	15 (26.8%)	3 (5.4%)	2 (3.6%)	56 (100%)
Swing	28 (28.6%)	39 (39.8%)	23 (23.5%)	7 (7.1%)	1 (1.0%)	98 (100%)
Night	3 (30.0%)	2 (20.0%)	2 (20.0%)	3 (30.0%)	0	10 (100%)
Multiple	11 (26.8%)	16 (39.0%)	10 (24.4%)	4 (9.8%)	0	41 (100%)
Total	58 (28.3%)	77 (37.6%)	50 (24.4%)	17 (8.3%)	3 (1.5%)	205 (100%)

the least liked. Whereas over 80% of doormen report liking all or most of their tenants, far fewer report liking their tenants' guests. Compared to supervisors, delivery people, coworkers, and maintenance workers, guests receive the "lowest" approval rating, even considering that a non-trivial proportion of doormen actively dislike their supervisors. The relationship between liking tenants' guests and shifts is also of some interest, reported in table 3.6. It is easier to burn people you don't like. No doubt, the fact that guests feel ignored by doormen contributes to behaviors on their part (walking in, being rude) that later come to provide the justification for the burn. This is an example of a self-fulfilling prophecy, where sets of beliefs about outcomes shape behaviors that induce the outcome initially believed in.[7]

It makes sense that guests are the least likely to be liked of all people whom doormen interact with. They come only occasionally, and they have little motivation to be polite. If unknown, they must be treated with suspicion and the legitimacy of their visit ascertained. And they are vulnerable. Unable to independently discover whether or not their host is in, they are at the mercy of doormen, who can rationalize slow service by reference to security concerns. And this is why many tenants try to circumvent the doorman by insisting that their visitors be allowed to pass without a security check. Here,

---

7. The most famous self-fulfilling prophecy in the sociological literature is the Pygmalion in the classroom study, described in Rosenthal and Jacobson, *Pygmalion in the Classroom*. Here, teachers were told that some students would experience an intellectual blossoming in the subsequent year on the basis of a new assessment test. But the test was simply a standard IQ test, and students were allocated to experimental and control groups at random. Not surprisingly, those students expected to have a blossoming increased overall IQ by more than thirty points in grades 1–3. Teacher expectations about the blossoming led them to attend to students differently. More disturbing than IQ gains — which reveals much about the plasticity of IQ — were teachers' subjective assessments of students, as curious, troublesome, difficult, and so on. Teachers subsequently rated previous high achievers who were not identified as bloomers as disruptive, needy, and troublesome. These students internalized the negative sentiments and began to become less attached to school.

there is a duality difficult to escape. On the one hand, the special request allows the doorman to assume a professional role, where professional is defined by the particular treatment of others. On the other hand, by making a special request of this nature, tenants further reduce the opportunity for their doorman to demonstrate that he is doing his job. Consequently, they are more likely than others to perceive him as idle or unhelpful at precisely the moments that service is required.

TENANT PERCEPTIONS

It is not uncommon for tenants to talk about their doormen. In fact, since they see them each time they come home, or at least expect to see them each time they come home, who was on the door and what they were or were not doing are routine topics of conversation. This is true even if the tenants claim to not really care at all. Lori, for example, notices:

> At night the doorman is not as available. Occasionally the door will be locked and you need to key yourself in because he is taking a break or getting food. I am not really sure what he is doing. During the day there is someone consistently there, but at nighttime, especially late at night, like around the hours of seven to nine. I am not really sure what they are doing. It does not bother me. Like I said, I do not need someone to open the door for me. I do not mind having to let myself in, but I just wonder, "What are they doing? Why are they not there for like a two-hour period of time?" I come home and he is not there. And then one of my roommates will come home and she will mention something to me about the doorman not being there. And I'll just be, "Well, where the heck are they?"

Tenants talk about their doormen with their partner, and if they have no partner, they will talk about them with their friends and neighbors. The talk frequently turns on a mix of wonder and complaint. Tenants wonder where the doormen are when they are not on the door. And they wonder why their doorman never seems to be around (except during the Christmas season, a topic I consider in more depth subsequently). They wonder what they do during their shift, since most of the time they seem to be doing absolutely nothing. And, of course, all of these seemingly innocent thoughts veil complaints about the apparent mismatch between presence and service. As noted above, the mismatch is driven by the stochastic nature of the work experience — the fact that clients can and do arrive with heterogeneous problems all at once, so as often as not when an individual needs them, they are busy.

The fact that Lori misses her doorman between seven and nine has more to do with the scheduling of the dinner hour than congestion per se, but the fact of congestion implies a second consequence that is of equal import. Doormen will be idle much of the time. In fact, they are likely to be idle most of their shift unless they are assigned (as they often are) to other tasks only indirectly associated with their main job — for example, polishing brass in the lobby. And so, most of the time when tenants see their doorman, the doorman appears to have nothing to do.

The deepest irony is that tenants are most likely to observe doormen either when they have absolutely nothing to do or when they are extremely busy. In the first case, they can only conclude that the doormen don't really do anything. In the second case, they are likely to feel slighted because their position in the queue was "not respected" and conclude that the doormen are "doing nothing" or "inattentive to their specific needs." A critical element of the job of being a doorman involves changing these perceptions. Oddly, in operations research, little thought seems to be given to understanding how servers shape clients. In sociology, by contrast, there is much interest in considering how server systems shape client behavior, for example, in workplace and laboratory studies. For those interested in the dynamics of professionalization, however, little attention has been paid to how claims to professional status shape client preferences and thus mitigate (by inducing distinction in client preferences) potential congestion.

The problem that doormen face with respect to tenant perception is especially vivid because doormen as servers are in a different relationship to their tenants as clients than, for example, airlines are to their clients. Whereas airlines can burn specific individuals scheduled on a specific flight by not passing on the delay to the aggregate group of travelers, doormen do not have such a luxury. If they are burned, passengers may not return to the airline, it is true; but if all airlines do the same thing, which they do, passengers will eventually find their way back. The problem that doormen have is that their clients will return, whether they burn them or not. And they will return right away. Worst of all, when they do return, because most of the time doormen have nothing to do besides their job — getting the door, watching the door, securing the lobby, and so on — the client is likely to observe them doing "nothing," thereby vividly reminding them of the previous "injustice."

There are a few things that doormen can do to shift tenant perceptions. These can be considered "coping mechanisms" insofar as they are things that doormen do to cope with server problems. The simplest thing is to try to manage the overall perception of the tenant by being attentive. This can involve the simplest of interactions — saying "Good morning" — or can stretch over into overtly obsequious service. Whether tenants want it or not, doormen will greet them when they come in and out. As Peter says:

> That is [a] second part of the job, be nice. You must not be down-trodden to people; you have to be bold and nice, and tell them, "Good morning," "Good afternoon," "Good evening," whatever; regardless of how many times they come in here, that's what you have to say — "Good evening" — every time. You have one man comes here five times a day, that's what you have to say. One man tells me, he says, "You don't have to tell me good morning." I say, "Well, that's my job, I'm sorry." That's what it takes [for] me to do.

When they are not otherwise engaged, doormen will thus proactively initiate contact with their tenants and try to engage them in conversation — usually about the weather, but also about the day that they will have, the building, or the traffic. And most doormen report that most of their tenants are more than happy to talk. So doormen initiate these conversations, whether they really enjoy it or not. As noted above, the most common topic is the weather. On a daily basis, more than 70% of the doormen report talking about the weather with their tenants. Most doormen spend so much time talking about the weather that they make sure they have the latest information before starting their shift. Angel says:

> The first thing I do, I am not even at work, I'm just getting ready for work at home. I turn on the weather station and I listen to the forecasts for the day, the week, whatever I can. That way I get to work and I can say, "It's going to rain this afternoon, but clear up at night," or whatever the news is. So that's my first job. It's pretty lame when the doorman doesn't know the weather, or if he doesn't know if a certain person is home.

Or more bluntly, Richie says:

> I keep good track of the weather, the time, the traffic, everything. So when you're going out, you call me and say, "Hey, how's the traffic?"

It's the little things like that. For example, we are not supposed to carry radios, but I always carry my little Bloomberger, which just tells me what I need to know. I think it's fucked up for someone to ask a doorman, "You know if it's going to rain today?" and the doorman say[s], "I don't know." I mean, you've got to know the fucking weather. Some of these other guys are fucking lazy, like they won't even stick their fucking head outside so they know if it's raining or not; if you are going to be a doorman, you have to know what it's [the weather] going to do and what it's doing now.

Second on the topic parade is sports (68.8%). More than half of our doormen report daily conversations with tenants on both building matters and current events. After September 11, doormen, like all others in the city, talked constantly about the World Trade Center, the victims, and the fate of the city. Doormen can talk about some kinds of contemporary events, but not all. The weather, news, traffic, and the state of the building provide generic elements of quick conversation that are stripped of content with respect to the revelation of personal views but signal an availability to be of service. In contrast, some topics are off the hit parade; under this rubric can be found the bigger issues of the day — politics, religion, cultural values, and so on. Tenants utilize the conversation openings provided by doormen in turn to ask for favors, to inform their doorman that they are expecting a package, dry cleaning, and whatnot. By initiating conversation when they are idle, doormen connect with tenants that they know will, sooner or later, discover them too busy to help. In this sense, the idle conversation of the lobby serves both as a depository, but more critically, as a signaling device, operating on tenants to shift their perception from "doing nothing" to "available for service." Doormen successful in effecting such switches have only to discipline tenants into developing preferences for specific services. This is more difficult.

TOO MUCH TALK

The problem with appearing ready to serve as a strategic deployment against the perception of idleness is that at times the conversation that ensues is onerous and a distraction from other aspects of the job. As Hans says about overly voluble tenants, "Outside [i.e., as a projection, not outside the building] we can be friendly and talk, but we have to do our job first."

Likewise, Felix describes unwanted contact with his tenants as "intense at times. People do get on my nerves. The hardest thing is trying not to show them that you are getting bothered."

In some instances, tenants spend long periods talking to doormen. More typical on the swing or night shift than the day shift, doormen recognize that they are not really being asked to "talk, but to just listen." They often see themselves as unpaid psychotherapists. Elbert describes one situation, of many:

> [A tenant asked if she could just stay with me], if I don't mind that she would stay right here and just talking to me because she has to spill her guts to somebody because it's craziness what happened to her, and then you listen and you let them talk, and if they trust you with problems of their personal life, it can be helpful, like a psychologist, I guess . . . you let them talk, and listen. And it, and it's fine sometimes, so they may be with you for a few hours.

About one old man who has no friends in the building, Billy says:

> I tell him to come down and talk to me if he is lonely and just wants to shoot the breeze, that I don't have much to say but that I am a good listener. So he comes down once or twice a shift and we talk a few minutes.

In some cases, routine small talk creates priority problems when events that need attention do arise. Tenants arriving with groceries may find their doorman engaged in conversation and consequently unable to get to the door; and doormen who use conversation to signal availability often feel unable to extricate themselves just when they want to. As Radzac says:

> See, like now, I'm talking to you about sports or something and this one comes in and I have to give her a wink or something just to tell her, "This one talks a lot; I'm going to be right there." So it's like all the time I'm saying one thing to you and another to her.

These winks can become encoded into specific relationships that tenants have with doormen. One tenant describes how, because he speaks Spanish with one of his doormen, they have developed a code largely inaccessible to other tenants. Using a reference to the TV show *Naked City*, which ends, "There are eight million stories in the Naked City. This has been one of them," his doorman says, "Another story [in Spanish]," when Richard sees him trapped in one of many long conversations. Such "special relationships" that doormen have with their tenants are not unique, although they are experienced as unique by the tenants, who tend to believe that their door-men are especially close to them, not thinking necessarily that they must be close to others as well. The successful doorman develops such special relationships with most of his tenants. The perception that doormen have special relationships extends beyond the relationship. Tenants in buildings where their doormen have worked for many years almost invariably feel that their building is unique. They are thus surprised to find that this is the case in most buildings. That tenants who talk with doormen feel that their relationship is special says something about the capacity of doormen to project closeness, despite the status differences that are always present. This projection is considered in more detail subsequently.

MORE MOVEMENT AND LESS TALK

The problem is that talk is cheap, as the saying goes. On average, though, neither small talk nor in-depth conversation with a few needy tenants is sufficient to counter by itself tenant perceptions that their doormen have too little do to or that they ignore them when tenants need them. To shift these perceptions, doormen generate services that they can do for tenants in their free time. They may appear to jump up to hand them their laundry, take an extra trip up the elevator to personally deliver a package, or rush outside to watch their tenants' car to make sure that when parked in front of the building, it will not receive a ticket. These small services are a constant feature of the workday for most doormen. Doormen do not articulate that they engage in these services to change tenant perceptions. Rather, they talk in terms of providing professional service. However articulated, these services often tend to go unnoticed by tenants, who perceive them as either building policy or simply the way that their doorman is (except around Christmas, when the prevailing rhetoric shifts to allow tenants to interpret small services as non-normative and motivated by the upcoming bonus). Even outside the Christmas season, the provision of small extra service is not always successful. Overtly obsequious service may backfire in some cases. Donald, for example, reports how in one case he "heard one of the tenants speak to another tenant, and I guess maybe I was too polite or something; she said, 'It's like having an English butler working here.'"

In describing what other doormen do, some doormen adopt a cynical attitude. Atzan describes coworkers in his building in relatively uncharitable terms:

> Certain doormen do certain different things for tenants also. Go the extra mile. You know, feed the plants, feed the cats, walk the dogs, wash windows. You'd be surprised what some of these doormen do just to make that extra dollar. It's a hustle, everything's a hustle, and this is one of them.

As noted above, this is a view that most tenants share on the approach of the Christmas season, when tenants read doorman behavior as bonus seeking. Doormen, on the other hand, report little seasonal change in their behavior. They are wrong; their behavior does change. But tenants are also wrong. Doorman behavior (increased attentiveness) changes not as an explicit attempt to bolster the bonus but because of very subtle structural changes in the temporality of work. As the holiday season nears, the pace and intensity of work increases. In the weeks before Christmas, the volume of packages increases, and even a slight change in the number of packages received for any given day creates new queuing problems for doormen. And longer queues make it more likely that they will be busy when tenants need something. Therefore, doormen are likely to compensate as best they can when they are free, so they take the time to deliver the packages, greet tenants when they enter the lobby, and initiate conversation. Many tenants perceive this as a rather obvious attempt to bolster their bonus. In contrast, the doormen see this additional service as necessary to compensate for the busy times of the day. I consider the bonus problem in chapter 6 in more detail.

Service and talk are the simplest strategies that doormen employ to shift tenant perceptions that they both do nothing and are unhelpful when needed. In reality, doormen cannot control the flow of events that enter the lobby, and so they are bound, like any server system, to be unable to serve everyone at the same time. This fact creates stress, since they have to make quick decisions about who to serve — and the priority schemes that they utilize will make some tenants unhappy. If they were always busy, tenants could become disciplined into adjusting to a first come, first served model, assuming that the door — like the pizza parlor, the grocery store, and the dentist's office — will get to clients when it is their turn. But because doormen are often seen without anything to do, tenants become frustrated that they are not available when they need them. The main "weapon" that doormen have to counter negative perceptions that arise from a misreading of the nature of the server system they are embedded in is to shape client preferences.

Grocery stores, dentists, airports, and other server systems also experiment with shaping preferences. For example, airlines develop systems for rewarding frequent fliers with shorter queues, and grocery stores induce different shopping patterns by linking specific servers to the number of items purchased. Consumers of these services make choices about their own behaviors based on the incentive structures provided by the server systems. In the absence of express lanes, people are less likely to purchase just one or two items in the grocery store. Since the average cost of each item in a small (less than ten-item) cart is higher than in a large cart, stores create incentives to attract small cart shoppers. These incentives, over time, shift purchasing behaviors.

In the same way, doormen try to develop over time their tenants' specific preferences for services. If they are successful, they gain some control over the temporality of their day; while they do not necessarily reduce stress, they do lay the groundwork for a claim of professional status. And this proves exceptionally important in the management of the lobby. Not all doormen are successful and some strategies fail. Shaping tenant preferences requires that doormen distinguish tenants on multiple dimensions. If doormen fail to distinguish tenants — that is, induce distinction — they can only treat them as equivalents, who are therefore subject to the presence (or absence) of the same formal rules. Thus, failure is first and foremost associated with a commitment to universalism and unwillingness to be particularistic with respect to conversation, service, greetings, and attention. In this sense, doormen who work to rule will fail. Another way to say this is that doormen must in relation to tenants renounce being an employee and claim professional status. The obvious tension is that, rhetorically, one aspect of professionalism entails a commitment to universalism. For example, doctors should treat all persons, whatever their capacity to pay for services. Likewise, one would consider lawyers who do a bad job for some kinds of people (those who cannot pay, those whom they do not like, etc.) unprofessional. But this is simply a rhetorical structure, for the salient indicator of professionalism is the capacity to act substantively against the demands of blind formal application of rules. Doormen commit to the professional norm to serve, but this commitment entails inducing differences among tenants so as to serve them better.[8] When doormen fail to differentiate across tenants, they are likely to develop negative attitudes toward them. This is often followed by exit, for doormen who seek protection from discretion must work to rule, an experience deeply frustrating for both tenants and doormen.

INDUCTION OF DISTINCTION FROM THE LITTLE THINGS

When guests arrive, doormen can hold them in the lobby and phone up to the apartment for confirmation that the guests are invited. Alternatively, doormen can send the guests on their way, phoning as soon as they step into the elevator. Or they can just send them up unannounced. When packages arrive, doormen can hold them in the back, bring them up, phone ahead, or keep them at the front desk. Videos can travel upstairs with or without warning or be held at the front desk. If cars come early to pick tenants up, doormen can call up to tell the tenant that their car has arrived or wait until the scheduled time for departure before calling. Dry cleaning can be laid out in public or stored in the back. When children come down to play, doormen can watch them or let them be. If while the parents are gone their teenagers had a party, the doormen can tell the parents or not. These small things and hundreds of others should seemingly be inconsequential. And in most instances they are. But they need not be. If unexpected guests are announced over the phone while they are downstairs, tenants who don't feel like socializing with them are caught at home and could feel trapped by the unexpected visit. Better for some would be prior warning that Mr. X and Ms. Y were on their way up. Tenants may want to avoid tipping their delivery person; if so, doormen might hold food and videos until after the delivery. Some parents may want the doormen to watch their children when they are playing out front; others may find that intrusive. The doormen do not care which preferences their tenants have, only that they have preferences and they know what they are. If tenants do not have preferences, doormen help

---

8. This brings to light a more general problem somewhat beyond the purview of this book. Is it the case that in all interacting social systems — especially those characterized by formal hierarchy — particularism in practice will emerge as a key "coping" strategy? This is certainly the case, for example, in graduate student training, even in the presence of unions. Without pronouncing from on high, one can safely say that where possible, humans will work hard to preserve substantive rationality through the exercise of discretion. The willingness and capacity to exercise judgment is at the same time a key element of professional status.

them acquire them. As Tito, who works on the swing shift in a small building on the Upper East Side, says:

> Right away, I try to ask what they want. Should I call after I send people up or before? What about their kids' friends? Do they just go up, or do I call? Relatives, people they always want to see, the whole works. If they don't care, I tell them some people I call up, others want them to go straight. If they don't know what they want, then I tell them what I like. For me, if I never seen the people before, I call up when they are in the elevator. If I know them and they come a lot, I call when they are in the lobby so they don't have to go up. But this is their choice, see. I get them to make a choice.

Training tenants to have preferences is interactive. Doormen may bring packages up to tenants and ask, "Would you rather I just held it for you downstairs"? Likewise, if kids come down to play, the doormen may call up to the apartment and say, "Hi, Mrs. X, this is the front desk. It's no problem for me to keep an eye on the kids. You want me to make sure they don't get off the sidewalk?" Repeatedly, doormen will work to find just that mix of services that tenants want. When they find it, they stick to it, often reminding the tenants that this is in fact what they want. As Bob says:

> I always say, "I got your package safe in the back just the way you want it." I want them to know I am thinking about them. Not leaving their package around on the front table 'cause they don't want others looking at it or whatever.

These little tricks of the trade provide the framework for inducing tenants to have and communicate preferences. The induction of distinction across tenants is important not because it provides better service — most of the distinctions are trivial enough to be within tenants' zone of indifference — but because it provides a solution to the management of time in the lobby. Or more precisely, because it begins to solve some of the problems associated with the experience of time — of too much and too little to do, and tenant perceptions thereof.

OVERVIEW

People do not often find themselves thinking or talking about all the people whose job it is to think deeply about how many people to put to work in some specific way in order to sufficiently provide for one service or another without creating too much redundancy. But there are a lot of those people and they are all trained in operations research. In operations research, such problems are commonplace and certainly complicated enough, once the possibility that the structure of service systems will shape client preferences is established.[9] One reason these problems are so difficult is that people are not so easily divided up. If a doorman is a little too busy and the busy period is random across the shift he works (rather than bunched in such a way as to allow hiring a part-time assistant), the only solution is to build in excess redundancy by hiring another doorman. Because employees are expensive, managers of server systems try to minimize the number of servers at work at any one time. This impacts the doorman's world, for doormen, like other service providers, struggle with the simple fact that clients arrive sporadically and with heterogeneous needs. This creates moments of intense activity and long periods of boredom and inactivity. But here ends the comparison to most other server systems, for the doorman's clients appear and reappear constantly. It is the clients who are the inescapable aspect of the doorman's daily work life. Because their needs are generally small, tenants often cannot understand why they are not met, especially since they see their doorman doing nothing most of the time. At the same time, while an enormous social gulf separates doormen from tenants, tenants are by virtue of the smallness of the services provided and the constancy of interaction very close to their doormen. This closeness is in part produced by doormen, who work to induce preferences for services and interactions with their tenants as part of their claim to professional status. But the closeness is also simply a product of the intense scrutiny that comes with serving as a border between the inside and the outside of the building. No tenant can escape for long without his or her preferences for friends, foods, movies, wines, and other services being noticed and recorded, and if absent, induced. The consequences of this fact are considered subsequently.

---

9. This possibility was considered previously. A simple example is that small-item lanes in grocery stores shape client behavior insofar as they strive, if close, to stay under the ten- or fifteen-item limit for the express lane. For doormen, known congestion at some times of the day, perhaps when the mail carrier is scheduled to arrive, may motivate tenants to report their problems either earlier or later in the day.

CHAPTER 4

Crossing the Line

I would like to think that if some huge black man came pressed against me to my side and I looked really freaked out that my doorman would know maybe something was wrong, or even just any big large man or somebody looking that they have never seen me with that they would question it and try to do something.

The previous chapter considered time management in the lobby and the tensions that arise from having too little and too much to do simultaneously. In this chapter, I shift focus and consider two substantive problems — crime and sex — that color the dynamics of lobby interactions. As noted earlier, most doormen consider that their primary responsibility in the building is to provide security. Analytically the term "security" serves a rhetorical function, encompassing a large array of services that are perhaps better described as insulation. In this broader sense, "security" serves to insulate tenants from the uncertainties of the street and thus absorb potential disorder. By absorbing disorder, doormen raise the prestige of tenants. As such, doormen provide a security service, in this general sense, much like the service provided by executive secretaries and butlers — the security is protection from uncertainty. Of course, secretaries and butlers serve single individuals, whereas doormen serve many people and some of these people are problematic for (themselves) and others. Many of them are interested in the others as objects of curiosity, enmity, or friendship. Some appear interested in the doormen as objects of fantasy. All of these cases pose special problems for doormen and their management of the lobby, and it is this set of problems (and their consequences) that I consider here.

If analytically one can say that security provides a rhetorical envelope for insulation, for doormen security also provides a ready justification for the decisions they make with respect to priority of service. For some tenants, security provides a convenient screen from which to justify the consumption of services. For other tenants, security is a real concern. Ferreting through these competing images is one of the goals of this chapter. With respect to security, the main problem I consider is simple enough: Why is security an important trope when security-related events rarely happen? This empirical focus on security provides just one of the various instantiations of a much more general theoretical problem. The theoretical problem that this chapter considers is at the broadest level how doormen and tenants generate and sustain their roles through interaction. It may seem odd at first to ask how doorman and tenant roles are generated through interaction, but as suggested in the previous chapter, while just residing in a building makes one a tenant, the content of the relation "tenant," and in this case its complement "doorman," is not defined, and one has to learn how to be a tenant in relation to doormen; that is, one has to learn how to have preferences, interactive styles, and so on. There is thus a dynamic process through which doormen help teach tenants how to be tenants, while at the same time tenants help teach doormen how to be doormen for them.

This mutual dance is common to all roles and role structures. It makes sense that it is so, since in the absence of clarity over the behavioral content of roles — that is, what people do when they express behavior that is consistent with their role set — it is simply impossible to know what a behavior means. The simplest analytic statement of this problem is that the meaning of an event is conditional on its position in a sequence of events, and therefore to understand what an event means, one has to locate it within a sequence that has a beginning and an end. It is the presence of a role structure — a set of understandings governing interaction — that provides for people in interaction (here, doormen and their tenants) these boundaries for the interactions they are experiencing, and hence a frame from which to share the same interpretation of the meaning of an event.[1] One could say, blithely, that cognition is distributed. Without a role structure within which one can locate the interacting parties, the meaning of a behavior is up for grabs. Thus, most fundamentally, this and the following

---

1. Consider the simple example of interpreting the meaning of a smile. It would seem at first that the smile is unambiguous — a socially acceptable way to indicate pleasure, joy, and so on. But all of us have had the experience, at some time in our life, of finding that the seemingly innocent smile, proffered by a stranger as a prelude to interaction, becomes somehow sinister and disturbing, and thus serves not as an indication of joy or pleasure but, instead, of malfeasance and perhaps horror. This transformation of the smile is the result of its placement in a sequence of interactions, for the same smile alone may mean something quite different than the same smile offered again and again, without any corresponding escalation of interactive content or in response to a proffered escalation of content in interaction.

chapter are concerned with the generation of role structures that make shared meanings possible.[2] It is also the case that the generation of a role structure involves the drawing of boundaries. In this chapter, we consider both the formal and informal boundaries that emerge between tenants and doormen, and the ways in which doormen and tenants define the boundaries of their joint world, in opposition to the street.

ALL VISITORS MUST BE ANNOUNCED

First and foremost, most tenants and many doormen agree that doormen are expected to provide security for their building. The standard enforcement mechanism is the ubiquitous sign: *All Visitors Must Be Announced*. This sign is ubiquitous because building managers (and tenants and doormen) believe that potential criminals are likely to pursue stylized strategies for gaining entrance to a building,[3] all of which involve *not* being announced. Thus, in the security briefing of one major apartment building on the East Side, doormen are advised that there are numerous ways that criminals try to gain entrance to apartments, using pretenses such as "I am expected"; "I have an appointment"; "I am Dr. X and have to see . . ." Managers also report that a standard strategy that malfeasants use is to mill around the entrance of a building until a group of tenants arrives. They then try to walk in with the group. Some doormen report hearing about such techniques as well, though no doormen reported ever having this kind of experience.

---

2. A shared role structure is just one element, of course. History, biography, and their intersection (as Mills, *The Sociological Imagination*, noted some time ago) are also important.

3. A quick glance at the *New York Times* over the past century suggests that while criminals generally follow simple strategies for gaining access to apartments (and so building managers are right to focus on some stylized strategies), there is a lot of innovation among the criminally inclined. One can read, for example, of one enterprising criminal who posed as a deliveryman. Pulling his gun from an empty box, he took the doorman to the back of the building and then, with compatriots, systematically robbed residents who entered or tried to leave the building. In one ten-minute takeover of a posh East Side building, this group of crooks made off with $1,312 in cash, $2,250 in jewels, and a Volkswagen (used as the getaway car). Three weeks later, the criminal developed a better plan that allowed him to jettison his compatriots. Pulling a gun on the doorman and locking him in the staff room, he next put on an extra uniform and ensconced himself at the front desk and greeted tenants with a cheerful "Good afternoon — I'm your new doorman," before robbing and locking them in a back room. Selectively collecting tenants as they came down the elevator netted five more victims, and within five minutes he had escaped with $175 in cash and $5,345 worth of jewelry. "Stolen Glemby Gems Are Officially Listed."

Bob, for example, says: "I once heard that some people followed someone in and got on the elevator and tried to hold him or her up. See, they were with them but they were not with them." Because this ("going in through traffic") is reported to be a common stratagem, building managers instruct doormen to be alert to the possibility and to challenge all visitors in a group, even those with a tenant, in order to ascertain whether or not they are in the same party. But management insistence on 100% screening poses significant interactive problems for doormen. They simply cannot *always* ask tenants if the people they are with are friends or not. It would be way too intrusive. But more important, it would signal exactly what they do not want to signal — that they do not know their tenants. Because knowledge of their tenants provides one of the central bases for their claim to professional status, inflexible adherence to the written rules would be professionally de-legitimizing.

So while doormen can listen and look for verbal or visual clues to see if the guest is wanted or not (if tenants are talking with or looking at their "guests," the doormen can assume that they are legitimate guests), such clues are often absent for a number of reasons. First, and perhaps most obviously, the presence of the doorman shapes the behavior of hosts and guests. Once in the lobby, many parties shift attention outward, toward the doorman, thus providing few hints as to the nature of the "internal" relationship. This is especially true for couples, who will tend to limit their intimacy upon entering the lobby.[4] Second, and most often the case late at night — and most noticeably for tenants who have an incentive to keep some aspect of their private life private — it is not uncommon to find that tenants often try to "sneak" guests past their doormen, especially if their guests are sexual partners who would prefer for some reason or another to remain anonymous, but more generally anyone they would rather not be publicly associated with. The irony is that the effort that tenants exert to build a privacy screen around their guests creates an incentive for doormen to look through the screen for a sign of a relationship. In the absence of such

---

4. Many buildings have closed-circuit video systems installed in the elevators, which doormen watch. A few doormen in these buildings report all sorts of sexual behavior occurring in the elevators (whether this is fantasy on their part or not is harder to assess and is considered subsequently). But most doormen will report that if the couple is alone, they almost always resume interaction once in the elevator, out of the "public" eye. Doormen can thus watch the elevator if they are in doubt about the legitimacy of a guest, but this is also a bit like closing the barn door once the horse has left.

a sign, doormen have to make a flash decision: Is the visitor with the tenant or simply using the tenant as a mechanism for entering the building?

To be able to answer this question with any degree of reliability, doormen have to invest heavily in building up a bank of faces and personalities that they can associate with each tenant. No one is too surprised that doormen remember the names and faces of their tenants. That they also remember the faces and relationship to tenants of their tenants' friends and relatives is more surprising. For each tenant, doormen develop elaborate theoretical schemes that allocate classes — or ethnic groups or social types — of people as legitimate visitors. The homogeneity of most buildings with respect to tenant social class and ethnic background minimizes the work involved, but it is still extensive. With tenants resident in buildings for long periods of time, the accuracy of the doormen's perceptions can be extremely high, consequently minimizing risk for all residents. While doormen often purport to have little interest in the personal lives of their tenants, the problem is that in order to do their job well, they actually have to learn quite a bit. The key is that by virtue of their everyday contact with tenants and their visitors, doormen develop theories about each tenant to help them make the kinds of decisions they need to make.

Before too long, tenants also come to realize that their doorman has a theory about whom they associate with and that the theory is generally accurate. At one level, this knowledge provides a comfort of sorts. Tenants can feel relatively secure that if they are indeed brought into the building by a criminal ("with a knife pressed against my back"), the doorman will realize "that kind of person is not who she usually hangs out with" and subtly intervene. At the same time, tenants come to realize that if doormen can do this, they know an awful lot about what kind of life they do have.[5] And this realization is extremely uncomfortable for tenants with things they perceive are worth hiding. And it is vaguely uncomfortable for all tenants, even if they do not exactly feel that they have something to hide. Tenants who feel uncomfortable about the knowledge their doormen do have still prefer

---

5. Most people are also uncomfortable with the idea that they can be "read like an open book" and would prefer to imagine that around them lies at least a small aura of mystery. When people come to think that their doorman can read them, there enters a certain subtly disturbing existential threat. But because they know their doorman, they can also gain comfort from the fact that he cannot really know them, playing therefore on the non-trivial social class and life experience differences that lie between them.

their knowledge to an alternative, having their neighbors (or some set of neighbors) know more than they already do.

SPYING ON THE NEIGHBORS

Many building managers faced with the high costs of maintaining doorman coverage twenty-four hours a day thought that an economical alternative might be closed-circuit television coupled with an automatic buzzer system for opening doors.[6] Such systems can reduce costs significantly, since in most buildings with doormen, labor costs constitute a quarter of the building operation budgets. When these kinds of systems were first introduced in 1967, building management could expect to save substantial amounts of money, up to $200,000 per year. In many buildings, savings could be substantially higher; now it is easily double this. For less than a couple hundred dollars per year per unit, buildings could set up special cable channels for tenants that enabled them to view the lobby and front door whenever someone buzzed their apartment for entry. This would allow tenants to check on their visitors with more accuracy than voice monitoring and also allow them to ascertain whether or not the guests they were admitting were theirs. While such systems were not designed to block access to interlopers trying to sneak into the building on the tails of otherwise legitimate visitors, they were designed to replace the essential security services of living doormen.

And they were popular with building managers, who sold the security provided by closed-circuit TV monitoring as "better than door service," since it was on without breaks or interruptions twenty-four hours per day, seven days a week. No longer would buildings be without "essential protection" because the staff were getting coffee or smoking a cigarette. Notwithstanding the rhetoric, security was never the main issue. Still, twenty-four-hour surveillance closed-circuit monitoring systems turned out to be especially

---

6. Almost all buildings now have closed-circuit monitoring of elevators, back rooms, and the lobby. In some buildings, doormen have been replaced by security guards whose function is to watch the camera banks. In buildings with video and doormen, the video is typically not saved, but there are exceptions to this rule. Saved or not, the increased reliance on twenty-four-hour video monitoring in buildings exposes doormen to significantly greater management supervision than previously. It is not uncommon for supervisors to watch selected tape in an effort to secure evidence that one of their workers was sleeping on the job, did not return from lunch on schedule, and so on, if they are eager to terminate them. Doormen may also watch tapes if they turn out to be especially amusing or, as they report sometimes, erotic, and they may share these with others in their building.

popular with some tenants, and this emerged as the central problem. Too many tenants turned out to have too little to do and consequently spent much of their time monitoring the traffic in the lobby. Long before executives at TV stations discovered that people would spend hours watching the minutia of other people's lives on reality shows, building managers and sales personnel of surveillance systems discovered that, as one cable official reported to the *New York Times*:

> The service was especially attractive to some homebody tenants who like to watch lobby traffic for hours on end. However, unmarried tenants and psychiatrists who maintain offices in apartment buildings sometimes object to a system that allows their neighbors to scrutinize their visitors.

Even tenants with relatively rich lives (people with friends and jobs) would find that the "lobby show" (as one described it) was relaxing and fun to watch. It was better than straight TV because one later got a chance to observe the celebrities (read: neighbors) off the set, on the street, in the hall, and even (for friends) in their apartments. Since the lobby show would be always on, it was possible to sneak a quick peek, just to see if anything was happening. Worse, people discovered that they could watch their closest neighbors in ways they had never been able to before. Hearing their neighbors in the hall, for example, one could grab a quick glance as they left the elevator and headed through the lobby, just to see what they might be doing that night, judging from the clothes they had on. Neighbors (those who live on the same hall) are bad enough, but the real nightmare came from the undifferentiated and completely uncontrolled surveillance of unknown people living in the same building.

Relatively quickly, then, first for persons with legitimate reasons to prefer some oversight with respect to lobby security (psychiatrists with offices on the first floor of residential buildings, for example, strongly objected to unknown neighbors observing the entrance and exit of their patients, but also divorcées, single people with active romantic lives, and so on) and subsequently for most people, the nonstop TV show, featuring them or their friends as stars, became uncomfortable.[7] Faced with the choice of having a

---

7. Typically, the absence of sound recording makes lobby videos more exciting to watch, since the triviality of most interactions one can observe makes it difficult to generate more interesting theories

single person monitor your personal life or multiple intrusive neighbors, most tenants strongly prefer the doorman. His knowledge is at least manageable, in large part because it is public (i.e., the tenant and the doorman are both present when the observation occurs, except for video monitoring). Because the knowledge is public, the doormen — unlike anonymous observers — also need to bridge the discomfort that arises from the tension between closeness and distance. So doormen work as hard as tenants to negotiate this tension.[8] In much the same way that one counts on their host to help collectively manage the embarrassment arising from an inconvenient slip of the tongue, tenants can count on their doorman to ease potential moments of embarrassment. That is what is meant by discretion.

CALLING AHEAD

As noted earlier, because doors are not always covered, it is often reported that malfeasants search for names of residents while the doorman is absent and then assert (when he returns) that they have come to visit one or another tenant. The "all visitors must be announced" rule is designed to block this trick. Likewise, delivery people are not to be sent to apartments without prior notification, and "doctors" who come to make house calls are also to be carefully screened (the latter probably with good reason, since anyone who thinks that they can get into an apartment because they are a doctor making a house call, an event whose frequency is relatively low, is a priori suspicious). Doormen are instructed to announce friends, relatives, dinner guests, children visiting for play dates after school, and so on. In theory, no one should get by without being announced, even if they come often. This rule poses interactive problems for doormen and also tenants, who often team up and resort to the peculiar form of duplicity with frequent visitors described earlier, sending them up in the elevator, for example, and then, as soon as the door closes, calling to warn their tenants of the imminent arrival.

---

about what might be going on. The monitors then provide a shell for the fantasy life of tenants, which is almost always more stimulating than the real life they are observing. This may be one of the reasons that it is so much fun to watch essentially nothing.

8. This is not the case with "tenant doormen." As noted further below, when we consider the impacts of the 1991 strike, tenants were generally less comfortable with having tenants who served doorman replacement shifts monitor their comings and goings than they were with their doorman. But more problematic was the tendency for tenants to officiously enforce identification rules, both with respect to guests and tenants, whether they knew them or not — that is, to not act as professional doormen.

The "all visitors must be announced rule" works to block entry to guests for those tenants who ask that the doormen adhere to the policy, but since many tenants prefer to have their visitors arrive unannounced, doormen are at risk — when they follow their tenants' preferences — of letting into the building the "wrong sort of people." Without a reliable theory to direct their decisions, doormen cannot decide which people ought to be announced and which ought to be let in. In the absence of a tenant-tailored theory, doormen make decisions on the basis of the two homophily principles at their disposal. The first is that the tenants' friends are like tenants. Since most tenants are upper class — at least from their perspective, and recall that doormen tend to estimate class upward for both psychological and observational reasons — their friends are likely to be upper class as well. Since class and race in New York City (and everywhere else in the United States) correlate strongly, doormen are much less likely to admit blacks or other minority group members without announcing them first.[9] Second, as noted earlier, since doormen are recruited from within ethnic networks and since blacks are underrepresented in those networks, doormen are much more likely to announce minorities than any others. They may do this, as in the case discussed previously, because tenants who prefer to have all visitors announced are least likely to have minority friends, or because in a context of uncertainty, doormen invoke the homophily rule to determine how to respond to building visitors, a rule that, because it is accurate most of the time, is remarkably efficient. Consequently, the perception that doors are closed more quickly to minorities is accurate. And this is true throughout the year; there are thus no special open or closed seasons. In this case, while doormen are not any more prejudiced than others, the exercise of small micro-preferences (of tenants or doormen) has quite striking global impacts. While the experience of racial discrimination appears to peak around holiday seasons, the practical reality of discrimination is relatively constant.[10]

---

9. Here one can see that the benefit of closed-circuit monitor systems is that they are not biased, even inadvertently.

10. Felicia Lee, writing in the *New York Times* (November 28, 1999) notes: "Now that the holiday season has officially begun, the city's social meters are clicking wildly. A cast of characters ranging from doormen to store clerks are busy flexing their prerogative of exclusion. . . . All my African-American and brown-skinned Latino acquaintances have stories. . . . The doorman who is so friendly to the other tenants harasses or ignores them and their black and Hispanic friends." Lee, "For Racist Slights, the Meter Is Still Running." Exactly why this should happen around the holiday

EXTENDING THE BOUNDARY OF THE PRIVATE

As there are many buildings, there are many systems for handling security. Here, I briefly consider one system — where guests or delivery people are unable to proceed to floors without a building escort — that relies on hiring staff to operate the elevator and installing door locks on staircase entries to floors, allowing residents to exit to the lobby in case of emergency but not to enter onto floors other than their own. Unless the management hires a dedicated elevator operator, the doorman function shifts predominantly from the lobby to the elevator. Because the operator needs to respond to all travel requests, thereby spending the bulk of his time outside the lobby, buildings with this system typically hire a dedicated elevator operator for the day shift and try to get by with a single doorman on the swing and night shift. Where doormen operate elevators, a different interaction regime often appears.

In such buildings, contact between tenants and doormen is more intense, since joint trips in the elevator force sociability between tenant and doorman when others are not in the car. If in other buildings tenants can walk quickly through the lobby, in doorman-operated elevator buildings, the temporal transit through the lobby is extended, often significantly. The elevator ride creates a new context for strategic interactions, as tenants may use the opportunity that other tenants as audience provide to engage with their doorman and, depending on the frame, perhaps express noblesse oblige or, more subtly, an "everyday, easygoing" personality. This experience of observed contact may feel too personal to some. Newcomers to the building often perceive too much closeness to their doorman relative to their prior experience in a doorman building with self-operating elevators. But this is a matter more of perception than reality. The doormen in both buildings know whom the tenant is seeing; the elevator just makes it explicit that he does. But the fact that the knowledge is explicit slices away one layer of ambiguity that helps preserve social distance between doorman and tenant, and therefore sharpens the nature of their relationship.

---

season is unclear, and in fact it seems unlikely that it spikes in any measurable way. More likely, the apparent peak during the holiday season is an artifact of increased visiting, the underlying behavior occurring at the same rate at other times of the year is just not noticed since a threshold is not reached. Alternatively, and perhaps driven by another dynamic — the difficulty of writing about discrimination in the *New York Times* — the holiday season was simply a device to get the article started, and everyone knows that the basic behaviors are constant across seasons.

The more significant change is that with the elevator operator, the boundary between the inside and the outside is elongated and extended; the
liminality of the lobby now extends to the floor. This is ironic, for the
purpose of the elevator operator is to preserve the floor as a private space.
But the cost of such preservation is the more visible penetration of the
doorman up into the world of the tenants.

ROUTINE TENANT MOTIVATIONS

Ask almost any tenant why they live in a doorman building and quickly
enough security comes to the fore. A small sample of responses to this
question should suffice to demonstrate the general point.

> When I looked for an apartment, I definitely made it very clear when
> I used a broker that I was looking strictly for doormen buildings, and
> I would say that I see them primarily at this time in my life, being a
> single woman, that they serve primarily the function of security for
> me, the feeling of security and safety mainly because they are there
> standing in front, and I come in late at night or even in the day or early
> in the morning, and I always know someone is going to be there at the
> door making sure that I get up safely and watching who is coming in
> and out of the building.
>
> I would say the security again, I really feel safe; I feel safer here
> than I do in my suburbia house that I grew up in when I lived with my
> parents, so in a nutshell security.

As noted earlier, doormen echo these sentiments, uniformly stating that
their primary function is to provide security.

> We are the security here, we are security, and, you know, since I been
> here I have no major problems, you know; I have no problems at all.
> I always keep my eyes on things, I do my job, I screen anybody who
> comes here, I notice everyone, I don't send nobody to go up there
> alone, they got to be escorted by someone, or special people that come
> through the door . . . visitors, family, and friends are coming through
> here, and no other people.

Screening, watching, noticing, and ultimately blocking access to all ("I don't
send nobody to go up there alone"), except as it turns out, visitors, family,

and friends; what is left implicit is "visitors, family, and friends that I recognize."

> The most important thing for a doorman in a building like this is do the things like security, which is one, that's the main one, that's the main thing, keep the doors safe from intruders, outsiders and stuff.
>
> It's a big, big responsibility. I mean, you're basically in charge of security, because you've really got to make sure that no one goes up unannounced or who's not welcome there. And we've got security cameras on the back door, so you've got to sort of keep your eye on that door. You've got people coming in as someone's leaving; you have to worry.
>
> If we wouldn't be on the door here, I would say at least once a week somebody would be robbed. I guarantee you that. I used to think, "Oh, a doorman, what a bullshit, stupid thing," but you know, no, it's not, it's a lot of security.

And on and on, interview after interview, security appears as a main theme. Oddly, only a few doormen can *ever* recall a single event at their building. In response to simple questions like: Has anything ever happened here? Has anyone ever tried to break in? Have you ever had to deter someone from trying to enter? and so on, most doormen — even those who have worked for more than twenty years — have never had an event occur on their watch. It is worth noting, in this context, that many doormen currently working now also worked as doormen during the high-crime period in the city. The fact that they cannot recall a security breach (from the outside) is therefore quite remarkable.

> Q: So you never had anyone try to get in?
> A: No, actually, no. [In] 2001 I'll have been pushing twenty years here. Actually, every now and then you'll get a strange person that will say does so-and-so live here. But whether you give them access or not . . . that you decide.
>
> Not forcibly, but at any moment someone could. I have a distress button in case I should need assistance quickly; as you can see, the boss doesn't always like to be bothered. Let's say I should need assistance immediately: I'm not armed or anything; it's not like I'm a cop where I

can defend myself. You know it's like the best I can do is press my distress button and that would be it. It's not like someone is going to come down and say, "You need help?" It's not that they don't care. They expect me to take care of the security; that's why I'm here; I lend a helping hand every now and then. The main objective is security.

See we have a black wood baseball bat hidden here on the bottom shelf; that's my helper in case somebody tries to get past me.

Q: Have you ever had to use it?

A: No, but there she is if I ever need her.

No, not yet, but they could anytime, so there are distress buttons and baseball bats and emergency alarms and video cameras; in short, almost all buildings have a machinery for protection. Most doormen have all this stuff but never feel like they are at risk to have to use it. There just aren't that many potential intruders. The exceptions to the general rule may be informative as well. Consider Danny, who reports:

Your basic job is security. What you need is to be an observant person, being someone who's not easily tricked . . . you know what I'm saying. Someone who's a little sharper probably than someone who's sitting in front of the door taking up space. I've had plenty of people trying to get into the building, giving fake names or wanting to go to the back and use the bathroom or things of that sort.

Here, the external validation of being a smart guy is catching people who try to be tricky. That other doormen do not observe tricky people could then be, as Danny suggests, because they are as dull as a hoe, but this seems unlikely. It is more reasonable to presume that nothing happens to them.

The mismatch between experience and thought is generally attributed to the uniform.[11] One idea is that criminals don't really try to get into doorman

---

11. Tenants also like uniforms. There is a sort of toy quality to their appreciation of them, in the sense that "they might as well get a cute one." "Yes. I do think that a doorman should have to wear a uniform. It looks nicer. It looks better, it is more impressive looking. I mean I am not really trying to impress anyone who walks into this building, and I could care less if they like this building or if this is a doorman building. But if you are going to have a doorman, you might as well have them wear a uniform." In fairness, other tenants have a different opinion, viz.: "The uniforms in my building are ridiculous — especially the hats — they should be paid extra for the humiliation of having to wear them." During the Kennedy administration, the *New York Times* ran a feature story on the transformation of the uniform, noting that "the epaulets, braid and trimmings once considered

buildings because they see the man on the door in a uniform and realize it is hopeless. As Bob suggests: "The uniform at night is really an act of deterrence. It cuts down on crime and it makes those lingering outside a lot less likely to wander into the lobby. With the uniform, they don't even bother to come in."

There may be come truth to this kind of claim, based on a counter-factual that cannot be actually observed, viz., in buildings of this kind, in the absence of doormen, crime would be higher. The presence of doormen blocks criminal activity, so the fact that doormen almost never actively block illegal entrance to the building is the consequence of their being there in the first place. One could, of course, consider crime rates in buildings that do not have doormen, but these buildings are in different neighborhoods, have different people living in them, and are under different surveillance from the residents, so the comparison is likely to be misleading. In any case, doorman buildings are without much crime, at least the kind of crime arising from the disorder of the street.[12]

TENANTS ON THE EDGE

But there are problems that confront doormen from disorder in the building. Doormen aid in the production of this disorder by training many tenants to prefer to have their visitors pass through unannounced. For tenants, there are a lot of reasons for this preference. First, some tenants feel that the "announcement" makes the visit too formal and changes the relationship that they have with their visitors. As Dunbar says:

---

essential for the well-dressed doorman are as outmoded as the comic-opera generals who wore similar outfits. The doorman's uniform of today is single-breasted, and it has the natural shoulder. . . . Either the three buttons of the Ivy League or the two-button style preferred by President Kennedy is the rule today." Still, in 1962 tenants were reported to invariably prefer fancier uniforms — going so far as to specify full-length dress tailcoats. One doorman, who was asked to wear a uniform trimmed with gold lamé to match the fabric under the marquee, was reported to have rebelled: "Do you want me to look like Liberace?" (Liberace, by the way, is famous for noting: "My clothes may look funny but they make me money.") "Well-Dressed Doorman Trades Epaulets for Ivy League Look," 187.

12. The fact that residents in doorman buildings are more concerned about security, all things being equal, than residents in non-doorman buildings also increases the difficulty of entrance and provides additional protection. Still, it is remarkable to discover how many people living in New York City in doorman buildings never lock their doors. Some go so far as to keep their doors unlocked but pretend to lock them for the doorman and others, so they ask (for example) for the doorman to keep the keys for their cleaning service workers, pet walkers, and so on, even if the doors are open.

> I want my friends to feel like they can just drop in whenever. The doormen know if I am home, and so if I am, I want them to just send them up to see me.

Ironically, Dunbar realizes, though, that if the doormen don't know where he is, that they should call to preserve (in this instance) a fiction of "openness."

> Yeah, if they know I am out, they should call, because otherwise it looks like they are just preventing my friends from coming to visit me. And anyway, they could be wrong. I might have come back and they just didn't see me or something.

Second, many tenants don't feel comfortable having the doormen know all of their friends, even if they are comfortable with, and appreciate, the fact that the doormen know most of their friends. For doormen, though, tenants who come to prefer doormen to use discretion in determining who should or should not be announced allow them to deliver personalized professional service. So many doormen thus help their tenants come to think that their preference is to allow some friends and visitors to arrive unannounced. This "training" is simple. Once doormen recognize regular guests, they often suggest to tenants (when they call) that they could "just send them right up since I know them now." Tenants thus learn that there are opportunities for specialized service — here, the recognition of their friends — that violate the posted rules. They can choose to play, or not. And this choice — whatever direction is takes — is what doormen look for.

Letting strangers in without calling ahead is a simple thing, but like all simple things can lead to bigger problems. Potential problems are why the rule is there in the first place, and these potential problems can be especially acute for tenants whose activities, in the main or part, put them on the wrong side of the law or normative behavior. These tenants create special problems for doormen, who are well aware of their tenants' behavior.

In fact, many of the crime stories involving residential buildings in New York appear to arise from instances in which doormen allowed access without announcement to apartments where illegal activities were going on because they knew that the visitors and tenants were jointly engaged in the activity. The problem is that there is (often) no honor among thieves, and bad things can happen when criminals are unsupervised. Thus, for example, in 1932 two men got past a doorman by pretending to be bootleggers delivering illegal alcohol to one of the tenants, H. C. Glemby. Carrying a burlap bag containing bottles, they absconded with $350,000 worth of gems and jewelry. In 1937, under similar circumstances — in both robberies the wife was out for the evening, a fact known to the crooks — two men pretending to be deliverymen got past the doorman on West Seventy-second Street and stole $50,000 in jewelry from Isaac Keller. Oddly, Keller's wife was Glemby's mother.[13] In the mid-1960s a tenant was murdered when a drug deal, conducted in an upscale apartment building, went awry. More recently, in an upscale East Side apartment, a doorman was suspended for allowing two men access to an apartment. Once in the apartment, they pushed the tenant around and threatened him. Here, the tenant was involved in illegal processing of identification cards. It is likely that the doorman, knowing the tenant's business, let the men up, assuming they were there to collect the altered documents they had paid for previously. Unfortunately for all involved, the operation had been discovered by the police sometime earlier and shut down. For the doormen involved, whether turning a blind eye to drug trafficking or facilitating the delivery of illegal liquor or the processing of illegal documents, those involved in illegal activities have a bad habit of associating with unsavory people.

Most doormen don't work in buildings where tenants forge documents or trade in illicit goods. Or if they do, their tenants are smart enough to avoid capture. Many, however, work in buildings where some tenants are involved in high-end prostitution. The general sense of building managers in the city is that most large buildings have "a working girl" in them, and that they make fine tenants as long as the traffic flow into the building or on the floor is not too high. For many women in the escort service, doormen provide additional security and protection beyond that provided by their pimp or service. The discretion involved is significant. Doormen have to both register the presence of and not see johns. Their exercise of discretion means that they put themselves at some risk, for it is always possible that something will go awry in the exchange going on upstairs.

In all of these instances, the doorman's knowledge of tenants' behaviors — the liquor being delivered, the presence of an escort business, or the fact that a document-altering operation was in existence — meant that they could not

---

13. Although the facts of these cases suggest an inside job, no reference to complicity of the doormen can be found. But explicit complicity is only in degree different from the implicit complicity of knowing that criminal activities are occurring and, for that reason, shifting one's gaze.

accurately "announce visitors" without implicating themselves in the operation. That much of the risk to tenants arises from their own (or a neighbor's) behavior puts doormen in a complicated relationship. They know what is going on, either because they are conduits for illegal information or because they have multiple opportunities to watch, yet they have to act with the utmost discretion.[14] They may also benefit directly, although few doormen will talk explicitly about the relationship between their illicit knowledge and the bonus.[15] With tenants engaging in illicit behavior, doormen exercise a protective role. The problem is that the protection they provide places the building at increased risk. The trick that gets them out of this bind is the management of the lobby, a problem I return to shortly.

LINE CROSSING

In pornographic literature, it is not uncommon to find, when they are mentioned, well-endowed doormen with buff-sounding names like Gary and Chad either (a) "taking off their gloves" and "delivering more than packages to their lonely tenants"; (b) surreptitiously watching, via video cameras mounted in the elevators and back rooms, their tenants with names like Monica and Bill have "sex"; or (c) discreetly directing elderly gentlemen to the buxom blond who resides in the penthouse apartment, perhaps courtesy of some mobster. Confronted with such scenes arising from the imagination of xxx-rated story writers, one might find it surprising that real doormen and real tenants are generally more boring than the Bills and Monicas of

---

14. Doormen's knowledge of the comings and goings of their tenants and their friends sometimes puts them in the limelight, whatever discretion they might otherwise exercise. Frank Caldwell, a doorman at 969 Fifth Avenue, was called to testify on the whereabouts of Doris Duke in September 1943 during divorce proceedings initiated by H. R. Cromwell. Likewise, Norval Keith stood by his story — against the sworn testimony of other eyewitnesses — that it was Vincent "the Chin" Gigante who shot Frank Costello (after saying, "This is for you, Frank"). "Costello Doorman Sticks to His Story," *New York Times*, May 17, 1958, 40.

15. One doorman was relatively explicit, though, noting: "[Here] are some transvestites — they go up in suits, they come back down, they're dressed as women, you never know. Things like that, they really bug you out. I had a guy, he was totally normal seeming, you know, he would have this second life, or something like that, where he used to like to get whipped, and chains, and all that crazy shit. Yeah. So he used to give me the trust. See, in that building, they used to have to trust you, because you can hurt them." In this instance, while blackmail is not explicitly mentioned, one got the feeling that the discretionary knowledge that the doorman did have rested in the background as a subtle threat. This was very unusual, though.

fantasy land.[16] Still, sex is present in both the conversations and thoughts that some tenants have about their doormen and that some doormen have about their tenants. And the problem of sex colors the dynamics of the lobby in important ways, whether "anything" actually happens or not.

A pretty woman crosses the lobby. The topic of conversation is priority service, how to manage conflicting demands, who should get served first if there is a pileup. Armando doesn't skip a beat, replying, "That one, you know what I mean?" But then he clarifies:

> Seriously, I wouldn't go to a party at her house, I wouldn't hang out, it just causes too many problems. Even if the opportunity were to arise, I wouldn't. It just causes too many problems. These girls you see every day. You can't have a relationship with them. It's going to break up eventually, and they're going to have guys coming in and out, in your face. Work is enough pressure without you having that kind of thing going on. Not that it wouldn't be nice.

On another day, in a small lobby, the conversation is winding to a close. Directly in front of the door is the elevator; Seymour is behind a large counter on the left. He is talking about this and that when two attractive women walk out. He interrupts the conversation and says hi, and then turns and says, quite out of the blue:

> I try not to with that. It's really not a good idea. I don't like to know much about them, and, you know, there's a flip side about that, they don't know too much about me either.

In response to a question about orientation and training, Roberto, who has worked in his East Side building for less than a year, says, "Yeah, in this building there is one rule. The super tells me: 'Out there it's under sixteen, in here, under eighty-five.'"

So the three messages here, echoed in other comments, suggest both an awareness of the potential sexuality of tenants and the clear risks of

---

16. It is possible, of course, that neither the doormen not the tenants trusted us enough to talk about sex. If one considers the national data (cf. Laumann and Michael, *Sex, Love, and Health in America*), it turns out that most Americans have relatively boring sex lives. There is no reason to think that doormen are any different, except that they are likely to be more traditional since they come from disproportionately Catholic and working-class backgrounds.

involvement with them. And this is almost always referred to as the line that doesn't get crossed.

> We used to have a doorman who was rather friendly, but he crossed that line, and that's one thing I do not do. We are friends; we shake hands, whatever, but as far as crossing that line between tenant and employee, that I don't do. So we know what boundaries there are. That tenant, she still lives here. She is not a flirt but she is very nice. He took it the wrong way. So he bought her flowers, wrote her a letter, and signed the letter instead of sending it anonymously. And she read that, she was offended, and her father was a lawyer, and he was fired two days later. You know, there is a fine line between tenant and doorman, and you have to be nice but not cross that line.

"Under eighty-five," "not a good idea," "a fine line," "better stay away from the juice"; doormen know that while they need to personalize their relationships with tenants, that such personalization has clear boundaries. While doormen may also fantasize about their tenants, from their perspective risk also occurs when tenants act on fantasies with their doormen. Either way the risk is that something will bring doormen and tenants together in ways that threaten the line. Bill, for example, reports:

> One night during the midnight shift, I was working on a Sunday, these two tenants came in and were a little intoxicated, and they proceeded to undress themselves in front of me . . . two females, and I had to stop them. So they stopped. I don't cross that line between tenant and employee. That was about it.

And Ryan relates:

> One day I was working the night [shift] and a lady here, I guess she was doing drugs earlier that night. It was like 2:30, 3:00 in the morning, and she came down here just in her underwear. What am I going to do? I approached her very nicely, I talked to her, and I grabbed her by the arm, walked her into the elevator, and took her to her floor. I helped her on her floor and I just closed the door and I locked the elevator down here so there was no way for her to come down here. If she wanted to come down, she would have to walk and I don't think she could have made it down the stairs. The next time I saw her, she behaved like nothing happened.

Note, though, that the line is really drawn around a specific element of the relationship, sexual contact. Tenants can and do share deep personal confidences with their doormen. And doormen put up with or actively participate in such confidences, without ever thinking that they cross over the boundary of professional behavior. Thus, Timoto reports:

> Sometimes people might come down in the middle of the night with a personal problem and they have to have somebody to discuss it with and some of them are very personal; even a wife may come down [saying] that she has a situation to deal with because of her husband or another situation that a person might come down because of the emotional trauma she's in. The emotional trauma she is going through she wants to give me the alcohol, a couple of bottles immediately to make sure that she's not going to get them.

And the absurd happens now and then, often potentially sexual, but clearly not. For example, Chris describes how a tenant locked herself out of her apartment and had to come into the lobby to get his help. Here, despite similar behavior, there is no mention of crossing the line.

> One time it was a tenant, it was kind of odd, she's down in the lobby, running, and she's in like panties and a bra, and she's running through the lobby. You know, she's hiding behind me, 'cause I'm fairly wide, and she's like, "Chris, get me the spare key!" She went to throw out the garbage and the door closed behind her, and she was trapped, locked out of her apartment, so she had to come down the elevator and into the lobby, and there's all these people walking by, and she's hiding behind me, waiting for me to get the key.

Tenants use the same "crossing the line" metaphor as well to describe doormen who seem to them too forward. Here, Lorraine, a young attractive woman who lives with two girlfriends on the Upper West Side, describes a substitute doorman as crossing the line, though she isn't quite sure if *the line* is in the rule book or not.

> I'm really not sure about the doorman rule book. . . . [W]e actually had a substitute doorman during the summer because the doormen went on vacation. And he was [a] younger fellow. He was like nineteen and he sort of like, I would say, crossed the line. One day I came in, and he said, "I was going to ask you out to lunch." Then I said, "Are you like

asking me out to lunch by saying that you were going to ask me out to lunch?" But that was the closest I ever came to personal activity with my doorman. But there was no actual lunch involved. But he definitely freaked me out.

[T]he one who sort of asked me out on a date, that was sort of strange and weird. And I actually said to him, "Isn't this crossing some sort of line in the doorman rule guide? Doesn't this go beyond the professional level?"

Of course, the line is written in the book and crossing it can get you fired, whether or not one has accumulated prior warnings. The union may dispute a termination on the basis of an unsubstantiated charge of harassment, but they will not be able to protect a doorman who has been caught line crossing.

Rules prohibit behavior that people would otherwise prefer to do if there were no additional costs associated with behaving in a prohibited way. Thus, to select a simple example, everyone picks their nose sometimes. It is a pleasurable thing to do. But the pleasure one obtains from nose picking does not typically outweigh the costs of the negative social sanctions one receives if caught picking in public. So people pick their nose when they think they are alone and they can just enjoy it. Many doormen and many tenants might very well like to have some kind of sexual relationship. The rule prohibiting such relationships provides the formal recognition that some people would like them and if they were not costly would have one if possible. Of course, most doormen are not interested in their female tenants, and many of those who might have an abstract interest do not need a formal rule to prevent them from initiating such relationships. For example, Armando shies away from involvements with tenants not because they are prohibited, but because he does not expect such relationships (if they were to occur) to last very long. Since his theory is that "it's going to break up eventually, and they're going to have guys coming in and out, in your face," he finds the potential cost of seeing one's former partner with other people too high.

Not surprisingly, doormen bear the brunt of the costs of line crossing. Why should anyone care if doormen have affairs with their tenants? After all, if a tenant has a torrid affair with the cashier at the grocery store, no one would think that anything untoward had taken place. Likewise, tenants could have affairs with their hairdresser, the teller at the bank, and their postman without raising too many eyebrows.[17] One idea is that such relationships are prohibited because doormen are supposed to stand in the same relation to all tenants, so that the presence of such a relationship destroys this equivalence and creates the possibility of playing favorites. The other idea is that doormen know too much about all the tenants in their building, and that special relationships with one tenant threaten the doorman's capacity for discretion. For this reason, ignoring the obvious power asymmetry, people tend to have a distasteful feeling thinking about their psychiatrist (should they have one) having a relationship with another patient.

Interestingly, people are not really bothered by the idea that psychiatrists have relationships, or that their psychiatrist (again presuming they have one) has a partner, so the issue isn't the possibility of pillow talk per se. The distasteful feature is the idea that their psychiatrist is having a relationship with someone who may know who they are and who occupy a structurally equivalent position to them. In this sense, one realizes that discretion is not really about "no loose lips"; rather discretion is about the capacity to segregate domains. Psychiatrists who have relationships are not a problem even if they talk about their patients so long as their partner will not likely interact with the patient. Thus, it is the interlocking of patients in a practice that makes discretion problematic. This interlocking of patients in a practice is significantly less dense (and likely of shorter duration, on average) than the interlocking of tenants in a residential building. Still, most people believe that what they tell their lawyer, priest, or doctor is confidential. Do they trust their doorman less?

The answer is yes. Tenants feel no shame about asking their doorman about other tenants, even if they would never dream of asking their lawyer to sit down and talk a bit about his or her other clients. The social class distance between tenants and doormen allows tenants the social space to be intrusive. Because they perceive that their doormen will talk to them about others, they also trust the doorman less than their lawyer or doctor. The problem is that while few people would ask their lawyer or their psychiatrist about their other patients, many people find themselves interested in their neighbors and more willing to consider it reasonable to ask their doorman about

---

17. Maybe if they had an affair with all of them, some eyebrows would be raised, but that is another matter.

them. Recall that such curiosity led to the demise of the video-doorman experiments of the 1970s and '80s. If all tenants have such curiosity, then they each have the same preference: that their doormen break confidences they have with others, but retain the specific confidences they have with them. Of course, this is impossible for doormen. Doormen need discretion in order to manage neighborly curiosity, and line crossing threatens their capacity in the eyes of others to act professionally. Even so, they still talk a lot to tenants about other tenants, and they certainly talk to their coworkers about the tenants they share.

DISCRETION

You've got to be secretive. Just between you and that person. You don't go around and tell any other people.

Doormen know that it is important to be discreet. Recall that they know a remarkable amount about their tenants from both direct conversation and indirect observation. Their knowledge is often quite fine-grained. If one of their tenants has a drinking problem, they know that, but also (even if completely useless as knowledge) what kind of alcohol they prefer to drink. In many cases, they know things about their tenants' households that the tenants do not know about their household. Does the adolescent daughter have a boyfriend? If so, how often and for how long does he come over for a visit? Does he only arrive when no one is at home? Does the babysitter have visitors after the kids have gone to bed? Does the cleaning lady leave early? Does the husband come home in the middle of the day? And so on.

Doormen recognize that they have this knowledge. If asked whether they would like to live in a doorman building, many doormen will, as noted earlier, often say no because they "are not impotent." But they will also say no because they know just how much they know about their tenants, and that makes them uncomfortable — or more precisely, the idea that someone would know that much about them makes them uncomfortable. For example, Donald says:

> I'm not used to it. I guess if you grow up with it, you'd be used to it, but I wouldn't want it. I mean, somebody checking your going, you know, in and out. You know, I'm just not used to that. Like they come and

say, "Is my wife home?" I say, "Yeah, she's here" or "They're not here."
[Showing a pad of paper with the apartment numbers and boxes on it]
We just put a check when somebody goes in and somebody goes out.

"It's not for me. When I go home nobody is watching me on the video.
I've got my privacy." Tenants don't know just quite how much supervision —
passive or active — they are under. If they did, they might be less comfortable.
This supervision gives doormen knowledge, but because this knowledge is
often inchoate, it does little more than contribute to the theory that doormen
have about each tenant, another small piece of data to work with. That is,
doormen know they have such knowledge, but they tend not to operate on
it. But these small pieces of data are often interesting to others, for their
own reasons, and one problem is that doormen do not always protect their
tenants' confidences, in part because they do not see their knowledge as necessarily interesting. So tenants have some basis for both their concern about
their own confidences and for their prying into the confidences of others. In
response to questions about celebrities and other news makers living in their
buildings, many doormen initially say that they are not at liberty to talk about
the tenants, but soon start telling you who lives where and what they are like.
Thus, in the course of this study, I learned a slew of things about celebrities,
their residences, whether they were assholes or not, and even how often they
visited their psychologists. One doorman, for example, couldn't help say that

KM, she is xxx in *All My Children*. She is a good person, a real good
person. Someone that is famous like that, you would think they would
be snotty, but she is a real good person. I met Roger Moore here,
Roger Moore. I met, what's the lady's name from *Gilligan's Island*, xxx.
She's old now. Grouchy, grumpy, she's the worst lady you will ever want
to meet.[18]

And, for one final example, another says:

Well, I'm not too at liberty to say. xxx comes here to see his psychologist. I mean he comes in a few times, and I was like blown away 'cause

18. Not all doormen spilled the beans, of course. Here, I have replaced names with initials and
removed the obvious identifiers of the celebrities, not to protect them, but to protect the commitment
to confidentiality we made to the doormen. Since one cannot deduce whether Roger Moore lives in
the building or just visited, his name is retained.

I had just seen his movie the day before. I told him I really enjoyed his work. He just walks by and no one notices, and I'm like saying, "Am I the only one who notices?" That was pretty cool, getting to meet him. I mean, I didn't really get to talk to him. I've seen him like four, five times. You know mostly I just call up and tell the lady that he's here.

Such indiscretion is not limited to celebrities. As noted above, doormen will often talk about news makers in their building, whether or not they are particularly famous. Doormen, in this case, reveal a certain pride that their building houses an important figure in ABC News, a partner in a major law firm, or a chief executive at a company like Pfizer. And they often want to communicate this to strangers. But infamous people work as well for conversation:

Well, I don't think I should say this, but it's funny to me because it's one of the tenants, she got caught selling drugs, somewhere on Fiftieth Street. She worked for the xxx, she was on the *Daily News*, the *Daily News* came over to the building, asking questions and stuff like that. I mean she's a fifty-year-old lady. She even got caught selling Viagra. [She was caught selling on the street? She was a dealer?] Yeah, she was an actual dealer, she had her customers, she makes her runs, and she was always in and out, she always has her pouch. Everybody in the building knows that she does it. She got caught this year in the summertime, everybody in the building knows about it, when they see her, they whisper about what she does, and stuff like that. All you can do is laugh.

Names of persons, even such modest details as whether they are good tippers or not, pleasant to be with, and so on, are not particularly revelatory and therefore mentioning them does not seem like an indiscretion to many doormen. But this is a slippery slope, and little details that spill out about tenants (who uses a syringe because they are diabetic, who "slaps their wife around," and so on) are just the kind of stuff that many tenants would both prefer that others did not know about them and, at the same time, would like to know about others. The fact that tenants are interdependent, in ways that patients at a clinic or clients at a law firm are not, provides enormous motivation for tenants to try to use their doormen as information fonts.

Because doormen work on developing, in the context of their own professional claims, personal relationships with their tenants, there is always a risk that such information will diffuse or, worse, the temptation to use this knowledge to signify the special relationship that they have. This leads many managers, and also tenants, to be deeply suspicious when doormen and tenants are seen having long conversations. While managers cannot prohibit such conversations, they can try to monitor them. Supers, for example, are often reported by their doormen to be watching them from their offices, ready to call if they appear to be engaged in too intimate a conversation with their tenants. The supers have a fine line to cross, however, for many tenants are happy about the building staff because they can talk with their doormen. What supers are attentive to, however, are signs of sexual relationships, and they can and will strive to prohibit sexual relationships from enduring. Why is crossing the line cause for immediate termination? The threat lies not with the relationship per se but, more broadly, involving the claim to equivalent treatment in the context of personal knowledge. Doormen, privy to information that may not even appear as knowledge to them, who are in personal relationships with tenants make other tenants feel uncomfortable — whatever their personal habits may be.

INTERVENTION WITH LIMITS

Doormen walk a tightrope when asked by tenants to do them personal favors. But almost invariably, under such situations, they will oblige. If asked to hide their bottles, or if asked to call if their husband is returning unexpectedly, or if asked to keep a special ear out for trouble in their apartment if their husband comes home drunk (and with a history of abuse), doormen are willing to help where they can. For the drunk husband, they may make a special effort to create a racket on the floor when they are taking away the garbage or delivering a package, just so it is known they are out there, should need arise. For husbands and wives involved in illicit affairs, doormen will help by calling up and announcing the imminent arrival of a spouse. They will not, though, try to redirect the spouse, even temporarily. And doormen will hide X-rated movies in the back room or their desk, if explicitly asked. But they will rarely directly intervene and try to shape the behavior of their tenants (or their tenants' friends) unless this behavior is specifically proscribed and poses serious risk to the building.

Sometimes, though, doormen will try to direct the course of events if they see they are heading in the wrong direction, but they cannot always succeed, especially if their intervention is not in the perceived interests of their tenant. James, working on the Upper East Side, describes how he failed to stop an older man from being fleeced by one of his tenants, a young woman working as a prostitute out of his building, and how later he could not help the man seek redress from the tenant.

> There was an old man having this young girl, and she took all his money [laughs], all his money away. So he had to move, he got homeless. He didn't have any money. See, she took all his money. And I tried to tell him. I tried, I tried, I tried to tell him, "Don't mess with her, she's, you know, no good, a whore." [After this happened, the man returned to visit the girl, but he had nothing left.] And so he came back to me, too, and I told her, "He wants to go upstairs," but she says no. So he can't pass in. If she had said to me to send him up, then I would have sent him up. But she said no. I was just trying to help him, you know, but he would not listen.

In other cases, doormen may be confronted with tenants whose own behavior is dangerous to themselves. Typically, these tenants laugh off their behavior as unproblematic for themselves or their doormen. For example, Rosemary says:

> I honestly think they probably think that I am crazy, because they just see me coming in, in the morning, wearing the same outfit that they saw me leaving in five o'clock last night. I do not know if this is really appropriate, but I am always drunk coming in and bringing in five football players with me.

But Eamon feels an obligation to the younger female tenants in his building because he imagines he is some kind of father figure for "the kids who are living in the big city for the first time." So he

> always says, "Be careful out there," when the young girls go out at night, but I don't think they listen to me anyways, because they are returning to the building after I leave at one in the morning most of the time.

The reality is, though, that as Eamon knows, they do not listen. Nor is he free to intervene more actively. For proactive advice threatens to dislocate the balance between closeness and distance that doorman have to retain, even if tenants threaten through their neediness, or curiosity, to shift the scale in one direction or another. The problem is simply that he cannot know too much, even if he does. Thus, he is free to provide generic advice only, for the moment that he allows specific behaviors to percolate out into the open, he risks breaking the symbolic discretion boundary, whereby each party may know that the other knows what they know, but both agree to, in Goffman's terms, preserve face behind the shield of the generic.

CONTRADICTORY DEMANDS

One thing that doormen learn after a very short time on the job is that some of their tenants are more problematic than others. Some are problematic because they are pursuing goals that put the door at risk, for example, low-level illegal activities. Others are problematic because they do things that indirectly threaten other tenants, for example, propping the door open in anticipation of a delivery (in the temporary absence of the doorman), and some are problematic because they have goals that appear to threaten other tenants. The latter arises more often than one might guess, and when it does, doormen are faced with one class of contradictory demands. An example of one situation might help put flesh on what appears to be an abstract problem. One tenant describes a complex encounter:

> They definitely looked after my safety. I had some woman in my build-ing who wanted to set me up with her son. I had never met the son; I had never met the mother — she had just seen me in the building and thought that I was perfect for her son for some reason. So they actually warned me, they came to me personally one day after about a couple of weeks because they were concerned because they knew that he had access to come upstairs because of his mother and so they looked out for me, and I think at that point I really realized that they were really looking out for my best interests and really did care about my safety, because they were concerned that he was just going to come knock on the door one day.
>
> It was a couple of days before the strike might have happened, the doormen thought they ought to pull me aside and let me know the situation because they were afraid that if they did go on strike that the son would just go and do whatever he felt like. I'm sure that he was a nice guy or whatever, but they just felt that they needed to tell me more so because it had been going on for like a month this little escapade; he had apparently seen me, knew my name, and knew my apartment number. I never knew anything about this, but right before

the preliminary strike was going to happen, the doormen, like two of them, just said, "We would like to talk to you," and I freaked out thinking they were going to ask me out. I couldn't imagine what they wanted to talk to me about, you know. I just sign packages and they pulled me aside and I'm thinking, "Oh my God, isn't this illegal to do this?" and I was so worried; they said, "When you come back from running your errands, we would like to talk with you," and I thought and I ran errands for like three hours freaking out because I thought, "What am I going to do?"

. . . [I] never flirt, so I felt like that would be just ridiculous for them to do that, but I just couldn't imagine; they seemed so serious. . . . I finally came back and they told me that there was this woman in the building whose son is, you know, and because of the strike that they were thinking that there would be no one on duty [and] they wanted to just warn me about the situation; they didn't think that it was anything that would cause alarm. They just felt that if I heard any mysterious knock on my door that I should use precaution.

Here, the door faced a peculiar problem. The mother was not a criminal and her son was not actually stalking the young (and attractive) tenant. In fact, he didn't live in the building and only came to visit his mother, which is generally thought to be a nice thing. All the mother had really done was ask who that attractive young lady was and to remark that her son was looking for a partner and that she looked perfect. These kinds of innocent comments are made all the time, and tenants almost always ask doormen about new faces in the building — "Who is that cute couple with the new baby?" "When did that guy move in?" and so on — without inducing the idea that these questions pose risk for the baby or the "cute guy." So here the door knew something about the mother, the son, and the attractive young woman — and the combination of that knowledge led to the warning, however unnecessary, as the doormen did not strike, the young man never knocked, and the mother asked no further questions.

One interesting fact is revealed, however: in this and in other relationships that tenants have with their doormen, there is a pronounced asymmetry in understanding. To make sense of this asymmetry, we need to consider more carefully the micro-dynamics of interaction between doormen and tenants — interactions that allow each to develop theories about the other. That doorman theories are better than tenant theories (for the most part) should come as little surprise. Doormen are successful to the extent that their theories work. Tenants, for the most part, can get their doormen a bit wrong and still get what they need, partly because doormen train them into developing preferences for what they need.

SUPER(VISION)

Can I ask you to step back? We are being watched here. The superintendent will get very mad. I know he is watching me. If you are too close to me, then he will think there is something between us here.

I'm the middle man; he wanted to see the supervisor and I had to call him regardless of whether the super wants to be bothered or not. Most of the time I have to notify him; he has to be notified, regardless. See he [the super] came out with a face — he is angry because I called him; it has nothing to do with you being here. But if I don't call him, then he'll be mad at me. And, actually, he is my boss, but actually the tenant is [the] bigger boss because this is a co-op and the tenants own the place. And who is stuck in the middle?

In the midst of the complex world of tenants and doormen are other actors who shape the ecology of the lobby — supers, delivery people, handymen, and union representatives. Of these, the super is the most important. Doormen, tenants, and supers all bring to the table and apply different theories and accounts to make sense of and construct the lobby as an interactive environment. Here, I consider only the role of the supers, whose impact on doorman-tenant interactions is the most significant.

As noted earlier, doormen owe their job in most instances to the super, for in most buildings it is the super who either directly hires doormen or whose recommendation is considered by building managers with hiring responsibility. In most buildings as well — but certainly not all — the super is always around, for it is quite common for supers to be given apartments in the building as part of their compensation package. Some of these apartments are quite remarkable — grand lodgings on upper floors worthy of *New York Times* stories — but the majority are small back-facing first-floor apartments that in the apartment status sweepstakes are ranked at the bottom of the distribution. In the urban legend world, tenants are often reported to fear their super, whose capacity to exert revenge for insufficient acknowledgment (around the Christmas bonus, considered in chapter 6) is thought to be boundless. As with all urban legends, there is in this legend some truth, for supers may respond quickly or slowly to problems in the building. For those who live in single-family houses, the need for a super seems hard to fathom, since only so many things can go wrong and need immediate repair. But in older apartment buildings with multiple units, the frequency of crises large and small is quite high. From little problems such as broken doorknobs, rattling radiators, and (for those with high ceilings) spent lightbulbs, the first line of responsibility lies with the super, who either directly repairs what he can or determines the priority order for the handyman.

The fact that apartments are piled on top of one another leads to larger problems. Almost all apartment dwellers have experienced how simple water leaks from a neighbor's clogged sink or shower drain, overflowing toilet, dishwasher, or backed-up radiator quickly ratchet into nightmares as parts of their ceiling falls in, walls begin to bubble with water, or floors become suddenly squishy, through no fault of their own. Most tenants can recall as well how services to their apartments from failure of the steam heat, AC, standpipe, or other systems in the building suddenly stop. If the home owner can expect a crisis requiring service in one or more of their systems once every year or so, one can see how in a building of one hundred units, two units could be expected (if independent) to need some kind of service each week. The problem is that most unit problems are not independent. Against this background, it is into this mix of interacting tenants and complex building systems comes the super, whose expertise is often quite remarkable.[19] Building emergencies are on their own schedule. They come as they please, and because of this, supers are on call in their building twenty-four hours a day, seven days a week. For some, the fact that supers are always "on" appears to induce an over-identification with the building that expresses itself in the dictatorial control some supers exercise over the activities of their staff. In this way, the building seems to resemble a long-distance sailing vessel from the eighteenth century. For the super and the captain can often come to feel as if they are in total control, and it is not uncommon to hear tenants and doormen criticize their super either for being a martinet — in the shadow of Bligh — or a brutal dictator. Tenants also frequently comment that their

---

19. A quick glance at the various courses offered by the union to help doormen become supers is instructive and indicates how complex modern apartment buildings are. Most tenants simply have no idea how their building actually works and only discover the complexity when something goes wrong.

super is lazy or useless. Yet not infrequently, tenants report that it is because of their super that they remain in their building. Thus, whether positive or negative, tenant attitude toward supers tends toward the extreme. This drift to the poles of the affective attitude space is the consequence of the contact structure that tenants have with supers.[20]

Because tenants see supers less frequently than doormen, and because they see them when they are vulnerable (e.g., something is wrong or about to be wrong with their apartment), supers have few opportunities to structure tenant expectations. In contrast to doormen, super contact with tenants is a small number problem. Perceiving that they have to invest in the super, many tenants try to influence their super's attitude toward them through manipulation of the bonus. While the bonus is considered in more detail subsequently, here it is important to note that in contrast to doormen, supers can respond to the bonus. Because the contact opportunities are fewer, both parties can code slight variation in response as a product of the "bonus intervention." Still, all things considered, supers have enormous latitude in structuring their relations with tenants, and thereby influencing the relationship that tenants have with doormen. They certainly have more latitude than do their doormen.

Since each apartment is likely to need intervention at some time, supers can ensure that they are in the middle of all decisions with respect to allocation of handyman, porter, or doorman time. Alternatively, supers can leave such allocation decisions to handymen or to doormen, who in some instances are charged with allocating the labor of porters. Super influence is greatest, of course, where they are intimately involved in all decisions, but such involvement comes at the cost of their being at the constant beck and call of tenants. Since it is impossible for them to be everywhere at once or to be always available, tenants and their doormen often find it in their interest to work around formal rules requiring super notification for routine jobs, such as getting the keys for the apartment, sending the ladder and handyman

---

20. While there are many instances where doormen have negatively charged relationships with their supers, these are the exceptions. It may help to remember that in many buildings the super is a member of the union, that in most buildings supers are responsible for hiring their staff, and that supers control overtime opportunities for their doormen. In such situations, it is not uncommon, then, for doormen to express loyalty, whether or not they exactly feel loyal. In contrast to tenants, though, extreme positions in the attitude space are less common. This is because supers and doormen interact a lot. In general, frequency of interaction mutes affective range outside of kinship groups.

up to change a lightbulb too high to reach, and so on. Thus, ironically, it turns out that by insisting on total control, supers create strong incentives for doormen and tenants to develop competing service relationships.

Such relationships are seen by supers as something to be avoided, and much of their energy is often devoted to supervision of doormen, ostensibly to ensure that they are "on the job," but often to assess whether or not they seem unusually close to tenants. Thus, in almost all buildings, supers try to influence the nature of tenant-doorman interactions, breaking up relationships that seem too close on some dimension or another.

Supers may use signs of such relationships to discipline doormen they are unhappy with or even to fire them, if possible. One such incident that a student interviewer, Laura, observed is worth reporting in some detail, here taken from her notes written on the night of her first interview.

> I went to interview my doorman at about 7:00 last night. He was out to dinner, and the doorman [Bob] at the desk at the time informed me that he would be back in fifteen minutes. I sat in the lobby and waited for him. During this wait, a couple of female tenants came down from upstairs and had a brief conversation with the doorman — who seemed rather upset — about how his grandmother was very sick and how his parents were both dead. The one girl whose parents had also both died when she was in her early twenties wrote her phone number on a piece of paper, handed it to Bob, and then stepped behind the desk to give him a hug. As she walked out of the building with her friend, she called out rather loudly that the two of them should go and get a glass of wine or something because she wanted to be there for him as much as she could. During all of this, several people have gone through the lobby and the doorman seemed to become more and more uncomfortable. After the two tenants left the building, Bob turned to me and to a woman who was sitting next to me (waiting for her dog to get ready to go for its walk) and announces that he's about to be fired. When the woman asks why, he says because the super's wife had just walked by and witnessed the entire scene and that she would think he was flirting. Shortly after, a young woman comes into the lobby and starts yelling at the doorman. "What did you do? My mother is flipping out." Apparently, this is the super's daughter [later called D]. . . .

After Mitch (the focal doorman) returned from dinner, things settled down a bit, but there was still evidently some tension in the lobby. At one point in the interview, Mitch whispers:

Can we hide the tape recorder behind the desk, because that's my super [and then], to make things easier, if he [the super] comes over here just tell him you're the girlfriend of one of my friends and that you saw me working and so stopped by.

Meanwhile, Bob was called away. When he returned, he announces that he was fired, saying, "It was nice working with you, man." The super is with him and suddenly notices me. He turns to Mitch and says, "I'm sorry but I don't recognize this young lady. She is not one of our tenants. Who is she, Mitch?" Mitch tells him I'm the girlfriend of one of his friends. The super turns to me and asks, "Really, which friend?" I packed up my bag and as I was leaving, Mitch told me that he was sorry the night went the way it did, but that I had wandered into the climax of a scene that had been building for some time.

A few days later, Laura finished her interview with Mitch, but not before she learned why Bob was fired.

How my night ended was truly the craziest part, for as I left for the subway I ran into Bob and D [the super's daughter], who invited me to join them for a cup of coffee, and at the coffee shop learned that they have been secretly dating behind [her] father's back. It was a sad evening, though, as Bob told me that this job was all that he had and that had he only joined the union, none of this would have happened and that he was "just being a nice guy" and that he hadn't been flirting. So I felt as though I had a sort of adventure and I made a couple of friends in a sense as the three of us stayed at a little coffee shop for over an hour talking about Bob and D and their trouble, life, and how they felt I would have an interesting report to return to my class after that night. . . .

Obviously, Bob and D were not as subtle and sneaky as they thought. Both the super and the super's wife knew about their illicit relationship. When presented with an opportunity to fire Bob for crossing the line with female tenants, they jumped at the opportunity.

Many doormen report, for example, that their super will be watching them when they talk with tenants, and that if he sees too much talk, he will come out from "hiding" and ask them to undertake some other task, for example, mopping or polishing, managing the packages, and so on. Recall in this context that Mitch's super was extremely concerned that he was talking too much with Laura — although in this instance, he was likely worried that Laura had witnessed the incident and therefore would be in a position to harm him.

Doormen thus often feel that they have to walk a fine line between being open to tenants and at the same time casting an image of distance or disinterest. It follows, then, that a central dilemma for supers is remaining engaged in the minds of the tenants, whose contact with the super is often restricted to just those moments when something goes wrong with their apartment. At the same time, supers recognize that the relationship that doormen develop with their tenants, and vice versa, plays a central role in defining the feel of the building, and thus shapes tenant satisfaction (or dissatisfaction).

Because supers must supervise, and because it is always the case that the formal rules that govern what the doormen do during the day do not reflect (and cannot reflect) what they really do, supers must also find the balance between adherence to formal and substantive rationality. The formal rules guarantee that doormen do not explicitly favor some tenants over others, and that doormen do not find themselves off the door or out of the lobby because they are providing a service to a specific tenant, thus leaving others not so favored out in the cold. At the same time, the substantive demands of providing professional service will mean that some tenants are treated differently than others. Like all managers, supers have to find the line that works best for their building and for themselves since, like doormen, they also depend on the Christmas bonus to augment their salary.

If supers supervise just a few doormen, they are unionized under the same collective bargaining agreements as their doormen. Consequently, they are in a somewhat awkward position — having line authority over staff, yet seen by staff and management as unionized workers. Consequently, staff size profoundly influences the supervisory relationship, not because small staffs enable more personalized attention, but because both parties are unionized. In general, union membership tempers super behavior significantly; and where supers are unionized, doormen report much more positive relationships than when they are not.[21] Super authority over doormen is also profoundly shaped by doorman tenure. While they may have

21. This is almost surely the result of unionization of supers, rather than a function of shop size and frequency of interaction. Supers with six doormen are not unionized, whereas those with fewer are. The quantitative difference in staff size is too small by itself to yield the qualitative difference in doorman-tenant interactions that one can observe.

formal authority over doormen, doormen with extremely long tenures tend to think of their tenants — with whom they have established enduring relationships — as their boss. Thus, it is not uncommon for doormen to note that they have hundreds of bosses, and that the super is just one of them. The simplified structure of the lobby in terms of formal organization therefore poorly represents the actual ecology one observes; for doormen with long tenures will try to uphold the specific relationships they have with tenants, even if such relationships contravene the (new) super's formal rules. The wary super recognizes that his influence over doorman-tenant interactions is shaped by doorman seniority and is less prone to intervene when he observes closeness that appears to cross the line.[22]

But as with doormen, supers have recourse to the rhetoric of security, rhetoric they frequently deploy when necessary to provide foundation for interventions that limit the discretionary space that doormen have for working with tenants. All interventions designed to make the super more central to the tenant world can be presented as security related. As might be expected, when such rhetorical devices are utilized, visitors to the building are the first to experience them, and this experience often results in the perception of social closure. And not surprisingly, such interventions are more common in larger buildings with correspondingly larger staffs.

OVERVIEW

Doormen and tenants both report that a doorman's main role is to provide security. The main defense is the rule that all visitors must be announced. This seems simple enough, but in practice, the world of the lobby is more complex. First, some tenants do not want their guests announced, and, second, visitors often enter the building on the heels of tenants. Doormen have to be able to make quick decisions about these guests, and in order to do so, they need to develop usable theories about their tenants; these theories tend to be accurate. Tenants are often concerned about how much their doorman knows about them, but the alternatives that they face — having their neighbors know more about them — are unpalatable. Consequently, they rely on

---

22. This is also the because older doormen are less threatening to tenants than younger doormen with respect to the probability of finding themselves in a relationship that crosses the sexual line. Consequently, supers are rational to invest more supervision time on younger doormen.

the doorman's discretion. One consequence of the exercise of discretion is that access by minorities is routinely made more difficult by doormen, leading to an institutional bias against blacks that each doorman claims is not in fact an individual bias. Aside from this, the fact that tenants are interdependent creates all sorts of problems for doormen, but also opportunities. Knowledge then is, as always, a double-edged sword. Doormen are at risk of having too much closeness with their tenants, especially when it would seem that tenants are at risk because of the knowledge that doormen have about them. There is in the end an interesting irony. Doormen are better than closed-circuit tvs because they reduce tenant interdependence. In order to do this, doormen must develop good theories about their tenants. So they must watch them and come to understand them. Yet once they do, the interdependencies between doormen and tenants, and tenants and tenants, may be expressed. This expression occurs in the lobby, the focus of the next chapter.

CHAPTER 5

Status Displays

Out here [in the lobby] is the zoo. We are the animals on display.

I n the lobby, tenants use doormen to pursue their own status aims. Doormen in turn use tenants to make status claims of their own, yet the struggle for coveted roles in the lobby is not a zero-sum game. Doorman gains are not necessarily won at the price of tenant losses or vice versa. In lobbies that work, tenants and doormen jointly construct a world that allows each to hold on to and enhance their status. In lobbies that do not work, tenant claims to status are thought by doormen to be illegitimate and are experienced as a lack of respect. In turn, tenants most often perceive doormen's status claims as "poor service." This chapter considers these interactions, both those that work and those that fail to work, with a focus on the ways in which tenants make status claims, how doormen work with or counter those claims and make their own claims, and, by doing so, jointly define the nature of their relationships.

In some buildings, doormen often feel as if they are on display. The experience of being on display seems similar to the way that stewardesses used to feel — as if their appearance was more critical than either the service or safety functions that they were trained to perform.[1] Consequently, as with stewardesses, many doormen, reflecting on their role, feel as if they are little more than fountains (or monkeys), adding aesthetic and social value to the building. More succinctly, they see themselves solely as conspicuous display items for the tenants to consume. This is especially true for those doormen working in class A buildings on the East Side (and Trump-style buildings elsewhere), but the sentiment runs even beyond these buildings, and the doormen who work in them often feel, especially those wearing

---

1. Hochschild, *The Managed Heart*.

fancy uniforms that limit their ability to "get my work done," that building management is primarily interested in their display functions. This is not entirely the case, even in Trump-like buildings, which most clearly articulate the culture of conspicuous consumption, but it does contain a partial truth, and others realize correctly that their work is — though not in whole, then in part — a form of status display.

Not surprisingly, in buildings where doormen are oppositional to tenants and where tenants reject doorman claims to professional status — ironically in those buildings where class differences between tenants and doormen are least marked — this sentiment is more common. It is true that some tenants think that doormen are just like the chandelier — something to walk by and not actively notice precisely because it is there. And it is true that doormen serve as signifiers of status in the building and that, in some sense, the signifier works "in the cross section," that is, just on observation of a moment. But doormen are not fountains or chandeliers. Doing the job right is hard work that involves interaction, and thus temporal process.

The critical interactions are those in which doormen provide services to tenants through their active engagement in conversation, in delivering packages, announcing (or not) visitors, calling taxis, providing security, and handling deliveries. At one level, as we saw in chapter 2, this active engagement is their job; that is, it encompasses the set of tasks that doormen have. But more importantly, the engagement provides the vehicle for the active articulation of dual status claims. For the doormen, there are their own status aims — principally, their claims to professional status. The tenants, and the services that doormen provide to them, provide the goods on which these claims operate. Tenants, in turn, use doormen and their services to articulate and lay the foundations for their own status aims. When status is expressed in the lobby, one can occasionally observe tension between tenants who use doormen as goods through which to enact their own status aims and doormen who counter on the claims of tenants and, in turn, make status claims of their own. More commonly, though, doormen build on the status claims of tenants to establish their own. In this way, tenants and doormen jointly construct a workable world of work.

This chapter considers these interactions. Neither doormen nor tenants think in terms of status claims, counterclaims, or struggles for coveted roles. While these are the problems to which interaction is devoted, the specific language used here is an analytic convenience. Rather than coveted roles, doormen think and talk about their interactions in the building in the idiom of respect. Likewise, tenants talk about doormen in the idiom of service. I first consider negativity and the idiom of respect, and then the language of service. Doormen feel respected by tenants when they feel they are treated as a professional — that is, as someone whose job involves substantive decision making. If doormen can train tenants into having preferences that allow the door to exercise judgment — which requires that doormen come to know and understand their tenants — they create room for substantive judgment. This enables them to provide a specific kind of service. The grist for such knowledge, and the micro-context in which tenants and doormen induce their collective roles, rests in trivial everyday conversation. In this chapter, these conversations are considered. They do not exhaust the scope of interactions. Whereas everyday conversation provides a foundation for explicit acknowledgment of "closeness," doormen and tenants cannot escape the service relationship. In the subsequent chapter, I focus in detail on the encoding of social distance and the service relationship through the bonus and tips.

NEGATIVITY (AND TENURE)

Day after day, often for years on end, doormen see the same people traverse the lobby, entering and exiting their buildings. As noted earlier, because different kinds of people choose different kinds of buildings, the doormen in one building interact with people who are often quite different from those in another building. They also come to shape those interactions, and in doing so they help to define the people who reside in the building.

Although it is difficult to obtain systematic data, tenure rates for doormen vary rather strikingly across buildings. In one building, for example, all of the doormen have worked for at least fourteen years, whereas in another, mean tenure is below five years. There are thus short-term and long-term buildings. These tenure differences may have a number of different sources. One idea is that all of the buildings have the same tenure averages, fifteen years or longer, and that observation simply captures the age of the building, with respect to the hiring of doormen. It seems unrealistic, just from sheer demographic exigency, but since one observes specific buildings only in the cross section, it is possible that the buildings one sees with short-tenure doormen had, just before one looked, all long-service men who had worked to retirement. Aside from the difficulty of imagining how such a process could resist the stochastic variations that govern death, illness, and geographic mobility (to mention just three of the many events that could lead to a vacancy), it is impossible to fully reject this idea. But it seems unlikely on face value.[2]

It is also possible, and seemingly more likely, that building tenure rates reflect management styles. Where supers are intrusive or difficult to work with, for example, the conditions of work could be expected to decay, and doormen may try to exit, thereby leaving vacancies for someone else to fill. If this were the case, we might expect to observe some kind of correlation between mean tenure rates and supers' characteristics. The data again are suggestive in this regard, for doormen with shorter tenures are less comfortable with their supers than those with longer tenures. But while there is a relationship, the cause of this association is unclear. Similar doormen could have different tenures because they interact with different supers, or, alternatively, doormen who have short tenures are different from those with long tenures; for example, one can imagine that some proportion of the doormen with short tenures are less easygoing than those with long tenures, and hence more likely to report conflicts with their supers. Or alternatively, to pick up the other side, supers may ride those who end up having shorter tenures harder than their older employees. In a cross-sectional design, it is impossible to disentangle causal order in arguments of this kind.

But both of these explanations — the first resting on chance distributions of hires and vacancies, the latter resting on stable traits among doormen or supers — seem less compelling than the simpler idea that doormen and supers, in interaction with their tenants, come to shape the feel of the building, and that in buildings where such shaping dynamics are weaker, doormen last less long and turnover is higher. If, as we suspect, job satisfaction is clustered by building, a simpler and more sociological set of accounts of the basic finding seems to have greater face validity. A whole array of mechanisms that would yield imbalanced tenures across buildings are easily imagined once interaction dynamics between tenants and doormen are included into the mix. We can list a few of them here. The doormen could have shorter tenures because the tenants are more demanding, perhaps because they are not being properly "trained," or perhaps because the status difference

---

2. This is a generic problem in the social sciences. It is likely the case that many variances observed in the cross section, or even across short periods of time, are artifactual — that is, a product of the observation window — and hence disappear over a longer time frame. This does not seem to be such a case, however.

TABLE 5.1. Proportion Tips of Annual Income by How Many of Tenants You Like

Tips	All	Most	Some	Few	None	Total
< 10%	39 (34.8%)	54 (48.2%)	13 (11.6%)	5 (4.5%)	1 (0.9%)	112 (100%)
10–30%	10 (18.9%)	35 (66.0%)	7 (13.2%)	1 (1.9%)	0	53 (100%)
> 30%	7 (38.9%)	8 (44.4%)	2 (11.1%)	0	1 (5.6%)	18 (100%)
Total	56 (30.6%)	97 (53.6%)	22 (12.0%)	6 (3.3%)	2 (1.1%)	183 (100%)

between tenants and doormen is too small. If the latter, doormen may feel as if they are being cast in a servile relationship. Or they could have shorter tenures because tenants, not in relationship with them, provide a smaller bonus at the end of the year, thus reducing one of the benefits of the job. In this light, consider the cross tabulation above (arising from the survey questionnaire) that suggests that there is, not surprisingly, a relationship between liking tenants and the size of the bonus. Though what causes what is unclear. Probably the truth lies in an interaction. This could also arise from another classic self-fulfilling prophecy: If tenants think their doormen will leave (i.e., it is a short-tenure building), they will give less as a bonus and doormen will be more likely to leave, thereby confirming the initial theory of the tenants.

It is also interesting to see that the relationship between the size of the bonus and doorman attitudes toward tenants' friends is similar, as indicated by the following cross tabulation. If doormen begin to develop oppositional attitudes toward their tenants, they are much more likely to find their visitors unpleasant.

One can think through a number of specific elements that, once in place, would conspire to yield short-tenure rates, on average. The core idea is that in such contexts, where doormen move in and out, the tenants emerge as the fixed element, with correspondingly more influence over the nature of their interactions with the door. In other words, their attitudes come to dominate. And this domination shapes the doormen's ability to define their jobs as professional, creating a less pleasant work atmosphere and leading to faster turnover.

As noted earlier, most doormen are, as they are fond of saying, "people people"; some are more so than others, and such feelings tend to be

TABLE 5.2. Proportion Tips of Annual Income by How Many of Tenants' Visitors You Like

Tips	All	Most	Some	Few	None	Total
<10%	34 (30.4%)	42 (37.5%)	24 (21.4%)	10 (8.9%)	2 (1.8%)	112 (100%)
10–30%	11 (21.2%)	17 (32.7%)	21 (40.4%)	3 (5.8%)	0	52 (100%)
>30%	4 (22.2%)	7 (38.9%)	4 (22.2 %)	2 (11.1%)	1 (5.6%)	18 (100%)
Total	49 (26.9%)	66 (36.3%)	49 (26.9%)	15 (8.2%)	3 (1.6%)	182 (100%)

associated with long service careers. In other buildings, specifically those where tenures are on average shorter, many doormen come to think of their jobs as trivial and their tenants as simultaneously helpless and arrogant, a combination that Spiro Agnew captured succinctly in the term "effete snobs." It is not surprising that charitable feelings toward tenants tend to be positively associated with tenure as a doorman. This is not because people mellow with age, although they may, but rather reflects the simple fact that people who like their jobs tend to stay in them longer than those who do not. In this case, one must like tenants to like being a doorman. So negative comments about tenants tend to come from those new to the field. If doormen hold negative attitudes toward tenants, they are also less likely to stay on in the job. And so tenure rates will decline, for the building as a whole.

RESPECT

The unhappy doormen talk a lot about respect, and they evaluate tenants in terms of the currency of respect. When respect comes to organize social settings, it is generally associated with an inability to segregate roles. Thus, in so-called honor societies — where kinship, economic, social, and political identities are tightly interwoven — being disrespected in one domain spills out into the other interlocked domains. Consequently, individuals feel that they must react to the smallest slight, in order to preserve their honor. The same dynamic seems to operate on the street. Much gang violence appears to be driven by the perception of disrespect. By contrast, consider our own situation. If we are insulted at work, we can return home without our core identity challenged, for our relationships within the family are disjoint from those at work. This capacity to segregate domains enables most people to sustain slight insults without feeling as if they must respond. But for youth in gangs, whose total social and economic identity is embedded within the gang context, such segregation is impossible.[3]

It would be convenient if doormen concerned with respect behaved consistently with this idea. But they do not. Rather, one would expect that if capacity to segregate domains were the core driver of the concern with respect, those with longer tenures would consider respect more salient than those with shorter tenures, since their identity as a doorman is more salient. But they do not. Rather, those whose concerns revolve around respect tend to have short careers as doormen and tend to think of the job as a stepping-stone to something else. They do differ as well from long-tenure doormen by virtue of their orientation to tenants.

These doormen tend to think that the tenants are arrogant and incapable. They express this in two ways. The perception and description of tenant arrogance are cast and organized in the language of class. Not being capable is often expressed and organized in the language of sex. Those who are incapable are seen as impotent or frigid. Those who are arrogant are seen as beneficiaries of inherited wealth, without corresponding effort. Because they see tenants in this light, they also believe that many tenants do not respect them in their ordinary behavior. Tenants, in this sense, need to do little to earn the antipathy of oppositional doormen.

In considering whether or not their own job is important or useful, or whether they would prefer to live in a doorman building, all things being equal, these doormen reject the idea that they perform a useful service. They cannot really see why they are needed. Their sense is that it is only the weakness of tenants that provides the rationale for their jobs. Here, some comments might provide a better sense of the antipathy these doormen have toward their jobs and toward tenants. First focusing only on comments articulated in the language of class, the following examples are typical:

> [The tenants are] arrogant people, snobby, trying to make you feel lower than them because they have a couple of dollars more than you, more than a couple of dollars.

> The main objective the people have here is to save money, as rich as they are.

---

3. Gould, *Collision of Wills*; Anderson, *Streetwise*; Goffman, *The Presentation of Self in Everyday Life*.

No, I don't have any problems with tenants, because I treat everybody the same, I try to treat everybody the same, but there's a lot of hypocrisy. The difference is they have money and I don't, and they let you know in many ways.

In describing tenants in general, doormen with negative opinions can easily lock in on social class. The fact that tenants have money, and often a lot of money, is not exactly the issue, though. This is the case in almost all of the buildings. What makes some tenants stand out? Two elements are salient. The first is that some tenants make the doormen aware of wealth. The awareness of wealth is, not surprisingly, more likely to appear where social distance between tenants and doormen is smallest, and where tenants are more likely to tip doormen for small favors, thereby inscribing the differences that do exist in a simpler currency. In this regard, there is some neighborhood — and building — clustering with respect to class antagonisms. Doormen working in large apartment buildings on the East Side — where the typical apartment is small, the clientele younger, and the money is "newer" — are more likely to read their tenants in class terms than those in established prewar buildings. In the newer apartments, one cannot help but note that doormen, who make $50,000 per year, are not, in some instances, too far behind in terms of income — not counting status and or income over the life course — than some of their tenants. The fact that they are on different trajectories is what counts in the end. Recognition that they are on different trajectories is typically expressed by distinguishing those who work from those who have inherited their wealth. Many doormen on the Upper West Side, for example, contrast their tenants with those on the East Side by noting "that here they are working people too." The hostility toward inherited wealth — for those who express such hostility — is not limited to males. Older women on the East Side living in less prestigious addresses are the frequent target of class-based negative comments.

The second salient idea is that doorman are more likely to articulate class hostility if their tenure is relatively short. There is likely a powerful selection dynamic going on. In buildings where class differences between doormen and tenants are less marked, tenant mobility is higher than in established buildings. In these settings where tenants are more mobile, doormen are less able to shape tenant behavior; consequently, they see tenants as uniform because a uniform tenant attitude shapes the mood of the building. I return to this selection dynamic shortly.

It is not uncommon that the same doormen who view their tenants as hypocritical and arrogant, and who attribute these characteristics to the fact that they have inherited their wealth, also see them as impotent. When asked whether they would like to live in a doorman building, many doormen say that they would not because they would not like their comings and goings under observation all the time. This response is much more common for doormen with longer tenures. But doormen who perceive that their tenants do not respect them say no for a different reason: because they believe that doormen are unnecessary. Doormen tend to value their masculinity, and consequently those who develop oppositional relations with tenants come to think of their tenants as soft, feminine, impotent, or frigid — in the sense that they cannot experience real life. Some comments along these lines may provide meat for the skeleton:

> Some people will stand there in the cold just 'cause they don't want to open the door. It's funny how the wealthier side is living 'cause you know it's kind of weird. There are a lot of weird things in the building as far as that. Sometimes they'll even ring the doorbell, and they'll just wait. All they have to do is open it, but sometimes I'm like on the intercom or working the elevators but they'll still stay there. It's like they're frozen or something.

Or some more penetrating comments in response to a simple question about their living in a doorman building:

> I mean, I really don't like a whole lot of people opening my doors. I'm a do-it-myself kind of guy.

> For what, I do everything myself. I'm not impotent, you know, I'm not a person that can't do it myself; I can walk, I use my hands.

> I don't think I would like to have [a] doorman. It is not necessary to have doormen. Can't you push your own button for your room? It just is not really necessary to have [a] doorman working.

In contrast, some tenants are seen as more capable. Rather than standing in front of the door waiting for it to be opened, some tenants will "try to beat you to the door so that you don't have to open it." In other cases, where doormen like their tenants, they are often described as able to do things for themselves. As Abdul says, for example:

I have a lot of them. I like a lot of them. As long as they treat me kindly, I'll treat them nice, know what I mean. I like kids. There's one tenant, in particular, that has a little girl named — I don't want to say her name. A little girl, she's very sweet and they're very kind, very nice. They always offer me things; we always talk. They do everything for themselves.

Abdul and most other doormen think their job is important. But doormen who believe that what they do is not useful ascribe impotence and frigidity to tenants. Once this door is opened, it is almost too easy to find examples of tenant impotence — that is, tenant inability to do it themselves.

DOGS

For tenants who are thought incapable, some of the greatest vitriol is reserved for their relationship to dogs. First, a vast number of apartment dwellers in the city own dogs. Many of them hire dog walkers to take their dog out for a walk each day. Doormen get to know the dog walkers and soon come to realize that the typical tenant drops from $18 to $20 per hour on walking their dog, while they earn just over $17 per hour.[4] So doormen come to think that tenants value dogs more than they value them. Nor are dogs as common where doormen live. This is in part because many apartments in the less wealthy areas of the city successfully prohibit pets. It is also partly because less wealthy people cannot afford dog walkers. While building managers in doorman buildings may prefer to prohibit pets, they cannot get away with it, for there is sufficient wealth, on average, in doorman buildings to warrant moving to buildings that do allow pets. But the major differences are in orientation, and here there are clear class lines that can be drawn; working-class people do not tend to see pets as members of their family. Instead, they see them as pets, as dogs, cats, gerbils, or whatever. In contrast, the upper class seems to have a different relationship to their pets. As Duran says:

---

4. Dog walkers in the city can make relatively significant money. If they take six dogs out for one hour, they pull in roughly $120. Since they can do this easily in a two- to three-hour shift, an aggressive walker will work less than six hours a day and make $1,250 a week. If they do not report cash payments, this translates, over the course of a forty-week year (many dogs go away for the summer), to over $50,000, or roughly $65,000 taxable income. Not bad, for an academic year, and certainly better than most doormen, not counting the absence of benefits and job security, and the fact that they have to pick up an amazing amount of shit.

They love their dogs. Most of them that don't have kids treat their dogs as their kids. Anything that happens to those dogs or, you know — but me, I never really liked dogs. But you have to try to learn to get along and like the dogs.

At one level, many doormen simply cannot understand the relationship that their tenants have with their dogs. For hostile doormen, these relationships appear luxurious and unnecessary, much like their own jobs. If they have dogs, they may like them and they may even consider them a part of the family, but doormen who find tenants incapable of doing anything see tenants' reliance on dog walkers not in practical terms of ensuring that the dog gets sufficient opportunity to "do his business," but as avoidance of getting one's hands dirty (metaphorically) with dog poop. They interpret this reluctance to get dirty as another example of frigidity — an inability to engage with the world. The dog walkers may also be too close to doormen, since they share on one level an equivalency relationship. Dog walkers absorb (pick up) dog shit. While we may see that doormen absorb the impurities of the street, thereby preserving the status aims of tenants, the negative doormen who see tenants dropping substantial cash on dog walkers simply see a bunch of people who are unable to manage by themselves. Then again, they see this already in terms of holding doors, calling elevators, and, in some older buildings, operating the elevators.

The inability to manage alone in the world outside the building reaches its apogee in descriptions of tenants who never leave. It seems many buildings have someone in them who has not thought to venture outside over a period of months or years, for no obvious reason, viz.:

There's a woman that hasn't left her apartment in six years. She gets all her food delivered, you know, everything. All she has to do is take out her garbage at night. You know with the way things are today, you can just call or go on the Net and have things delivered. I mean, I haven't even met her. I speak to her every day on the intercom. I mean, she's not that old. Probably about fifty, but, you know, I've been working here for about two years and haven't met her. I mean, she's never had anybody [over] when I've been here.

Doormen describe others similarly trapped. One senses that the trapped serve as a trope for doormen who are in an oppositional relationship with their tenants, for otherwise one would have to imagine that there is an agoraphobic epidemic in the city (though how one catches it is another question). Whether real or urban legend, for the doormen who do not like their tenants, the trapped women are like all the rest of the tenants, essentially incapable of getting it on, of doing it by themselves.

For doormen, sex is an idiom for discussing class, and class antagonism is articulated in the accessible languages of the street: sex and disrespect. As noted above, doormen also talk about class more directly, in terms of the distinction between inherited and earned wealth. The focus on class — even if limited to just a small proportion of disengaged doormen — is unusual. In contrast to many workers in other sectors of the service industry, doormen often think in terms of class. While it is tempting to account for this simply by virtue of the social distance between doormen and their tenants, similarly situated service workers do not share the same sentiments, by and large — for example, workers in upscale clothing boutiques, whose clients may drop a clerk's weekly earnings in a single shopping spree. The same could be said for receptionists in large firms whose typical clientele live in the buildings that the doormen work at. As considered in more detail subsequently, the language of class exerts itself when doormen see themselves as unskilled workers providing uniform service rather than as skilled professionals exercising substantive judgment about their clients' wishes. For doormen who look out and see an undifferentiated mass of elite tenants incapable of even opening a door for themselves, it is easy to understand how class emerges as a salient issue. The tenants, in this sense, appear as effete snobs. Many of them are, no doubt, but doormen who fail to distinguish tenants tend to have short careers. In part, this is because they have a greater probability of leaving on their own, but also because their inability to exercise substantive judgment will induce substantial tenant opposition that management, in the end — despite their commitment to rules — will feel bound to respect.

SELF-CRITICISM

Among older, more established doormen, the sense they have of the younger generation is often that they are the cause of their own unhappiness because they do not value their job as it should be valued. Nor do they see the younger generation going the extra mile for their tenants because they are professionals, but because, instead, they approach the job as a "hustle," where the goal is to extract bonuses through the provision of special service. Age here serves simply as a proxy for orientation. In this instance, younger doormen are those whose orientation to the job is not as a career but as a stepping-stone to some other career. Thus, Donald, who has worked as a doorman for more than twenty-two years, says about his coworkers:

> I think doormen — they look down upon themselves. They think that people look down on them, and I think that most of the people have an inferiority complex. I don't see that through tenants. I think tenants look at the workers and hold them equal, [though] not everybody. The better, the higher-quality people don't look down on them, on the people, and the lower-quality generally have hang-ups about them, their personal inferiority complexes, so they try to make up by putting somebody else down. I think most of the time the doormen do look down on themselves, and they think they are being looked down on. I don't think they are being looked down on so many times. But I think they generally have reason to be looked down on. So, personally, I don't consider myself less than any of the tenants.

And Arnold, who has worked in his building for more than a decade, in response to the question about wanting to live in a doorman building, says:

> Yes, I would. They don't even know everything, for example, tenants who moved out from here, long time ago, two, three years ago, they don't even know that they receive a package that was delivered here. They never know. But on my way, I might drop it off. It happened probably fifteen times. They'll never know that I was ever involved. I don't know if the other guys do it, but I do it and others probably do it too. So, these are things which do happen.

To escape class warfare, doormen have to come to see their tenants as individuals. Of course, this is exactly what they must do in order to provide professional service as well. The key skill is to be able to both differentiate tenants, so they do not appear as a congealed mass of the upper class, and to latch on to the professional norm that asserts that whatever their particular behavior pattern, one must stay in role. Thus doormen must switch back and forth from informal particularism to formal universalism, depending on the tenants with whom they are dealing. As Angelo says, describing tenants who just passed by and then considering some of the others in his building:

> He's nice and she's nice, they bring you things, say hi, they stop, talk to you, ask how you're doing, and they take time out of their busy

schedule just to talk to you, they even sit down and talk. There are people who just keep walking and walking, even though you say hello, or something, they don't say anything. They just keep walking. But maybe they just have it hard. You have got to just be kind to all them whatever their moods are.

Relationships with tenants are distinguished on multiple dimensions. Tom, for example, calls some tenants by their first names, others with an honorific. The distinction he makes is not about respect; that is, he tries neither to signal respect nor to interpret tenant use of his first name as necessarily signaling respect. Instead, the line is drawn in terms of professionalism.

> They tell you [management] don't call somebody by their name like "Frank" or "Jack" or whatever. Of course, we don't always keep it that way. For example, Mr. Wien, no, I call him "Jack." I would call him "Jack." There are some of the people that I would call "Mr. This" or "Mr. That" even if they call me "Tom." Just because they call me "Tom" it's fine, they can do it, but it's not that it is respect, but it is more professional. It has nothing to do with respect. It is the professional way to call them. . . . It's [a] different type of relation. A person that never talks to you, that just says "hello" or don't even say "hello" you . . . those who will, you get more personal — you even have certain subjects to [talk about] or you will know from other signs that it will be more proper to call him, so after that it is even improper to be so formal.

At the same time, the class gulf between tenants and doormen needs to be understood. As Donald notes about his tenants:

> They have it so much that they don't flaunt it so much. They just come down on a regular level and [talk] about the weather or something like that. Of course, people don't act like it [important people]. They are so used to it. It doesn't make any difference.

ASYMMETRIES OF DISTANCE

So far I have implicitly presumed that the distance between two individuals is symmetric, in the same way that the distance between New York and Los Angeles is the same, whether one starts out on the East Coast and travels west or vice versa. If we see persons as bundles of attributes such that each individual is represented as an inhabitant of an occupation, religion, party preference, educational attainment, and so on, it is possible to meaningfully assume that the distance between them is symmetric. Thus, for example, the distance between a vice president of manufacturing and a mail clerk is the same whether one starts with the mail clerk and travels to the vice president or vice versa. Likewise, the distance between a Catholic and a Protestant — whether represented qualitatively or quantitatively — does not depend on the starting point. This does not mean that all Catholics and all Protestants are equally distant, or that all vice presidents of manufacturing and mail clerks are equally distant. Catholics are much more distant from Protestants in Belfast than they are in Bangalore, and when it was possible to become a vice president by starting off as a mail clerk, mail clerks really were closer to vice presidents than they are today. The symmetry assumption simply means that for any two individuals — for example, a Catholic vice president of manufacturing in Belfast and a Protestant mail clerk in Bangalore — the distance between them is the same. And it is the same whether measured well (which is not a simple problem) or measured poorly. In this regard, we can say that while social distance depends on the relevant social, temporal, and spatial contexts, symmetry does not. Symmetry is an analytic construct revealed absent the moment we focus on actual interactions between people.

While assuming that symmetrical social distance is appropriate for some sociological problems, symmetry assumptions appear unwarranted when the focus is on understanding social interaction. In socially situated interactions, the distance between two individuals is rarely the same from both directions. This is easy to see within organizations. Secretaries may have doors to protect them from the public, but they almost never walk through their manager's office on their way to their desk. Assistants take messages for managers, whether personal or professional, and managers may joke with assistants in ways that assistants cannot joke with managers. Managers frequently inquire about an assistant's personal life — "Everything going okay these days?" Rarely do assistants have the same license. And in social interactions, those in positions of power can much more easily embrace some distance from their formal role than those who are subordinate, assuming thereby the posture of one who is easygoing and relaxed. While the relaxed and easygoing subordinate may be thought insufficiently committed to the project at hand, the charming executive is just a good guy. In organizations, being easygoing is a state more easily occupied by bosses than by staff. In this regard, it is always useful for those in power within an organization to remember, as Goffman pointed out, that social grace is a product of power, not an attribute that produces power.[5]

While easy to observe within organizations, such asymmetries in inter- action dynamics are not restricted to firms or workplaces. Similar dynamics shape allowable and unallowable interactions between doormen and tenants in the lobby, thus giving rise to asymmetries in social distance. And as with the case of managers and assistants where those with highest status are allowed to be closer to those with lower status, tenants are allowed to be in- teractively closer to doormen than doormen are to their tenants, in general. Tenants who appear to know their doormen well may, for example, tease them upon entry into the lobby, by pointing out that the doorman either is or is not working. For the busy doorman, one might overhear a jocular "Finally caught you, huh," or "I guess the super is here," and so on; whereas for the idle doorman, it is not uncommon to hear a tenant say, in a teasing sort of way, "They sure got you working hard today." If unremarkable, this kind of teasing provides a framework for the tenant to step out of role and thereby bridge some social distance to the doorman. Conveniently, while providing a bridge, the "joke" also solidifies the distance between doormen and tenants and brings to relief one of the interactive asymmetries that govern the world of the lobby, for it would be inconceivable for a doorman to greet a tenant with a joke about their working hours; for example, to the tenant who leaves the building late one morning, few doorman could actually say, "Got an early start at work today, I see," or to the tenant returning home early in the after- noon, perhaps directly from the gym or a tennis game and therefore in sport clothes, "Working hard as usual," even though these are "equivalent teases."

If at the office the rules that induce social distance asymmetries restrict the interactive range of subordinates to the benefit of superordinates, the lobby is different. Doormen have slightly more interactive flexibility. Their closeness to tenants allows them to interactively penetrate the tenant's pri- vate sphere, thus inviting an opportunity to bridge the social distance gap through a form of familiarity. While it would be inconceivable for a doorman to comment on the legitimacy of a tenant's compensation — the analogue of "So they finally got you working today," the doorman can legitimately ask residents, "How was your evening?" upon their return, or more invasively, "How was dinner?" after a take-out order, or even, "How was the movie?"

---

5. Asymmetry in social distance is discussed with respect to role distance in Goffman, *Encounters*.

after a video delivery, in the latter two cases suggesting that his taste in movies and take-out is the same as theirs, thereby closing the distance gap considerably.

The tables can be thus turned a bit. In some instances, tenants and doormen are each able to "exploit" interactive asymmetry in social distance because the lobby is simultaneously the place where doormen work and the entry to where residents live. But in the end, the cards are held by the resident, who can refuse the doorman's gambit and simply refuse to answer questions that appear somehow cheeky. For this reason, perhaps, doormen rarely initiate such exchanges — only when the resident steps into a "teasing role" do doormen orient conversation with respect to the practical activities of tenants. All other things equal, doormen will stick to familiar scripts for conversation, scripts that signify nothing but the fact of a relationship — conversation perhaps not too different from the conversation of those married couples who talk of nothing important.

Doormen must be able to switch frames quickly, and to handle as well the switches of others or settings.[6] One of the ways in which this switching is achieved is in ordinary conversation, in just talking. I consider switching dynamics in some detail subsequently. First, it helps to get a flavor for the type of talk in the lobby, since it is often the small talk that makes the big problems go away.

SOCIAL DISTANCE AND TRIVIALITY

A short stay in any lobby, fancy or plain, reveals that the typical tenant-doorman interaction is brief. It appears hardly capable of sustaining a relationship. There seems, in short, to be little "beef," as Mondale once complained. What are the alternatives, and what role does such conversation play in shaping the boundaries between doormen and their tenants? One idea is that conversations are trivial because the social distance between doormen and their tenants is too vast to be routinely crossed by conversation meaningful at the level of personal expression. If doormen are wondering about how to pay their bills and tenants are wondering about their country home, one could imagine that there was a gulf that conversation could poorly

---

6. The discussion of switching here, and subsequently, is largely based on the interesting work of Harrison White on "netdoms." Cf. Mische and White, "Between Conversation and Situation."

bridge. There is some evidence that this is the case. Many tenants have little understanding of the life experience of their doormen, and, quite clearly, many doormen recognize that there is a substantial gulf between them and their tenants, a gulf that prevents "authentic" understanding from developing. For example, in response to questions about how much money their doormen make, most tenants have simply no idea for the simple reason that they have never thought about it.[7] Tito, for example, who lives on the Upper East Side, thinks:

> Maybe $22,000 or $24,000 a year — no, that is too low, nobody can live on that, so I guess it has to be some more. But I don't know, they could have two jobs so maybe $30,000 is better.

While Robert across town says:

> I honestly never really thought about it. I assume they make minimum wage. I don't even know what the minimum wage is. I would say maybe on average $30,000.[8]

One could multiply such statements over and over. The same tenants likewise often have no idea where their doormen live, how they get to work, what time they leave in order to be on the door on time, how they live, and so on. It is not that they do not care in the abstract, for many tenants report that they have extremely good relationships with their doormen, relationships that they value, think about, and work on. But these relationships tend not to be particularly revelatory of the everyday lifeworlds away from work of their doormen. Nor need they be — for the tenants at any rate. But not thinking about how people live is quite different than thinking about it and coming to the conclusion that they live differently. Tenants are more likely to be

---

7. In cooperative buildings, by contrast, most residents have a better idea of the salaries they pay their doormen, since wages compose a non-trivial component of the monthly maintenance fee and they attend relatively carefully to the use of the fee. Renters indirectly pay for their doormen as part of their rent (e.g., calculated as $14 per month for the rental units controlled by Columbia University). They are often stunned to discover that they pay for their doormen — in conversations with my colleagues, many of whom live in doorman buildings, most simply never imagined that the rent they paid had a line item associated with doormen, assuming instead that "they just come with the building," like the hot water, views, and lobby maintenance.

8. For the record, the minimum wage is now $5.15 per hour in New York. Assuming a forty-hour week, for fifty-two weeks per year, this translates to $10,712 per year, so while the logic that got him there was faulty, the picture was a little bit clearer.

associated with the former, doormen with the latter. That is, doormen think about the way their tenants live.

Doormen are more likely than tenants to recognize the enormous social gulf that lies between them and their tenants, but as suggested above, this recognition comes from active engagement with their tenants' lives, rather than disengagement. Their engagement is selective, however. Doormen know how their tenants live, what they eat, where and when they work, what they do for leisure, and so on. This knowledge is based on observation of the public behavior of tenants and is filtered by the complexity of reading distant class codes, many of which as noted earlier may be obscure. The observations that they do have lead them to think that their tenants are wealthier than they are. If the perceived or real distance is too vast, doormen simply accept the fact that, at the level of meaning, they cannot relate to their tenants. As one doorman on the East Side says about a former high-ranking government official who lived in his building:

> Yeah, he was a very nice man. Considerate man, you know. But how do you relate to a billionaire?[9]

Also on the East Side, in a cooperative building where it is rumored that hundreds of millions of dollars in net wealth are required to gain acceptance by the board, one doorman sums up his tenants by noting that "most of them are not like us, they live here sometimes, but they also have houses in London and Hawaii, places like that, you know."

This class distance does not prevent conversation, however. Nor does it prevent niceties — that is, daily greetings and nods, and helpful chatter of all sorts. But it does mean that the conversation will likely be about generic topics. But is that unusual? If conversation topics are generic, it may simply be that the conversations that are thought in theory to be vehicles for breaking down boundaries between persons sink to the lowest common denominator, and therefore rather than increasing social connections across disjoint

---

9. The nice guy has now passed away. Actually, he was not a billionaire. Doormen tend to overestimate the class position and wealth of their tenants. This is both because they are invested in their tenants' status and because they are privy to the consumption behavior of their tenants. Since the consumption patterns that they do see and the social events that they observe — wine purchases, dry-cleaning utilization, food orders, parties held, guests arriving, and so on — are the moments in which (practical, everyday) wealth is expended — from their perspective — tenants appear to spend money liberally.

groups serve instead to solidify the boundary that lies between them. The triviality of the conversations one overhears between doormen and tenants may simply be an expression of the role structure that they are embedded in[10] or, alternatively, an expression of a more generic fact: that most conversations are in fact about matters that sound trivial to outsiders. In either case, one would need to be careful to assert that either out of such triviality authentic relationships would have a difficult time emerging, since these contents characterize the relationships most often considered authentic, or that triviality is the consequence of status differences. Consider, by comparison, the conversation at events designed to introduce similarly ranked people to one another — mixers and cocktail parties. Here, one observes the same radical truncation of conversation topics to just those trivial contents shared by all present: the table display; the snacks, cheeses, and foods available; the bar and the setting; the clear or overcast evening; traffic; and also "life," but here as well in its most generic form, "What do you do?"[11] There is thus a comparable descent to the common denominator, the shared world of the table, the apartment, guests, food, and so on. It is therefore not status differences per se that generate trivial conversation topics.[12]

Rather, such conversations occur between strangers positioning to learn more about one another. Since cocktail parties and mixers work — that is, they introduce people to one another — it appears that it is exactly when

---

10. Although not typically considered by sociologists when they try to ascertain the structure of core discussion networks, most conversations that people have with others, even those close to them, appear to be on trivial topics. Cf. Bearman and Parigi, "Cloning Headless Frogs and Other Important Matters."

11. The latter question cannot be answered in depth, for conversation that explicitly reveals something of the personality is considered tactless. Most of us have observed, after all, that awkward moment when, after asking someone what he or she does, just to fill the time, they actually begin to answer.

12. The same dynamic occurs in exceptionally close relationships between status equals, say, in marriage. Here, we observe a strange reversal of mechanism but the same outcome. Reserved for the marriage partner are just those topics, fears, and slights one received at work, the failures, concerns, worries, and so on that cannot be shared with others. The greater the intensity of the relationship, the greater the danger that this descent into the personal will swamp the relationship with the most negative aspects of the self, seen from the perspective of the self. Oddly, as the relationship intensifies, the selves that compose it become smaller and more generic — and once again, one can learn little from the content of conversation. Between these two extreme points, where form dominates content, one can find meaningful conversation in settings that are freed enough of the conventions of form to allow for the free personality to be expressed. But these are neither the conversations nor the settings that doormen have with tenants. Cf. Simmel, *The Sociology of Georg Simmel*, for more insightful discussions of this issue, as well as Waller, *On the Family, Education, and War*, for the insight that the marriage partnership descends into triviality.

content is stripped to the most generic that some kinds of information about people is most clearly revealed. What is revealed is social status, or, more accurately, trivial conversation provides one of the key lubricants for the articulation of status and the search for coveted roles.[13] Trivial conversation also makes possible fresh starts and new situations, allowing for shaping new roles and interaction dynamics. Here, the goods that doormen work with in conversation are not different than those that others work with at mixers and parties — they are the micro-level stuff of everyday life. Doormen talk to their tenants about the weather, traffic, the street, the neighborhood, the building, Chinese deliverymen, menus, bicycles, sports, and life. In these conversations, they are constantly switching from one level of familiarity to another, depending on the tenant. To see this process more clearly, one has to consider how switching dynamics operate.

SWITCHING

In all sorts of public places like the lobby, a cocktail party, a queue in the grocery store, or a crowd at a street protest, people often engage in relatively trivial conversations with one another — that is, they find them-selves making conversation.[14] Some basic data on conversation patterns with tenants are reported in the following table, which considers whether or not

---

13. As Joel Podolny notes, one can imagine, as a thought experiment, what would happen if we turned off the sound — this is, after all, what happens when we first enter a busy room with many people engaged in their own conversations that we are not privy to (Podolny, personal communica-tion). In other words, can we learn anything from simply watching flow? First, we may discover that it will make little difference to our understanding of the dynamics we observe. In fact, our perception of the social structure of the mixer may be better without sound. In the mixer, we can observe some people on the outskirts of the room watching (they may be like us, late arrivals, checking out the scene), and then others in the center of small groups, all eyes turned toward them. In motion, some people drift into new groups without impact, whereas when others drift into the group, those closest make room for them and orient immediately to their presence. Others appear to try to enter small groups, but with less success, standing just on the outskirts. Without sound there is much to learn about social standing, who might be profitably talked to, whose attention is difficult to obtain and hold, who might be best avoided (for fear of being trapped), whom others avoid, where others appear to be trapped, and so on. At the very least, one can find the social winners and the social losers very quickly. This should not surprise us since all conversation is equally trivial at such events; there is nothing that distinguishes one content from another, and, so, the sound just provides a distracting background noise, like music in the mall. In fact, one might imagine that the sound is simply a form of social lubricant useful because it provides a rhetorical distraction. What we learn from soundless observation at the mixer is what is immediately useful to us, the relative status position of others at the setting we are observing.

14. Mische and White, "Between Conversation and Situation."

TABLE 5.3. Shifts by Conversation Topics with Tenants

Shift	Sports	Weather	Politics	Building matters	Other tenants	Your family	Their family
Day	35	42	29	30	12	26	25
N = 57	(61.4%)	(73.7%)	(50.9%)	(52.6%)	(21.1%)	(45.6%)	(43.9%)
Swing	74	73	56	57	34	42	40
N = 97	(76.3%)	(75.3%)	(57.7%)	(58.8%)	(35.1%)	(43.3%)	(41.2%)
Night	7	5	4	5	3	5	5
N = 10	(70.0%)	(50.0%)	(40.0%)	(50.0%)	(30.0%)	(50.0%)	(50.0%)
Multiple	25	27	21	26	11	16	16
N = 41	(61.0%)	(65.9%)	(51.2%)	(63.4%)	(26.8%)	(39.0%)	(39.0%)
Total	141	147	110	118	60	89	86
N = 205	(68.8%)	(71.7%)	(53.7%)	(57.6%)	(29.3%)	(43.4%)	(42.0%)

shift structures conversation topics. Cell entries indicate the number (and corresponding percentage) of doormen who answered "yes" to any of the topics. Shift makes little difference. This comes as no surprise, or course. Making conversation is something that people seem to do. But why to they do this and, equally important, how?

One simple answer to the why question is that everyday conversation — whatever its content — provides an important mechanism for getting things done and learning about the other. In contexts where roles are unclear, conversation is the primary mechanism for establishing a role structure — that is, a set of behaviors that can be expressed within the relationship. Where roles are relatively fixed, conversation allows individuals to express their side of the role structure, thus encoding mutual expectations more deeply. And finally, conversation is the mechanism that people use to get action, to switch roles. In this latter sense, everyday conversation provides the raw material for new opportunities — both profitable and risky. Consider by way of example our colloquial use of the term "situation," in the sense of "that was a tough situation" or "the situation was fraught with difficulty." What do we mean when we say these things? First, the situation — whatever it is — is separated from the "non-situations," whatever they may be that provide their counterpart. If there are to be situations, there must necessarily be a population of situations, and if people know they are in a situation, they must have some sense that they are not in one, at other times.

It is easier to define the non-situations, for they conform to our most common experience of everyday life. Non-situations are those moments (one cannot really call such moments "events," for the canonical experience of life cannot be an event, which presumes some temporal and social location) in which highly predictable and clearly governed (stylized) interactions occur. With respect to doorman-tenant interactions, non-situations are those in which both parties conform to the highly stylized behaviors associated with their respective roles. The sociological problem is how do such roles come to be shaped and agreed upon? Each party brings some set of expectations to the table. Considering the closeness-distance axis, these expectations are closer to the distant than the close side. But the reality of the job, the fact that doormen know so much about tenants and that tenants come to realize that doormen know so much about them, constantly pushes them toward the closer pole. Everyday conversation provides the vehicle for stabilizing roles in the context of such tension. But it is also the vehicle for the induction of situations, for uncertainty and challenge.

First, consider the stabilizing effects of everyday conversation. As Goffman noted long ago, everyday conversation is timeless and without social significance.[15] In everyday conversation, the interactive future is absent; no one has a stake in the outcome, and specific contents of conversation carry no significance, either for other contents or the interactive parties.[16] In everyday conversation, interacting parties accomplish nothing directly because they have no goals, but the fact of conversation serves as a social lubricant, allowing individuals to enter and exit settings, and traverse from one setting to another, thereby making it possible to get action. One need only recall from personal experience the tensions that appear among persons occupying the same social space when conversation is completely absent — for example, in the waiting room of a child psychologist, an HIV testing center, or an employment office — to understand this lubricating function. But lubrication is

---

15. "Thus conversation, restrictively defined, might be identified as the talk occurring when a small number of participants come together and settle into what they perceive to be a few moments cut off from (or carried on to the side of) instrumental tasks; a period of idling felt to be an end in itself, during which everyone is accorded the right to talk, as well as to listen and without reference to a fixed schedule; everyone is accorded the status of someone whose overall evaluation of the subject matter at hand — whose editorial comments, as it were — is to be encouraged and treated with respect; and no final agreement or synthesis is demanded, differences of opinion to be treated as un-prejudicial to the continuing relationship of the participants." Goffman, *Encounters*, p. 14.

16. This accounts, by the way, for the often experienced sensation that in trivial conversations, people find themselves roaming from stereotypical topic to stereotypical topic, vegetarianism here, the new movies out there, without any predetermined plan, yet ex post facto, roughly the same across actors.

also sticky, and everyday conversations can quickly turn into situations when one of a number of different things takes place.

The things that can disrupt the routine of conversation are far too numerous and heterogeneous to enumerate, but for our case, one can observe relatively robust patterns. Here, I distinguish three. First, everyday conversations about trivial topics presume that the population of topics is, for both doorman and tenant, "acceptable" and transposable, that is, equally vacuous. This agreement on the terms of conversation is what Harrison White refers to as a domain, analogous to our everyday usage of "discipline" when describing an academic field of study — that is, a discipline should be seen as a shared set of conversations.[17] Against this background, a conversation can descend into a situation when there is an asymmetry in perception about the underlying domain rules. When people jump from topic to topic, not all topics can be selected; some are not "fair game." As Ann Mische and Harrison White note, "Within the bounds of a given conversation, we might say that all acceptable topics are equally available, but not all available topics are equally acceptable." We can call this drift into difficult topics "endogenous drift."

Second, conversation networks that exist in specific interaction domains induce a relationship between the discussants — the conversation relationship. If the domain boundaries are strong, there need be no change in the underlying network ties (conversation partners) that give rise to conversation. But if the boundaries are weak, ambiguity over the meaning of conversation can arise. It is not uncommon, for example, for romantic relationships to develop out of such network ties. When new network underpinnings intersect with conversation domains, situations can arise. The innocent remark can be interpreted as flirtation or harassment, and if the discussants are imagining that they are in different "domains," difficult and embarrassing situations occur.[18] We can call this dynamic "network switches."

Third, situations can occur when an exogenous shock to the system takes place. Such shocks tend to shatter the agreed-upon disciplinary definitions

---

17. Mische and White, "Between Conversation and Situation." Just to be clear, one tends not in sociology to discuss joules and ergs. But in chemistry such discussions are quite common.

18. Goffman spends much time on the social organization of embarrassment. In his case, he focuses primarily on the embarrassment that arises from the conjunction of two separate domains. This is why the capacity to segregate domains is critical for Goffman, for without this ability, identity is difficult to sustain. Goffman, *The Presentation of Self in Everyday Life*.

of domains, with respect to both comportment and interactive behavior. Obviously, in this context, the events of 9/11 and its aftermath threatened to wreck havoc on formerly quite carefully established interactive domains. I consider each of these challenges in turn, focusing first on situations arising from asymmetries in perception about the transposability of conversation contents; second, on situations that arise from the introduction of new network foundations to the domain; and, finally, to challenges arising from exogenous shocks, both large and small.

Endogenous Drift

As discussed in chapter 3, doormen have stock-and-trade conversation about the weather, traffic, sports, the neighborhood, and life. In general, these conversation topics are transposable. Our thoughts about the traffic (bad or good, worse or better, always the same); the weather (cold in the winter; warm in the summer; breezy, hot, humid, or nice); sports (teams losing or winning); and the neighborhood (changing or not, for better or for worse) carry few implications. More interesting, the topics themselves are independent. Opinions on one carry no implications for opinions on another. And finally, these thoughts are timeless. By this I mean that while they make use of time (one day the weather is hot and the next it is cold; one day the team wins and the next it loses), the opinions held are not arrayed in a temporal sequence. Another way to say this is that it does not matter on which day it is hot or cold, or on which day a team wins or loses. In this sense, there is a suspension of time. Each day is the same, whatever the goods (cold or hot, winning or losing) there are to talk about. The characteristic feature of triviality is this suspension of time; and the characteristic feature of trivial conversations is the transposability of topics.

Against this background, it is odd to discover that doormen often have conversations with tenants that stick to just one or two topics, rather than range across the whole set. That is, with one tenant, doormen will talk about the weather, while with another they will talk about sports. One explanation for this restriction of range is that doormen, in first contact with tenants, experiment with the topics that work, and then stick to those topics in daily interaction as a way to organize them into sets. Here, since topics are equivalent with respect to meaning, and since they serve to index the fact of the relationship rather than build the relationship, a simple learning model would lead to truncation of range. Tenants, too, may have similarly truncated conversation topics with many different people they encounter — discussing topic A with person Y, and topic B with person Z — as a product of the same general process.

While the central utility of conversation is to index the fact of a relationship, it is still odd that topics exchangeable across similarly situated individuals are in experience not exchanged. One idea is that truncation of range is a strategic response by both doormen and tenants to the dangers of endogenous drift, which can easily induce situations. While it is hard to imagine how talk about weather or talk about sports can be threatening, it is much less difficult to imagine how talk about politics or fashion could lead to endogenous drift. The nature of conversation, though, is such that topic domains cognate to each other can without proper boundaries easily spring up in unanticipated ways. Thus, on unusually warm days, conversations about the weather can descend into conversations about appropriate dress without either party realizing that they have trespassed into more difficult interactive territory, where values come into play. Likewise, simple conversations about sports can quickly descend, if not into comments about social fashion, into discussions of work ethic, high salaries, or ethnicity. Each of these topics — dress, wages, ethics, and so on — poses potential interactive dilemmas for doormen, whose valuations may be quite different than their tenants. Likewise, tenants may be uncomfortable hearing that huge salaries paid to individuals are wrong, whatever their merits as ballplayers or celebrities.

Consequently, both parties often work hard to police the boundaries of conversation domains. And the simplest form of policing is to stick to routine scripts. While the script content may vary across tenants, for doormen commitment to script mitigates against potential drift. Thus, conversations tend to be more stylized than one would otherwise imagine, except where relationships become more intense. By intensity, though, one simply means that they become personal, that is, directed to the actual inhabitant of the role, rather than simply as the instantiation of the role — in this case, tenant. To be clear, the problem is not solely that some topics tend to involve values whereas others do not (or at least not so explicitly). The problem is that asymmetries in perception about the equivalence of conversational domains — as neutral or as possibly difficult — can be quite pronounced, especially as one crosses social class, ethnic, and social experience boundaries. Fox hunting, for example, may be a natural thing to talk about if one is in the English upper class and it is a perfect day for hunting fox (whatever that may be). But it is not necessarily the first thing that comes to mind for most workers, who may imagine that the day (whatever it is) is perfect for a quick trip to the shopping center. Whatever the specific topic domains, the fact that they are organized by social class and experience means that the potential for such asymmetries in perception between doormen and tenants is quite high.

Network Switches

If one thing bothers doormen more than anything else, it is the common experience they have of being socially unrecognizable to tenants when they leave the building. In conversation after conversation, doormen, whether oppositional to or positively in tune with their tenants, hate the fact that when they meet tenants on the street that most tenants "don't even bother to say hello" or "just walk by like I don't exist." This sense of being ignored deeply challenges the idea that they have a special relationship with tenants and forcefully creates the sense that the tenants are snubbing them, thereby reproducing the class differences that through everyday conversation they have glossed over.

Doormen may be right to imagine that some tenants do not want to make this switch for fear of status loss. For example, Peter says:

> Say I'm walking down the street and I see one of my tenants. With some I'm going to say, "Hi, Mr. Bean, how you doing," or whatever. This guy just ignores me, like he just looks right through me. See he doesn't want to show that he knows someone like me. But when he comes in the door, I got to say the same thing and he is going to say "hi" to me back, you know. Like here it's okay for him. Even if he is a hypocrite, I have to be always polite.

But before we consider this, it makes sense to focus on other interpretive possibilities. A few things are going on here, some social and others perhaps more cognitive. One important fact is that there is deep asymmetry in recognition. First, tenants are rarely if ever in neighborhoods where doormen live. Consequently, chance encounters with doormen on the street are more likely to occur in the tenants' neighborhood (when the doorman is at lunch, arriving for work, shopping immediately after work, or running an errand) than in the doorman's. When doormen are in the neighborhood — even if not exactly at work — they are in a work frame of mind. So they are thinking about work. And this thought leads them to think about tenants. Thus, they are more likely to see tenants and therefore acknowledge them.[19] In contrast, when tenants are in their neighborhood, they may well be thinking about home, but they need not be. They are as likely to be meeting friends, conducting business, shopping, or entertaining. Since they are not thinking about doormen, they are less likely to see them or — and more problematically, for doormen — *recognize* them out of their work setting. If tenants were in a doorman neighborhood — and they knew that it was a doorman neighborhood, which they do not — tenants would look for and see doormen. But they are not and they do not.

But more than asymmetries in recognition processes arising from cognitive frames are taking place. Doormen see tenants on the street when tenants are embedded in networks different than at home. These networks may be actually enacted — in the sense that the tenant is with someone when seen — or not. Tenants hurrying from one shopping trip to another, heading for a meeting, getting ready to visit a friend at a coffee shop, or whatever are embedded in streams of activity with network underpinnings even if alone. The doorman who sees a tenant on the street crashes into this network, and when he greets the tenant, he is asking the tenant to make a network switch; in White's language, to zap from one show to another.

At the same time, there is clearly something beyond cognitive demand operating on tenants, and doormen are often right to imagine that their tenants — even those most friendly in the context of the lobby — are at some pains to ignore them in public, for fear of status loss. One could always try to assess whether this is the case by asking tenants, but none would admit to avoidance of their doormen. They simply don't see them. In this sense, since we know that people tend to see those with whom they are status equals, the fact that doormen do not register indicates something about the transposability of the relationship beyond the lobby. And these relationships, from the perspective of tenants, are not that transposable, on average.

Doormen also need to zap across social distance, for they come into repeated contact with "derelicts" and homeless people, who use the resources of the street to survive. Almost every doorman I talked to works positively with the homeless, that is, allows them to go through the garbage, collect plastic for recycling, and help with simple tasks. The price of not collaborating is a potential mess, but I believe that the main motivation lies in their

---

19. Consider by analogy the common experience of buying a new car (or even a pair of glasses) and suddenly seeing just that car or those glasses everywhere, where previously they had been almost invisible.

valuation of the homeless activity as work. While tenants see the unemployed sifting through garbage, doormen see workers.

> You know, they go through the garbage looking for something of value they can sell on Lexington Ave., so I'll tell them dig, but just don't make a mess. They have to make a buck, too, so I don't like chasing them away; the guy is trying to survive. . . . So as long as you don't make a mess, do what you want. Once I see them tearing it up and making a mess, then I have to stop them.

When doormen zap across contexts to see homeless recyclers as workers, they are obviously achieving something that for the most part they perceive their tenants are less able to do. Certainly, most doormen are uncomfortable with tenants in sharing the fact that they collaborate with homeless recyclers to make both their jobs easier. Since doormen understand this, they also have a sense that their tenants, for all their worldly achievements, are socially less able to navigate the shoals of complex city life. This understanding in turn feeds back to their assessment of tenants as individuals whom in many cases need help just getting things done. Doormen also see tenants as persons who can get some things done in other contexts, for example, providing introductions of other careers, helping with legal advice, and so on. Zapping across realms of cognitive experience, and across prior conversation domains, is a risky enterprise, for it makes demands on the relationship that it may not sustain. As Eugene, a doorman on the Upper East Side, told me about a tenant who lives in his building, a tenant with whom he has developed a rather striking animosity since a failed zap:

> That guy says he is for all the little people. He writes all these editorials about people who have to work for a living. But when I had a problem and asked him to help, he told me, "I don't have anything to do with stuff like that." So you know he is a real motherfucker.

In this instance, and others, the network switch — here, the doorman tries to embed himself in some way into the perceived network of the liberal tenant — fails and creates tension in the relationship, a tension the source of which is likely mysterious to the tenant. The danger of network switches is that such misreading of the relevant network structures is quite common. Very few people have a great grasp of the networks of their peers. For example, few people can really wrap their minds around the first simple rule, which is that on average their friends have more friends than they do.

Since such misreading is common, what is a structural impossibility for one actor is easily perceived as an affront or unwarranted demand by another. Doormen and tenants work to constrain their relationships in ways to block such network shifts from becoming corrosive. Most of the time, the shifts are subtle and have little impact on either party. Sometimes, though, the shifts cause rifts that are difficult to breach.

Exogenous Shocks

Ignoring for the moment the events of 9/11 — which I consider in more detail in the conclusion — there are many moments in the life of the building when an exogenous event shatters the calm of the lobby and threatens the interactive routines that have been established. These events can be as simple as a minor car crash in front of the building, the excessive beeping of an irate driver, a construction mishap, or the appearance of graffiti on the building wall; or as disruptive as the use of the lobby for election voting, the elevators going out of service, a power outage, or conflict between tenants spilling into the public sphere. In these moments, when ordinary building life is challenged, the nature of the doorman-tenant relationship is under pressure. Recall that the doorman's main job is to absorb such disruptions so that they do not impact the tenants. Against this background, when such a disruption occurs, the doorman is in a sense thrown out of role. The car crash may bring doormen and tenants out into the street to observe or help; if the latter, the doorman will need to leave his post, asking a tenant to stay behind to make sure that the building remains secure. The appearance of graffiti means that whole new conversation topics — previously defined as off-limits — suddenly come to the floor. These topics are much more likely to be value-laden than small-talk topics that may have characterized the relationship between a doorman and his tenant. Such topics may open up new possibilities for personalizing the relationship or create tensions from obvious competing value schemes. Either way, they are new. Likewise, legitimate disruptions such as occur when the lobby is used for election voting lead to new conversations, as well as a diminution of service. Since such shocks are in some sense part of the routine of the city — even if buffered by doormen — each doorman and each tenant is likely over the period they interact together to have experienced many moments where — however briefly — established role structures appear up for grabs, and thus without clear interactive guidelines.

It is also the case that we observe social structure because it is capable of surviving such exogenous shocks, and doormen and tenants, as with others, rely on established routines to bridge such moments, defining them as liminal — that is, outside of the usual relationship domains. In most instances, such interactive strategies — coding the event as unusual, as "That was strange," "It's a weird city," or "One sees just about everything these days," for example — suffice to return the interactive parties to their baseline. In some cases, though, such shocks, even if sealed over by attempts to define the event as out of the ordinary, reveal aspects of personality that either or both parties would prefer not revealed. This is much less a risk for tenants than for doormen, for tenants (as doormen know) reveal much of their personality indirectly through their everyday life — their comings and goings, their food and movie orders, the packages that arrive for them, and their visitors. While tenants may feel exposed by rapid shifts in the outside environment, their exposure is minimal, and the information projected about them is minimal compared to that revealed in everyday life. Doormen, on the other hand, are at some risk, for they may reveal emotional states inhibited by their usual emotional management. At the same time, exogenous shocks to the system can induce doormen's status in the eyes of tenants. This was certainly the case in the days immediately following 9/11. The increased centrality of doormen in times of crisis — large and small — can thus transform their relationships to the tenants, but such transformations tend to be short-lived, and, except for unusual cases, interactive scripts return to the routine, along with the roles that underlie them. In this regard, the struggle for coveted roles, while making use of exogenous shock, is in the end determined much more strongly by the routines that govern interaction and conversation. One critical routine, encoding much of the micro-process described here, is the bonus, considered in some detail in the next chapter.

OVERVIEW

The social distance between doormen and tenants is often enormous. Doormen who succeed — that is, doormen who stay in the job for a long time — see their jobs as professional rather than servile. Doormen who come to see themselves as servile begin to believe that tenants treat them as such — that is, that tenants fail to respect them. They also develop antagonistic attitudes toward their tenants. Much of the nature of the job, once framed as servile, supports such casting. Tenants become people who cannot open doors for themselves. They appear as weak and unable to cope. They have and pamper silly small dogs. The men are impotent; the women, helpless. Doormen distinguish themselves from tenants by valuing their autonomy and independence. They can open doors themselves. They don't need people to help with their bags. They can change light bulbs and cope with odd events. Cast in the language of sex, doormen come to see their tenants as feminine (the men) and frigid (the women). They see their tenants as the beneficiaries of an unequal system that rewards incompetence through inheritance. In short, they see social class.   ·

In contrast, doormen who can effectively frame their activity as a profession do not see tenants as undifferentiated representatives of the upper class. Instead, they see specific people with whom they have specific professional relationships. Conversation in the lobby is one of the principal mechanisms deployed to make this perception stick — to index the relationship and, therefore, reduce alienation. The fact that most conversation is not revelatory of personality — that it serves an indexical function — means that doormen and tenants can grease the wheels of everyday encounters, encounters always tinged by the vast social distance that lies between them, just by making small talk. And so successful doormen make small talk with tenants. This chapter considered the nature of this talk and the strange finding that most tenants and most doormen talk about one thing rather than range across the entire domain of trivial topics. I suggested that such restriction of range was the strategic response of doormen and tenants to block threats to established roles arising from network switching or conversation drift. By limiting discourse domains, doormen can successfully navigate between the shoals of too much social distance (limiting all interaction) and too much closeness — breaking out of role.

CHAPTER 6

The Bonus

We definitely have anxiety with how to tip and everything. The first year we lived here, we had never lived in a building with a doorman before and we did not know what was customary. So a couple of my friends who work in the office live in really nice buildings on the East Side who tip in like the hundreds of dollars to their doormen. But I do not think that they expected that much of a tip, but we thought that we should give them something and we baked cookies for everyone and the staff. We thought that was something a little more personal — we took time to do that. We were definitely a little bit nervous about it, but I think it was all right.

— TENANT, Upper West Side

Cookies are nice but I don't want cookies. Cookies are for kids, and I am not a kid.

— DOORMAN, Upper West Side

Sure. My wife and I had a discussion. We kicked it around for a couple of weeks before [we] actually figured out that we were going to drop [to] the building superintendent and a couple of other people more money than the other people, like I said there are seventeen people and the majority of those people are not — they are just building workers, people who work on the building, maintenance or handypeople. So, yeah, it takes a little time to figure we are going to drop two to three hundred dollars to these guys.

E very year after Thanksgiving, merchants pull out their Christmas displays, the business section of the *New York Times* focuses on the retail picture for the year, children start actively campaigning to see Santa Claus, building supers suddenly become more visible, and doormen *seem* to improve their service. Most buildings start to sprout holiday displays, and tenants, especially newcomers to New York City, begin to experience a peculiar anxiety over how much the Christmas bonus should be. They don't attack this problem without help, of course. The *Times* runs an almost annual article on the standard tip across the various grades of workers one might find in a building — super, concierge, doormen, porter. Local newspapers —

the *Spirit* on the Upper West Side, the *Resident* on the East Side — join the fray and offer more specialized guidance. But strangely, rather than reduce anxiety, the apparent presence of norms for others simply heightens concerns. Leaving aside, for the moment, newcomers, whose ignorance allows them a certain freedom to commit social errors without approbation, talk about the Christmas bonus is reserved for close intimates — like income, it is more private than sex. As one tenant reports:

> I never asked anyone. Why? We know people in the building, but the people I feel comfortable asking don't live in the building. If I asked, I would worry that they would ask in return, and I am not sure I would want to share that. It would be for fear of being embarrassed that it is not enough — that I should do more. And I don't want to have to think about that.

But at the same time, there is often also a strange undercurrent that runs through the buildings, an intensity of interest in exactly what one's fellow tenants may be doing this year with respect to the bonus. So while it may be the Christmas spirit, one can also notice increased talk in the halls, by the elevator, and in the lobby (when the doorman is not around) between tenants often too busy at other times during the year to so much as acknowledge their shared presence in the elevator. They want to get to the issue at hand — how much to give — but it takes some social lubrication. So for a while, the buildings take on a cheerier and friendlier light. It is a means to an end, though — getting the right information? Perhaps, but giving the wrong information could also be more accurate.

The dilemma tenants face is clear enough. The expectation is that doormen ought to get a bonus. So should the super. The conflicts when one comes to think about them can often be deep. The bonus is never not multivalent in the eyes of tenants. It is both a gift, a way of saying thanks, an obligation, and yet also a sign of expected reciprocal attention and an expression of social power. These contradictory meanings make the bonus difficult to talk about, and tenants often squirm in their seats (or cognitively) as they try to describe just what it means. For example, one tenant in an Upper West Side cooperative moves in the space of seconds from describing the bonus as a gift — "and I like giving gifts" — to a vehicle for achieving attention, to a moral commitment, to social justice abstracted from the building entirely:

It also gives me more power. For a certain time of year, the help focuses on what we are doing. It's nice for them, too, aside from the demeaning aspect, because it feels like free money. I feel good about it, but at the same time the whole thing is demeaning them. You get caught in the system, and you can't find the owner and demand he give them a higher wage — the moral situation is unfair because we are the human beings. The burden is on me to help. It ought not be on one to rectify the situation, but it is.

There are two public ideas about the meaning of the bonus. They appear quite different at first glance, and alone, neither accurately captures the real dynamic that is going on, but it is useful to start with them because the trick of the bonus — the way the bonus works — is that it unifies two simultaneous perceptions of temporality. On the one hand, the Christmas bonus is often represented as the acknowledgment of all of the assistance received during the past year. Because the norm is to not tip for little favors that are, in any case, potentially a part of the job description, tenants think about the Christmas bonus as a giant summary tip of sorts. Whereas tipping encodes the relationship too starkly as a service relationship, because the number of small favors is endless, the Christmas bonus symbolizes the value of all the little services over the past year. Call this the straight-service or post-payment model. Doormen may also define the bonus as a summary tip, on a post-payment model, in whole or in part. Asked what he likes best about the job, for example, Eamon says:

> Christmas bonuses! Christmas, Santa Claus, Santa Claus is coming to town. You know why, not because we are greedy or anything; we service them well. Come Christmas they are supposed to take care of the service they have received during the year. Am I right or wrong? We give them good service; this is our time now. I know that in bigger buildings with a hundred and fifty-five units, these guys can make eight, nine, ten thousand dollars. Right here I make about four, but I know guys that laugh at me when I make four because they make eight. It's not unusual for a tenant who likes you to give you a check for five hundred dollars.

Tenants also often think about the bonus in part as a post-payment for services previously consumed during the year. As the tenant quoted earlier who feels that the burden to provide a living wage should not rest on him says:

> It's a conflict. It means a nice gift and I like giving gifts, but for them it's not a gift, it's a chunk of their salary, so it's not extra, it's integrated into their wage, their expenses. At the same time, it's fun to get a bonus — it's potent psychologically. It's less fun to have that money evened out.

One might think that if the bonus were simply the summary of not-given past tips, that individuals would not experience so much anxiety about the size of their gift. Those who could anticipate such anxiety could easily record the number of times each specific doorman helped with packages, delivered dry-cleaning, or called a taxi; decide what the appropriate tip for each service would be; and pass that sum, or some fraction of it, along at Christmas. But it isn't so easy. Breaking the whole into its component parts is difficult practically. What would the appropriate tip be? And what are the "tippable" activities? More problematic, decomposing the summary bonus into a whole array of heterogeneous micro-services is psychologically as difficult as breaking down the minimum payment required on a credit card into the constituent purchases that compose it. Facing this, the post-payment model is often reported to be no more than a generic "thanks" — a bonus not tied to tied specific services — even if tenants often give different amounts of money to different doormen.

On the other hand, the Christmas bonus is often represented as a pre-payment or down payment for the next year, an advance on the services to be received. Here the bonus is simultaneously a pure gift — for it is given in advance of service — and a hedge for service in the coming year. On the one hand, if this was the model, tenants could easily reduce anxiety by doing what the gas company does when it calculates your monthly gas bill for those months that the meter reader cannot gain access to the meter — estimate the number of favors in the upcoming year as a function of the number of favors received previously. Since tenants are in the best position to estimate needs, given expected changes in household composition, the only tenants with anxiety should be those new to the system. This prepayment model then appears to be the same as the post-payment model with a year lag, presuming that the doormen who work at Christmas are still likely to be serving one in November. But this is a narrow interpretation, for the pre- and post-payment models involve completely different psychological orientations and temporal foci. In fact, the trick of the bonus is that it is both a pre- and post-payment. It is easier to see this if we think first of tips and then move to their cousins, the bonuses.

THE BONUS AS A TEMPORAL PRISM

Tips are given for services received in theory. I eat at a restaurant, where a waiter serves me. At the end of the meal — if social convention dictates — I pay my check and leave a tip for the service. At the hairstylist's tips are expected, but there is no clear relationship between the value of the tip — as a proportion of the total bill — and the perceived quality of the haircut. I may need a taxi at the hotel. The doorman may signal to the waiting cab to come and get me. This service benefits the hotel by keeping taxis from clogging the entryway, yet I may still feel obliged to hand the doorman a dollar or two. Good service is theoretically rewarded with a higher tip, poor service with a lower tip, but as the latter case indicates, in many instances the client has no foundation from which to base assessment of service received.[1]

Economists often find that tipping is a challenge to standard economic theory. The paradigmatic challenge is usually posed in the form of a question that appears in its starkest form when repeated visits are not expected, for example, in a roadside diner somewhere that the guest does not intend to ever come back to. Specifically, many economists wonder why consumers leave money for strangers when they are not required to, will not derive material benefit from doing so, and will not return to benefit from their tip. The simple answer that most people have to this question is that tipping is norm governed and that people most often behave in normative ways. This may be

---

1. There is a large literature that shows that the relationship between the services one receives and tip size is very small. In theory, tipping systems are solutions to information asymmetries. In restaurants, where managers cannot monitor the behavior of workers, structuring compensation so that it is dependent on tips places clients in the role of supervisors, thereby ensuring better service. But clients are poor discriminators. In restaurants, small tricks of the trade are known to influence tip percentage. For example, even if "posh" clients might feel it tacky, waiters know that by introducing themselves ("I'm Sarah, and I'll be your server tonight!") they increase their tip roughly 2%. Waitresses who sign their names and put smiley faces on the bills increase their tips by over 1%; waiters who do the same are penalized. Michael Lynn, "Seven Ways to Increase Your Servers' Tips," *Cornell Hotel and Restaurant Administration Quarterly* 37 (June 1996): 24–29. These tricks of the trade operate on the margins, though. The big action determining tip proportion rests in the norm. This fact is recognized by the state as well, which considers a large component of the tip as taxable income — that is, the tip is construed by the state as a right, as versus a favor — as "payment of money actually due." For the legal status of the tip, cf. Zelizer, *The Social Meaning of Money*.

because violating normative behavior makes people feel bad or because following norms makes people feel good about themselves, or both. For whatever reason people tip strangers, the fact that they do so simply means that all behavior is not meaningfully treated as if it were economically rational.[2]

But if all tipping is not rational, some tipping may be — especially in contexts where repeat visits are expected. One obvious idea is that people tip today in order to avoid bad service tomorrow. If seen in this light, the tip is not a payment after the fact for services received, but a prepayment on services to come. In this light, some tips are rational — those that are hedges for future services — and some are irrational — those that are simply normative responses to the provision of service. The bonus is a form of tip, but it is not just a tip. It is something better, and it is something better because it serves as a temporal prism; simultaneously a post-payment for services that were received and a prepayment for services that are to arrive.

PRE- AND POST-PAYMENT AND THE PSYCHOLOGY OF THE TIP

People prefer most of the time to prepay for things they want to consume in the future. This preference is not rational. That is, it violates economic rationality. And so it creates problems for economists. The rational consumer should not want to prepay for services in the same way that he or she should not tip servers that they will never see again. In theory, if payments are delayed, the consumer gets a better consumption experience. And the longer the delay, the better it is.[3] But most people do not follow this rule. The classic case is how people approach their summer holiday. If people are given a choice — to pay for the holiday in six monthly payments one for each month *before* the vacation or pay for the holiday in six monthly payments *after* the vacation, people prefer the former, even though it is irrational (it

---

2. Much behavior is governed by social norms. Why this is the case is the more interesting question. One idea from economists is that the causal direction is actually the obverse and that norms appear to solve economic problems. Here, tipping is seen as a decentralized solution to problems of supervision and monitoring. That may be true, but it does not solve the general problem posed by irrational tipping — potential free riders, for example, tend not to switch strategies because they have a commitment to solving problems of market failure, asymmetric information, and so on. If they are rational actors, they will let others solve the supervision, monitoring, or information asymmetry problems they have.

3. If there is any doubt about this, imagine buying a lawn mower today and being able to delay payment for as long as one wishes. Theoretically, one could delay until death; thereby enjoying the lawn mower the whole time one was alive for free.

is irrational because they could invest the money they did not prepay and therefore earn interest, reducing the cost of their vacation). Why do they have this preference?

The general idea from behavioral economists is that people tend to evaluate both payment and consumption prospectively — that is, they look to the future, not the past. Consequently, most people would rather prepay first because at the moment they pay, the pain of payment is reduced by the idea of the vacation they are about to have and, second, because while they are on vacation they can enjoy it without thinking about the future payments that they will have to make. If they already paid, the vacation is experienced as if it were free. Paying after the vacation means that their enjoyment will be reduced by the thought of the unpaid bills waiting for their return. Worse, when they do pay after the fact, they have nothing to look forward to, no future pleasures wait to lessen the pain of payment — and so paying is experienced as if it were paying for nothing, as versus getting something for free.

Against this background, consumers thus have a psychological preference for prepayment. Since they have this preference, they may also have a psychological preference to think of some kinds of payments for services as prepayments. The tip for the hairstylist can be seen as a prepayment for the haircut to be received next month; the tip to the pizza deliverer can be seen as a prepayment for more rapidly delivered pizza next time; and so on. Even if the tip is rhetorically construed as a post-payment — a payment for a service already consumed — it can be experienced as a prepayment, as a hedge against future services if they know they will receive future services. The repeat tip — the rational tip — is a prepayment. It is a prepayment because the client considers the tip as a hedge against potential bad service. The bonus is a prepayment par excellence.

But prepayment as a preference runs into an awkward fact. Consumers would prefer — all things being equal — to never pay for items that they consume, or to delay payment for as long as they can, so that they can enjoy the consumption of the item without having to pay for it. Put more starkly, if people prefer to prepay, why do people use credit cards and prefer to use credit cards and buy more stuff when they use credit cards since credit cards are all about post-payment? How can consumers prefer prepayment and yet simultaneously buy more stuff when they can pay for it later? The behavioral economics literature has a good answer here too. Credit cards decouple the pain of purchasing something from the enjoyment of consuming it. Imagine buying something. No matter what it is, thinking about the future payments that one has to make for the thing that is bought will lessen the pleasure of consumption. But if payment is psychologically separated from consumption, the attenuation of pleasure caused by having to pay is reduced. Credit cards are the magicians of decoupling. They achieve this both by increasing the time period between purchase and payment (no interest or payment for twelve months) and by combining many purchases into a single payment (the minimum payment).

The credit card bill itemizes the items purchased. But the bill is for the total amount or the minimum payment. Because individual items are combined into the total (or minimum) amount due, the moment of payment is completely decoupled from the specific consumption act. As magical, the fact the one can pay for anything by credit card means that the typical credit card bill covers a wide spectrum of commodities. The more diverse the specific things consumed are — a dinner, a ticket, a new printer, some books, a visit to the cash machine, the hairdresser, and so on — the greater the decoupling, for the heterogeneity of items makes it impossible for the consumer to associate a specific item purchased with the specific payment that they are making. Thus, decoupling takes the pain away from buying and leads people to buy more than they would if they used cash.[4] With credit cards, consumers get the pleasure of consumption without the pain of paying.

If tenants construe the bonus as a summary of the heterogeneous services that they have received over the past year, then the bonus is a decoupled post-payment. The specific elements that make up the value of the bonus are decoupled from the total paid. The heterogeneous services — packages delivered, doors opened, kids watched, taxis called, bags brought out, groceries brought in — are bundled together so that it is impossible to account for the value of any specific service. As one young mother of two children says about the bonus:

> We make a decision about how much we can give, which is pretty much based on how much we can afford, how much we can give, and not what they have done for the past year. We don't tip during the year, so it's a thank you for everything you have been doing for the year. I don't give different amounts. Everyone gets the same amount, except the super.

---

4. There is a logical contradiction of sorts. If consumption and payment are decoupled such that the pleasure of consumption is not reduced by the thought of payment, then the pain of payment is not reduced by the pleasure of consumption. And it is for this reason that people experience their credit card debt as particularly alienating and aversive — even though they still spend.

As important, the payment is temporally decoupled from the receipt of the service. Thus, the bonus is a decoupled prepayment, or put another way, simultaneously both a post-payment and a prepayment. It is a prepayment because it can be construed as a hedge, as a prepayment for services to be received; it is decoupled because it can be construed as a post-payment for heterogeneous services already consumed long ago. The temporal decoupling provides a vehicle for distinguishing the bonus from a tip, that is, from a routine expenditure. The bonus may be routine, but by temporal decoupling, it enters the world of social, rather than economic exchange, and can thus be construed as a gift.

The bonus rests discursively on the seams of two contradictory temporalities — the past and the future. How is this remarkable feat accomplished interactively? The interactive trick rests on the fact that the bonus is rarely acknowledged explicitly. Even if it is given at Christmas, it does not happen at Christmas. The bonus is the tip without time. As the tenant quoted previously who is torn between seeing the bonus as a gift or as moral obligation to rectify inequality says, his contribution is never acknowledged.

> Around that time it seems they must have gotten it. You look for signs of people looking a little more flush. You can detect people acting cheated or misused. I don't see this. There is an extra friendliness that lasts several weeks past the holidays. It's never acknowledged explicitly, no; but I take that extra friendliness as an acknowledgment. But it could be, now that you have me thinking about this, just that this extra friendliness or extra pleasure or happiness has nothing to do with the tip — they need to reflect people coming in. So if people are acting happy in holiday time, they have to also.

His experience is not uncommon. Most tenants report that their cards are not acknowledged — or more precisely, that while their cards may be sometimes acknowledged, the money is not. Tenants are not unhappy about this, necessarily. The explicit acknowledgment of the money is awkward. It is awkward because the quantification of a qualitative relationship is too naked to sustain the ambiguity necessary to make the lobby "work." If individual acknowledgment is rare, generalized acknowledgment is more common. Thus, in many buildings, especially on the East Side, tenants are greeted after the Christmas holiday with a public note by the elevator thanking them for their generosity. In one building, tenants give cards to doormen indirectly and are thanked en masse by such a public posting.

> We put cards in a big box in the lobby, separate cards for each person.
> We get a "thank you" posted to all tenants by the elevator.

A box is not uncommon. On the one hand, it solves the practical problem tenants have of trying to find doormen to give money to, allows tenants to give money to unseen workers, the night doorman, as well as porters and cleaners who may work odd hours. And it solves the interactive tension of encoding the relationship through quantitative exchange right at that specific moment. The box (or other system for giving without interacting) allows the bonus to slip through time. The box facilitates a specific kind of timelessness — drawing the bonus into the social world. Equally so, the envelope and the card insulate the money from the profane world of economic exchange, helping to transform the cash into a gift, into something demarcated from ordinary exchange. And crisp new large bills unsullied by prior exchange help as well to distinguish the money in the bonus from regular money — and thus declare that this bonus is a gift, independent of instrumentality.

While the rhetoric of the bonus is that it is either a pure gift or is in some way keyed to service, either from the past or expected in the future, it is possible that the bonus has little to do with either. One idea is that the bonus is a signaling mechanism and that tenants and doormen use the bonus to signal and negotiate status. Consider the idea that tenants, concerned about their status in the building, fear making the kind of error that would lower their perceived position with the staff. Giving too little is obviously potentially damaging. Oddly, so is giving too much. The signaling takes place in a context where doormen know that tenants have only a vague idea of their annual salary and tenants know that doormen are aware of the relative value of the apartments they occupy. At the same time, the doormen believe that they have an accurate read on the incomes their tenants bring in, extrapolating first from the rent or sale price of the unit and secondly from the "lifestyle" they observe. Their read is generally biased upward. Since they most often observe the public side of everyday life, there is a tendency to read the public (arriving in taxis, dressing up to go to dinner or work, packages delivered, dry cleaning received, etc.) as accurately reflecting the private side.[5] Tenants, on the other hand, tend to estimate doorman

---

5. Tenants are also engaged in the same exercise — trying to determine the wealth of their neighbors. Though there is homogeneity by building in general, there are still big wealth differences.

income as a function of their own income. Consequently, wealthier tenants' estimations are significantly upward biased, whereas middle-class tenants tend to underestimate doorman wages. Further complicating matters is the general tendency that doormen have to elevate the status of their tenants, if only to subtly elevate the often inchoate sense that their job is in some ways more important than it might be if the tenants were just completely ordinary. At the end of the day, however insulated from the profane world of exchange, the bonus is a number — and something happens to relationships when money is exchanged.

POSITIONAL PREFERENCES

Doormen of course prefer large bonuses. Tenants would prefer to give bonuses that are significant enough to make sure that the doormen and the super don't consider them cheap, but not so large as to be wasteful or to appear tacky. Even if there were not a direct relationship between the size of the bonus and service provided (there is, but it is weak), and therefore tenants did not have to fear service withholding, most tenants would prefer not to occupy the lowest position in the bonus sweepstakes, all things being equal. This is also the case in numerous other contexts where rationality gives way to status concerns. Here, for example, tenants would prefer to give $50 and be in the middle of the bonus distribution than give $50 and be at the bottom of the distribution, even though the actual value of the gift remains the same. This preference, and the obvious mathematical fact that someone has to occupy the lowest position — it would be better if it were someone else — creates upward pressure on the bonus, pressure that is conditioned at the upper levels only by the fact that giving too much also carries risk. At the same time, tenants do not want to give $50 and find that they are on the top of the distribution.[6] And this balancing act keeps things from spiraling out of control.

Like doormen, tenants use the evidence around them — the most important of which is apartment size, view, and history of recent renovation.

6. This is a classic instance of so-called auction regret. The winner of an auction knows immediately one awful thing: they paid too much for the item, relative to all the others' valuations. Such dynamics are worse in pre-bid auctions, where the dynamics of bidding cannot be observed; and it is one of the reasons that charity auctions often take this form — the auction regret that the winner experiences is couched in the language of a philanthropic donation.

The closeness of the relationship means that excessive giving is easily interpreted as an attempt to transform an employer-employee relationship into a master-servant relationship. While one garners status from giving, for the bonus, as in love, too much giving can lower the giver's status and delegitimize the intended meaning of the gift. Too large of a bonus carries an uncomfortable odor, so somewhere a balance has to be struck. The balance between too much and too little is derived from the distribution of other bonuses in the building, since the meaning of the gift is conditional on its position in the whole population of gifts — $500 means one thing in a building of other $500 gifts and quite another when the next largest bonus is $50. Tenants know this, although they rarely articulate it; preferring instead to rhetorically key the bonus to service. But this keying is a device, little more. It is a signal that is essentially local — having little currency beyond the building.

The optimal position for each tenant in the bonus sweepstakes is right at the top of the pile, but within close range of the others'. Little is gained from being in the middle; aside from avoidance of the bottom. The bottom quartile of the distribution is obviously exactly where tenants do not want to find themselves. The dilemma is that it is impossible to know how to position oneself without learning about the expected behavior of the other tenants. And this is why, around Thanksgiving, tenants start to position themselves to learn what their fellow tenants are intending to do. Eventually, they will have to start talking. The staff often facilitates the talking by sending a little card around the building, wishing the tenants a happy holiday season. The card often lists the names of the staff, their positions in the building, and not infrequently, their tenure. Tenants may use these cards as an invitation to strike up conversation with others, often indirectly and often focused on whether or not they (their new "friend" in the building) know one or more of the staff listed. This trick — asking if the neighbor knows one of the doormen — is more than a simple entrée to the conversation, since knowledge of doormen is a particularly valuable currency in the building, and not to be taken lightly.

(SO-CALLED) OBJECTIVE ADVICE

Before conversation starts, tenants can always consult the *New York Times* or other newspapers for advice. They do so at their own risk, though, as the messages are not always clear. In 1965 the *Times* reported, "The tipping custom is the most confused thing that ever was," quoting Ralph Guild, then vice president of Brett, Wycoff, Potter, Hamilton, specialists in apartment management. A paragraph later, they confuse the reader even more, writing:

> In Manhattan's luxury apartment houses it is not unusual for a tenant to give $100 to the superintendent and at least $20 to members of his staff, which consist of round-the-clock doormen, elevator men, handymen, and porters.

But then, a sentence later, they write:

> [A] superintendent of a 150-apartment luxury-class building could receive $700 to $800 in tips at Christmas time, while the doormen could get $300 to $350, in addition to tips received the year-round for getting taxes and doing other favor[s] for tenants.

So, somewhere the math got very mixed up, unless one imagines multiple supers and a staff of more than fifty. Simple math from the first sentence suggests that the super should receive $15,000 in bonuses, and the doormen $3,000 to $5,000. Working back from the second sentence yields a different recommendation; assuming the same 150-unit building, each household should give the super $5 and the doormen $2 to $5 for the year. A typical family we discover, just a bit further on, living in a moderately expensive building on the East Side could expect to set aside $80 to $100 for Christmas tipping. In 2002 dollars, this would be roughly $400 to $500. With guidance like this, it is no wonder why people feel especially helpless, and even experts admit that the whole affair is "confusing."[7]

In 1972 the *New York Times* couldn't help but notice that "a sense of status, a sense of guilt, and a sense of uncertainty enter uncomfortably into the annual tipping problem." In a year when the economy was slowing down, and at the start of the recession, the general advice was to hold back. Sonia Kamsky, who lived at the Imperial house on Sixty-eighth and Lexington, was planning to do just that; cutting back from $380 for the eighteen employees of the building in 1970, to $220. Or maybe she just didn't tell the truth. The article hints that Sonia is not alone; and in any case, if others would follow her (and their suggested) lead, she certainly would not be alone.[8] But one

---

7. "Tips on Tipping in Apartments."
8. Rejnes, "It's Time to Pass the Bucks."

has to wonder if, even back in 1972, Sonia might not have been telling the truth. There would be good reasons for her to lie, as we will see.

In 1975 the *Times* was more helpful; they clearly tell tenants what not to do and why. First rule: Don't ask the doormen. If you do, a more generous bonus will certainly result. According to the *Times*:

> . . . An employee's psychological attack goes like this: To one group of tenants — and he knows which one — a doorman will lament about how many people forgot him and how terrible he feels to find his work unappreciated. This heart-wringing tale will make the questioner feel that at least he or she will do right by the poor soul. Result: A more generous tip. To the other type the doorman will, with equal cunning, confide that he is so lucky to be in a building where the residents appreciate him and with surprising generosity too. Result: A competitive spirit emerges, a desire to out-tip the Joneses.[9]

Note that the *Times* presumes that doormen know what kinds of claims will work with which tenants, which is a good insight, since doormen can read their tenants' psychological orientations well. The *Times* introduces some ambiguity, though. Are tenants concerned with what other tenants will think or with what the doormen will think of them, relative to other tenants? Here it is important to fix one idea: while it sounds clever to say that doormen will induce a competitive spirit among tenants, the tenants are not so interested in what the Joneses think about them. They are interested in what the doormen think about them instead. The competition is in this sense asymmetric.

In 1975 the *Times* tried a new tack beyond considering doormen strategies. Consulting the etiquette expert Elizabeth Post, the *Times* reported that the fiscally challenged tenant can try gifts of "warm gloves, a bottle of wine, etc." But this is not really recommended, since "what most building employees really want in an otherwise warmhearted season is cold hard cash." So how much to give: here, the numbers are few and far between. The president of J.J. Sopher, a building management firm, suggests $20 to the super-intendent, $10 to the doormen, and $15 to the porters. An unidentified tenant suggests somewhat higher bonuses: $35 for the super and $25 for the

---

9. Rejnes, "The Art of the Christmas Tip."

doormen/elevator operators.[10] In 2002 dollars, this would be around $60 to $100 for supers, and $30 to $75 for doormen and other staff. Strangely, these figures suggest little change from the first set of figures recommended in the mid-1960s, despite relatively constant (albeit low) inflation.

The children of the tenants in 1965 to 1975 are now tenants themselves. Like their parents, they could turn to the print media for assistance. In 2000, a quarter century after the last article considered here, the advice is more specific but equally unhelpful:

> There are two things to consider when you're determining how much to give. The first is building size — the smaller the building, the larger your bonus should be. The second is the level of luxury. Lawrence Vitelli of Insignia Residential Group, which manages some of the highest-priced properties in the city, says supers at its big buildings routinely get between $100 and $300 from each tenant, and at small buildings, $500 to $1,000 is not unheard of. But chances are you won't have to shell out that much. For most buildings, $30 to $50 is appropriate for doormen, $50 to $100 for supers. Support staff like handymen and elevator operators are in the $20-to-$30 range. Adjustments should always be made according to seniority, and if you're planning on doing any kind of renovation in the upcoming year, it's in your best interest to give the super more than usual.[11]

Adjustment for seniority does not mean that tenants who have been in the building a long time should give more or less. It does mean that staff with long tenures should be given more, independent of service, than staff with short tenures; though why this is the case, when the underlying argument for the bonus rests on the down-payment model (Planning to do renovation? Maybe give a bit more), is unclear.

If the general advice is consistently unclear, the historical pattern is very clear. First, there is significant change in the value of the recommended bonus. In constant 2002 dollars, the average recommended bonus declined significantly over time. Second, the advice is increasingly less helpful. The

---

10. Rejnes, "The Art of the Christmas Tip."

11. Brian Farnham, "Tipping Points: If It's True that Money Talks, What Are Your Tips Saying about You?" *New York Magazine*, August 21, 2000.

spread of the recommended values, even though the absolute value has decreased, has increased significantly. One would expect that the spread would
decline as the absolute value declined. Third, there is remarkable stability
in the language used to talk about the meaning of the bonus. Is it a reward
for service well done, or is it an inducement for services to be provided? The
Times waffles throughout. The last sentence of the 2000 recommendations
is clear: for those planning renovations, a bribe is necessary. Likewise,
in a perverse twist on the traditional down-payment model, Jodi Wilgoren,
writing for the *Times* in 1998, makes the case for seeing the bonus as a special
kind of down payment, not for service, but to avoid negative outcomes. Here
the bonus is presented as an anticipatory hedge against a shakedown; in
Wilgoren's world, the doormen are a cross between the Sopranos and the
squeegee men who offer to wash your car windows.[12] No one really wants
them around; the bonus makes sure that they do no harm, forgetting completely about the promise of service. It's like the old days of Halloween when
"trick or treat" carried an implicit threat: no candy and we egg your house.
In this context, Wilgoren notes that

> while most people interviewed in Chicago, Seattle and Nevada said they
> tipped out of guilt or habit, many New Yorkers were motivated by fear.
> At one Manhattan parking garage, the holiday tote board shows that
> the guy in space 41 gave $450; other regulars might well wonder what

---

12. Maybe there is some reason to worry that not tipping your doorman could lead to bad outcomes. After all, this is what happened to C. Bai Lihme, who resided at 950 Fifth Avenue in 1927. One
morning while Mr. Lihme was at his weekend house on Watch Island, the doorman John Healy, George
Tiernan (the elevator operator), and a friend took the elevator up to Lihme's apartment, snacked on
a ham found in the icebox, drank some whiskey and Canadian ale, and systematically destroyed the
apartment, smashing a "Welte-Mignon organ, with pipes ingeniously concealed behind tapestries
and sound passages curiously covered with wrought iron decoration, so that when played in the salon
on the twelfth floor, its music could be turned on or off in any of the other rooms of the triplex
apartment which runs from the twelfth to the fourteenth floor"; destroying a priceless chandelier,
porcelain, and glass; ripping Flemish tapestries from the sixteenth century; and, perhaps, worse,
slashing a Van Dyke and decapitating a Rubens. When arrested — and after being escorted to the
police station in his "gray livery gloves, gold buttons, and braid" — Healy justified his actions by
complaining that he was expecting a bonus and better tips than he had received. In an editorial the
next morning, the *New York Times* noted: "Such a story should have some outstanding moral. But
it's hard to say exactly what it should be: whether that apartments should be kept strongly locked,
that employees should abjure strong drink when on duty, that doormen should be kept contented by
increases in salary and tips to suit, or that grievances should be worked off in other ways." "Servants
on Spree Wreck Lihme Home, Ruin Art Treasures"; "A Strange Case of Vandalism." This case is
extremely unusual; and one cannot help but notice that the number of instances in which doormen
have been arrested for robbing tenants is surprisingly low.

could happen to their cars if they failed to return the envelopes left on their windshields. Likewise, some veteran city dwellers say, ignore the Christmas card from your building's superintendent at your peril.[13]

The reality is that nothing written about the bonus escapes the same rhetoric, even if the advice jumps around. From seeing the bonus as compensation for past or future service, or avoidance of a shakedown, columnists and pundits seemed trapped in an interpretive frame that encodes the bonus as an economic transaction. It is really a social transaction, in which ambiguity over valuation and ambiguity over timing and value of the return gift are the central elements. We may be able to make some progress if we rethink the frame and focus on the sociological significance of the bonus. Shifting frames should, at the least, make sense of the fact that the value of the recommended bonus has declined over time. It will also help us to understand why many people lie when they report how much they give, often reporting less rather than more.

THE BONUS AS A MECHANISM FOR ENCODING DISTINCTIONS

Let's ignore the economic "meaning" of the bonus, forgetting for the moment whether it is a pre- or post-payment. Sociologically, the bonus is a simple mechanism to define two relationships.[14] The first is the relationship between tenants and doormen. The bonus encodes the status distinction between doormen and tenants. The second is the relationship between tenants and tenants. With respect to tenant relationships, there are two frames of reference, first the frame for tenants thinking about their neighbors, and then for doormen thinking about their tenants. The first is simpler. In talking with other tenants about how much they give, tenants navigate between two sources of potential embarrassment — giving too much and giving too little. Giving too little is just potentially embarrassing. Many tenants feel

---

13. Wilgoren, "Tips Grease for the Gears of City Life," BU9.

14. One could also imagine that the bonus is a mechanism to induce status distinctions among staff. Despite what tenants think, doormen do report talking about the size of their bonuses with some of their coworkers, but this talk is generally deployed as a disciplinary mechanism against doormen who are perceived to suck up to tenants too much. As in all work settings where there is a significant piece-rate element to compensation, there is a tension between individual gain and rate busting. The structure of this compensation also varies by shift; doormen who work the day shifts do much better than those who work either the swing or night shifts.

conflicted about the bonus — they know that they should give and that it is right to give and that giving should make them feel good, but at the same time they often feel that things are tight all around and especially at Christmas, when they have numerous competing obligations. Still, as one tenant on the Lower West Side told me about her neighbors:

> I would be embarrassed, I guess, if I didn't give the right amount. Some of this is just me, because I am obsessive, you know. I wasn't — I was brought up to do the right thing. But I also don't want them to think I'm really cheap, even though they don't really have any idea how tight things are right now.

Nobody wants to be embarrassed, and giving too little is potentially embarrassing. So is giving too much. The mental gymnastics can be quite complex. Tenants who rhetorically construe their gift as a gift — that is, as "thanks" — express concern about their neighbors; they tend to describe their neighbors as motivated by anything but altruism. These tenants worry that their neighbors will think they give too much; it is because they construe their neighbors as instrumental — as people who give bonuses not to say thanks, but to get better service or garner status. If their neighbors think this, then they are likely to interpret their gift as instrumental.

> I want to give them a good tip. They do a good job. I want to thank them for that. And they thank you, too, you know, they appreciate it, so they thank you. It's little things like a nicer "good morning" or just unusual things. But others think that it is a putdown of them, of the doormen, if I give more than the suggested amount. Like, "What are you trying to do?" They don't want to give, so they think that if we give it is because we want something back. But that's different. So you don't want them to think you think that you are superior to them.

If one's neighbors are not altruists, it is better to underreport than to be exactly accurate, especially if one imagines that they are on the high end of the distribution, which is where altruists end up and instrumental givers want to be. But not all tenants are altruists. It is not accidental that many tenants question the motives of their neighbors. If we focus on the bonus as a mechanism for encoding status distinctions among tenants (in the eyes of the doormen), we can understand better why when tenants tell their friends and neighbors how much they give, they may often underreport rather than overreport the value of their gift. Why would tenants, concerned about their image in the eyes of doormen, underreport their gifts, risking the approbation of their neighbors? One possibility mentioned above is that tenants do not want to be seen as instrumental by their neighbors. The second idea is that they are trying to influence their neighbors' contribution, for instrumental reasons.

It is clear that purely instrumental tenants perceive that it is in their interest to maneuver for local advantage over their neighbors in order to reap status benefits from the doormen. To be in a position to obtain this advantage, though, they need to figure out how much money their neighbors are giving. This is why they talk to each other or, rather, establishing what others give is the ostensible reason tenants report talking to other tenants about the bonus. Strangely, if they thought about it more carefully, they would realize that they talk to each other not to get information, but to give it — and often, to give bad information. What they often miss is the fact that, like them, everyone has an incentive to provide bad information.

Consider the problem as it unfolds. Each tenant is trying to decide how much to give. They want to give as little as possible. They want to avoid the bottom quartile of the distribution, they would prefer to be at the top, and they recognize that they gain proportionally little from being in the middle — but all things being equal, it is better to be at the top of the middle than at the bottom of the middle. Against this background, and looking forward to the upcoming year, tenants will find it in their self-interest to *understate*, when asked by others, the size of their bonus in the previous year. Consider the problem that tenants have when they try to ascertain, or when someone else tries to ascertain, how much money they give to their building staff. Here is what one tenant says:

> I don't really tell the truth about this. If someone in my building asks me how much I give to the doormen, I try to find out how much they gave the year before and match that amount. If they say $50, then I tell them I gave $50 too. If they say $25, I say I gave $25 as well. If they are new, I tell them I gave a little less than I really did. If I don't really like them, I tell them even less. This is because if I tell them how much I give, then they will give more than that and then instead of being one of the better tippers, I become one of the cheaper ones. No matter what I tell them, they are going to give more than me, because that is what they are trying to find out anyway. They just want to know how much they should give to make them look good, and no more.

The logic is simple: if all tenants give around $20, much is to be gained by $25 (and the marginal gain for $50 is minimal, and $100 is so out of line that it looks like an attempt to purchase favor, or in any case accomplishes nothing since one can get to the top of the distribution at a significantly lower cost). If I want to give $25, it is in my interest to tell others I give $10 or $20, so that if they follow my advice, I will look good at minimal cost. But if we assume that everyone pursues the same general strategy, then it is obvious that the advice seekers will also try to gain advantage by slight overpayment. Consequently, the tenant who stated she gave $20 should assume her neighbor will give $25, and so she should give $30. If there were a constant relationship between the amount actually given and the amount stated as given, one would quickly observe a rapid escalation of bonuses. But if the stated amount remains relatively constant over time, this pattern has the unintended consequence of slowing down the natural escalation dynamics that govern such bidding systems, although increasing (slowly) the gap between the real and the claimed bonus. Real bonuses will increase slowly over time, whereas the stated bonuses will remain relatively steady. Consequently, the misrepresentation gap will increase, all things being equal. And here, as it turns out, lies the explanation for the historical patterns we observed in newspaper advice columns.

Recall that the key findings are that in absolute terms the bonus has declined and yet (even considering the smaller absolute base, which ought to lower variance) variance has increased. The decline is associated with the steadiness of the claims (after all, newspapers can only learn what people give if they tell them), and variance is associated with the increased gap between claims and reality. The micro-mechanism at work then is simple. Tenants may say, and some may believe, they are asking for information when they set out to ascertain what their fellow tenants are contemplating as their bonus, but really they are engaged in providing bad information. Each tenant risks being considered cheap by the other tenants, but if all engage in the same general model (which is to understate their bonus from the previous year), they jointly construct a world in which everyone is cheaper than they really are. Hoping against hope that they convinced their neighbors to hold the line in the bonus game, each tenant adds a little more to the kitty. Because they cannot subsequently find out if their neighbors did the same thing, they then try to read the behavior of the building staff to ascertain if they got it right for the year. One of the key ways they read this is to ask their neighbors if they know specific staff, since they presume that such knowledge arises in part from special attention on the part of the staff. Tenants know that this is a relatively weak proxy, if cheap to exercise. Still, the little cards distributed each year make it easy to start conversations with other tenants about the bonus.

The best information comes from watching the doormen. But watching creates a whole set of new problems. The bonus encodes distinctions between tenants for doormen, but doormen are also savvy enough to create ambiguity so that reading their behavior is difficult and designed to be hard to interpret for tenants on either end of the giving spectrum. Before we consider the doormen, we need to consider one interesting innovation that tenants created in the unrealistic hope that it would solve the bonus problem once and for all. Like most simple fixes that rely on commitment to collective goods to succeed, this fix — the introduction of pool systems — also fails in most instances. The reason for the failure of pool systems is relatively simple: given an opportunity, tenants will free ride. Perhaps oddly, the free ride does not involve withholding pool contributions, but in giving more money to the doormen — just outside the confines of the pool.

POOL SYSTEMS

The tenants who live in the same building tend to be similar in social status. This similarity, whether at the high end of the wealth/income distribution or the low(er) end, leads some tenants to try to tackle the local status game head on by devising a cooperative tipping strategy. Consequently, in some buildings, especially cooperatives, tenants agree in advance to collect money into a pool and then divide the total under an agreed-upon formula for distribution to the building staff. Managers of rental units may also seek to put into place a cooperative pool bonus system, in order to buttress formal bonuses that they may routinely allocate to staff. Some doormen will report not liking this system, stating that it reduces the overall value of their bonus. This is not actually the case. Generally, cooperative bonus systems increase the total amount of the bonus by raising the floor. The reason the pooled bonus plan is not preferred by some doormen is because some component of the bonus must subsequently be reported as taxable income since it is officially organized by the building cooperative, thereby reducing the real value of the bonus by roughly 25%.

Pool systems are designed to rationalize the bonus, reduce anxiety for tenants, and more explicitly link doorman service to the value of the bonus, at least in aggregate, pooling both time (here a year) and staff. Typically pool values are allocated as shares by seniority (like wages on a whaling ship), but in some instances, if organized by a management group, merit-based bonuses are put into place.[15] But pool systems typically fail to work the way that idealists imagine. They certainly fail to reduce anxiety. In fact, tenants in pool-system buildings appear to be the most anxious.[16] First, if the value of the pool contribution is left up to them, tenants have an incentive to provide the minimum to the pool. This minimum is essentially what they think they can give without the residents or managers responsible for collecting the money thinking they are too cheap. Since they can only establish what this amount would be through conversation, they have to go through the same process as if there were not a common pool. If the pool amount is defined for them as a range, which is often the case, tenants contribute the stated amount, but this amount is most often a lowest common denominator. The pool sets the minimum contribution; it provides just the baseline. After the baseline contribution, tenants have the same incentive to try to distinguish themselves from others, to raise their status in the doormen's eyes, and possibly to thank the building staff and ensure service for the next year.

But the psychology of the pool is complicated. First, formally the pool does tend to lower the value of the bonus — as declared income for doormen. Looking on the formal side, consider the following tenant, whose friend lives in a pool building:

---

15. By pooling contributions across staff, management (or tenants) lose the capacity to use the bonus as an explicit monitoring-reward system. In restaurants, pools for tips theoretically create incentives for all waiters to assist others, thereby increasing client satisfaction. Given stochastic server-client flow problems as described in chapter 2, the pool makes sense as a strategy to alleviate momentary busyness, thus guaranteeing that multiple clients can be handled simultaneously under the same priority scheme. But the flow of work is too uneven to warrant pools from the doormen's perception.

16. This could, alternatively, be a classic instance of endogeneity. It is well known, for example, that people who have the most fears — say, about contacting a sexually transmitted disease or of being murdered — are at significantly less risk that those who have no fears — simply having fears leads people to engage in behaviors that protect themselves from risk. In the case of STD transmission, for example, not having unprotected sex. In the pool case, those with anxiety are those most likely to take the time and effort to organize a pool system, ostensibly for their own self-defense. But the pool does not stop people from making individual contributions. Thus, those anxious about others getting advantage through generosity — the reason for introducing the pool — find themselves as anxious as ever. Since we can assume that only the truly anxious have the energy to organize a pool, the fact that pool-system tenants are anxious may simple be a stable trait — hence, endogenous — rather than caused by the presence of the pool.

My closest friend lives in another doorman building, but she gives one check into a pool and it is divided up across the doormen. I like that system because there is not a specific amount attached to my family and me. [If your building had a pool, would you give the same amount?] I would give less. I guess I would give about 30% less. It's a strain for us.

The anonymity of the pool would result in a 30% decrease in the value of the bonus. Logically, then, 30% of the bonus — in her mind — is associated with the social pressure of having the doormen know that she specifically gave a bonus. While Louisa would not (if faced with the choice) give extra to doormen — "not in my building I wouldn't" — others are less constrained. In fact they want to give more, so that they are recognized.

The trick of the pool is that many people give twice, less to the pool, and then more on top. The pool fails to solve the problem it sets out to solve; instead it may enhance it, which is why pool-based buildings yield on average higher bonuses than buildings without a pool. The problem takes the form of a distorted expression of the free-rider problem. Tenants have an incentive to break the deal that they established as a device for protecting themselves against each other (or that management created to induce cooperative work among employees) by engaging in side deals (individual tips) with doormen.

Consider Jane, who lives in the Village:

I try to be fair and you know I'm always thanked. I do give people their tip and it is certainly not anonymous, it's in a card with my name on it and you know a little wish for happy holidays. When in another building it was an anonymous pool, I always gave the guy on Saturday extra.

Lori, who lives in a large co-op on the Upper West Side, reports:

The other building that I lived in, in Philadelphia had a pool where you put in a box. I didn't actually like that because I felt like I was paying money and they didn't know who it came from, and I wanted to hand it to them so they saw my face and knew it was from me; it is kind of like you are just throwing your money away with the pool. I would put in a hundred to the pool, which is not very much if you think about how much each doorman would get, and then the ones that were always there I gave them a separate envelope. When that time comes, they certainly are a lot more helpful; they start working a little harder.

One young tenant on the Lower East Side, Amy, is even more explicit:

> We have a pool in our building. We are asked to give $50 for all the staff. Then the total is divided up according to how long a staff member has worked in the building and also his position. I do not know the exact division. Now with five doormen, one porter, and a super, the $50 does not go very far. So I always give everyone a little more money, just from me, so they know I understand how much they mean to me.

The doormen appreciate the bonuses they receive on top of the formal bonus, of course. Oddly, Amy (and most other tenants who add to the bonus) fails to appreciate the fact that many of the other tenants in the building are doing the exact same thing, just so the staff will be sure to remember *them* when, perhaps, they might need a special favor, or just to show how much they mean to them. Even the *New York Times* notes that the opportunity to free ride on the pool (after all, unless participation is required by the building management, the staff cannot tell who gave what and have to assume that each tenant contributed the requested amount) is hard to resist, though they at least resist the temptation to actually endorse the practice.

> Some people insist on the personal touch. George Gorham, a doctor who lives in Manhattan House, a block-long building on the Upper East Side, hand-delivers about 25 checks to the staff instead of giving a lump sum to a fund that distributes largess.[17]

The doormen in this case are not too different from wait staff, who generally prefer to work in restaurants that impose an automatic 15% gratuity for large tables as this guarantees that the bottom doesn't fall out. Doormen with seniority in the building prefer pool systems not because they guarantee the bottom, but because the pool raises the bottom without altering the microdynamics that shape bonuses in the building. The only downside is that the pool component is generally reportable as taxable income. Consequently, doormen make money on pools when additional compensation rises roughly 25% above what the baseline without pools would be. It invariably does, because independent of the cost of the pool (which if not voluntary is keyed to mean building income), each tenant has a micro-incentive to add "just

---

17. Kerr, "Holiday Tipping."

a little bit extra" to indicate their appreciation (or to avoid the presumed shakedown).

As John, a doorman on the Upper West Side, says:

> We have seventy-six families in this building, and they all contribute $100 to a pool for the staff. We each get shares of the total, depending on seniority. So we don't get that much officially. We have to report this to the IRS. But we always get more because most apartments give each of us more — under the table. And sure I know who they are and what they gave because I know they want me to remember them.

Wilson, a doorman on the East Side, echoes the same sentiment. But there is a twist. The anonymity of the pool makes it difficult to assess who gave what, if anything.

> In this building, management gives a year-end bonus. It is not a Christmas bonus, but a year-end bonus. They collect money from the tenants for the bonus and then write a special check for you that comes with a card. The tenants don't have to give money to the management and I don't think very many do, but see I don't know if they did. But the tenants do sometimes give us a Christmas bonus, and so that makes up for the small bonus we get from the management. I know those that gave a bonus then, but maybe others are giving money to the management bonus and I can't see it. So we have to thank everybody, see.

Actually the ambiguity is not so problematic. Though Wilson and others cannot see through the management pool to ascertain who gave or not, they know enough already since those who do not contribute on their own, in addition, need not get special attention.

PEAK SERVICE

Tenants give bonuses that are real, in the sense that the dollar value is objective and fixed, but the *real social value* of the bonus is unknown to them. Since the information they receive from other tenants about the size of their bonus is likely inaccurate, they cannot really assess whether they "gave enough" without some feedback from the staff. So tenants watch their doormen for signals about the value of the bonus they gave. The doormen have a number of problems with respect to feedback. First, they do not want to appear as if the tenants own them; so changing behavior in the face of an unexpectedly large or small bonus is impossible. Second, they don't want the tenants who gave them a smaller-than-expected bonus to draw the wrong conclusion. In this case, the wrong conclusion — I gave the right amount this year — could be the product of no change in service or poor service.[18] And finally, they don't want the high givers to think that they were somehow too high; but this desire to retain ambiguity has to be balanced by some indication that the high rollers were "in the right place." This is quite a tightrope to walk. In aggregate, it is best walked with one's eyes closed — that is, without explicit acknowledgment.

The tightrope is crossed by playing on the duality of the meaning of professional service for doormen. On the one hand, professional service is linked to personal service. On the other hand, professional service is linked to the consistent application of uniform policies. Both rhetorical frameworks allow doormen to publicly declare that the bonus has no bearing on the service that they give, day after day, year after year.[19] By rhetorically rejecting the idea that the bonus is tied to service, doormen hold the line on the relationships that they do have with tenants through the assertion of professional distance. This assertion means that tenants do not "own them," either because the bonus was extraordinarily large or because it was woefully small.

Perhaps, ironically, the after-holiday claim to professional status is buttressed by shifts in behavior over the course of the year. As noted before, tenants perceive that doormen are more solicitous just before Christmas than at other times of the year. This perception fuels their attitude that the doormen are walking away from the professional claim and signaling that there is a relationship between service and the bonus that everyone knows is

---

18. One can easily see how giving too little can appear to tenants as giving too much. Imagine a system where doormen perceive the bonus to be a reward for the prior year and tenants see the bonus as a down payment on service for the subsequent year. A small bonus at the end of the year may be associated with poorer service in the following year, thereby allowing tenants to think they gave too much. In any lag system such as this, the possibility for self-fulfilling prophecies is very strong.

19. This is a real sentiment, that is, doormen report that it is true for them, and we have no reason to think that the self-reports we receive are only strategic. There is no reason, by the way, that real sentiments cannot also be strategic. In general, what we call strategic management in business is management that shapes the self-interests of those who are managed so that they are in line with unit goals. In this instance, the real sentiment that service is delivered professionally independent of the bonus has an affinity with the tangible interest doormen have in increasing compensation.

"in the air." Bill, a tenant in a medium-sized mid–West Side building, thinks that the shift in behavior is so obvious that it is embarrassing.

> After Thanksgiving, the doormen decorate the building, get the lights up. They also change their style a lot. Like before they get a package, they put it on the big table in the lobby, but right before Christmas they start to hand-deliver them to each apartment. It is totally transparent that they want you to give them a bigger bonus. Where are they in the summer? They think we are really stupid, like we have such a short memory.

But the proof might be in the pudding; Bill tries to give a "decent bonus," because no matter what extra they do during the holiday season, "the real thing is that the doormen work hard the whole year anyway."

Equally possible is the competing hypothesis that doormen use the weeks before Christmas to signal that they can step out of the professional role because they have a special relationship to their special tenants. The claim to professional role behavior makes anything they do that is slightly unusual "special." The test might be what happens after the holiday. If the operating model is enhanced service just for the bonus, service ought to decline after the holiday season. Doormen who imagine that their tenants really are like chickens (creatures with a two-week memory) should rationally withdraw extra services immediately after the holiday, since it won't yield a dividend in terms of the subsequent bonus. But they don't. In fact, most tenants observe that if anything, doormen step up their service delivery after Christmas, and that they sustain a heightened level of personal attention for some time.

> Okay, the thing is, I know my bonus "works" because I get better service and faster. The other day I asked my super whether he had any wood glue that I could borrow to repair a crack in the floor. The next morning, the carpenters arrived. If I hadn't given him a good bonus, he would have just told me what kind of glue they used.

The fact that service peaks after the holiday is ascribed by those tenants who give large bonuses as a product of the bonus. It is a self-fulfilling prophecy. Nor can these tenants rest too easily. Doormen will provide observably better service for all of the tenants during this period. For those who gave small bonuses, though, a peak in service provides the foundation for the claim that the apparent transparency of heightened service before Christmas was actually just professional behavior. By not slowing down, doormen get to

write the end of the sequence and therefore redefine the pre-Christmas ac-
celeration as simply "doing their job" or "expressing the holiday feeling." As
long as the "decay" to normal service is slow, the doormen can preserve the
ambiguity over the actual meaning of the bonus. What makes this possible is
the unusual content of the claim to professional status.

When other groups strive to claim professional status, the simplest foundation is to assert a set of norms that give rise to behaviors that are equivalent
across all persons. Doctors ascribe to norms that guarantee the facade of
equal treatment across social classes. Librarians provide reference assistance to all people, even if their requests seem unusual. Police are supposed
to give tickets to all speeders, not just those in jacked-up cars. The idea
is that doing medical, library, or police work involves doing work that is
uniform across all the clients one encounters. In contrast, doing doorman
work means that the content of the work shifts across tenants. The work
involves knowing what the tenants like and providing that service. Since the
claim to professional status is keyed to the delivery of a particular service,
doormen can simultaneously pursue a particular reward (the bonus) without
risking either loss of professional status or becoming a "creature" of the
giver. But they can only do this by denying the significance of the bonus —
which they do.

In discussing the bonus, Chris, a doorman on the Upper West Side, says:

> Yeah, they get the list. They ask for the list because before they go
> on their vacations they want to give you your money and stuff like
> that, your envelope. So that's how they basically do it. I guess they're
> comfortable with it, the president, they like the idea, that they don't
> have to tip you all the time. They're really no complaints from anybody,
> 'cause some people, they make a lot of money. The doormen make a lot
> of money. Let's talk money, some of them take home at Christmas, four
> to five thousand dollars. One of the main doormen took home seven
> thousand dollars. They can't really complain, I mean, people, you
> know, they do look you out, they give you money. I'm not complaining,
> you know. I'm there to provide the service; they don't have to give me
> anything. That's my job; I get paid every week, you know, I'm happy.
> They don't have to give me anything, you know, that's part of the job,
> providing the service, you know, that's what I'm there for.

Nor can doormen reject bonuses, however small. As with customers
in restaurants who signify their discontent with the service by leaving an

exceptionally small tip (thereby trying to indicate that they know the norm and violate it by leaving a symbolic amount of money, five cents, a dime, etc.), tenants will also hand doormen they find have performed poorly envelopes with just one or two dollars in it. As Frank says, it doesn't matter:

> You were on my list, you didn't give me anything, but if they don't give you anything, there must have been something you did, or something that happened that they don't want to give you anything. Usually people give you something, even if it's ten dollars. They fired a couple of guys because when people used to give them stuff like envelopes for the service, they used to send it back upstairs like they didn't want it, so they used to get fired for that stuff. You have to take it regardless. Even if it's a dollar, you have to take it.

The mistake these doormen made was to not deny the significance of the bonus. The right thing to do would have been to just take it, as Frank said. But just taking it is different from just saying thanks. It is just that — taking it. The dilemma doormen face is that they need to be in a position to deliver personal service, in order to legitimately expect a bonus. So they need to train their tenants into perceiving either that the generic service they provide is personal or to develop preferences of their own. This is perhaps most easily seen when we consider how newcomers (to the building) have to be trained by doormen in order to have preferences. Until the doormen can train newcomers, they are at a loss.[20] As Felix says:

> When someone new moves in, we have to decide whether they want us to call every time someone visits them, what to do with their packages, whether they need advice or not, and so on. They don't even know must of the time what we do. A lot of time I have to say we don't do this or

---

20. Newcomers pose other problems in terms of interpretability of the bonus. Newcomers to the city either seem to assume that they have to tip extravagantly for service, or they are completely unaware of the bonus tradition. Very few really get the whole picture until they have lived in the city for a year or so. Often, newcomers distinguish themselves by unjustified largess. Kathryn, the president of an activist lobby who moved from Washington to New York in October, says: "I had heard that I could expect to go through $400 tipping the people who helped me move in. So I gave the super $80, even though he didn't do anything, the doormen $20 every time more furniture came in, and like that. . . ." Such generosity carries little weight since some doormen may see newcomers as sheep just ready to be fleeced. The generous gift, even for doormen, has less meaning outside of a comparison set. And if the comparison set is newcomers, either they give nothing or too much.

that, but I also tell them: you need something different from what we do, just ask.

The problem for Felix, and the other doormen, is that in order to pro-vide professional service, in order to sustain the claim for professional status, they have to be able to deliver personal(ized) service. If tenants fail to develop — or perhaps more accurately if doormen fail to develop in their tenants — preferences, doormen cannot deliver the kind of service they want. Here, the rules and regulations of each building, when the trash should be put out for collection, whether forms ought to be filled out for repair requests, what to do with guests, and so on, provide the raw material for the generation of personal relationships since special service delivery has to be built from within the existing constraints and opportunities of each building. In all buildings, doormen are officially instructed to use for-mal salutations — Mr., Dr., Mrs., Ms., and so on — when addressing tenants, but they quickly learn who wants to have a more personal, and ironically more professional relationship, signified by the use of informal salutations. Likewise, as noted earlier, doormen help their tenants develop similar pref-erences for announcing visitors, receipt of delivered food or videos, and so on. The process of developing preferences is lengthy and involved, and is one of the reasons that doormen (and tenant) turnover is so rare — since both sides come to interpret the specific relationship that they have as unique — creating barriers to mobility for tenants and promising increasing returns to doormen with long tenures.

Doormen also use the rules to distinguish tenants in terms of service provision for seemingly more pragmatic reasons — to help nice tenants or to hinder those they consider to be assholes. For example, while Felix cannot tell his tenants whether or not their spouse is home, since his building does not require him to mark the exits and entrances of each tenant, Roberto can, although not all tenants in his building either know that their entrances and exits are recorded or have use for such information.[21] Sometimes, though he imagines that they do — or would if they knew it was possible. Here, for example, Roberto imagines that he has helped one of his preferred tenants,

---

21. Surprisingly, not all tenants in buildings where such information is routinely collected know that they are being watched so closely and would be upset if they realized this information was collected on them.

aware that he keeps track of tenant comings and goings. Whether he actually helped him is another question.

> So once Mr. _____ comes home early for lunch and I know his wife is home with some other guy because I've got both of them on the list here, see like this. So he asks is his wife home. And because he is a nice guy, I say no she just left and so he leaves, too, because she isn't there. Some other people are assholes and I wouldn't do that for him, I'd just say, "Yes, she is," and let them figure it out.

Rickie also distinguishes tenants in terms of necessary versus preferential service.

> See, you don't have to do the extra, you just do the job that you have to do. So to give an example, if people don't look at the [package] list to see if they have something, I will come and let them know. Now if someone is giving me a hard time month after month after month, I let him find it — that's why we have a list. And he may have that package sitting there a couple of days. I don't have to let him know. You still do the work, but you withdraw the extra.

Working to rule is one of the ways that doormen discipline tenants if they fail to deliver appropriate bonuses. The explicit claim behind working to rule is that uniform policies guarantee professional — that is, undifferentiated — service, although as the doormen know, their professional status derives from the particular local knowledge of the micro-preferences, however constructed, of their tenants. Consequently, if doormen work to rule, service provision can be delivered formally under the rules, sustaining the rhetoric that they do not work for the bonus, while simultaneously disciplining tenants who should know better. Note that the tenants who do not know better, that is, those tenants who simply expect doormen to work to rule, are unlikely in any case to give large bonuses. As Duran says: "You make little allowances not going exactly by the rule because going exactly by the rule would be stupid."

Working to rule is stupid strategically with respect to the bonus. It is also stupid substantively, and doormen who make bad substantive decisions are at risk of losing their job, even if they are working to rule; or perhaps more precisely, because they are working to rule. On example should suffice to make the general point:

One of the workers here, he used to work the midnight shift and he got fired, because the super gives us rules and we have to follow those rules, and the rule is do not leave your post when you are working the midnight shift. There was an incident that happened upstairs, an emergency, someone fell down and hurt themselves and they called the ambulance and they buzzed down to the doorman, the doorman said, "Look, I can't leave my post." He says, "Yeah, but I want you to bring the ambulance guys up the back." He says, "Fine, when they get here I'll do it. But I really can't leave my post. Send down your son and then I'll go up." From what I understand, he sent down his son and he did go up. But they wanted it through the back freight elevator. And he's not supposed to run it, either, that's our rules, not to run the back elevator in the middle of the night. So he did do it, and the stretcher didn't fit through the back. So automatically, he had to come back down and go through the front. And the lady complained that he took so long and he hassled them, because he didn't want to go up, and he got fired for saying, "No, I can't leave the door." Technically, yes, that's a rule, you can't leave the door in the middle of the night. Would I do it? Would I stay at the door? No. To the point where I don't give a fuck what the hell my boss says. They're the tenants; they're paying my salary. Now they got a problem, I say, "Look, I did you a favor. I went upstairs. I left the door."

TIPS

Some doormen also receive small tips throughout the course of the day. No tenants tip their doormen for opening the door, of course, but for other small tasks they may do so. Thus, tenants returning from a vacation with luggage may try to slip their doorman a few dollars for his help carrying the baggage from the street to the building or loading it on a baggage cart that is stored in the back room. Likewise, tenants may tip a doorman for calling a taxi for them, watching that their car does not get ticketed if parked illegally out front, or keeping an eye on their kids who are playing in the lobby or on the sidewalk in front of the building. These activities are not part of the standard job description and so tenants can construe them as out of the ordinary, even if, as we saw in chapter 2, they are routine for doormen. And at the same time, while routine for doormen, they are not routine for each tenant, since no single tenant returns every day from vacation, while returning vacationers may be a daily experience for doormen in a building with 150 units. This fact creates an asymmetry in perception about what is a normal event in the course of the day, and the dual views thus induce some ambiguity about norms. Many tenants respond to this ambiguity by tipping, or trying to tip. In general, doormen report discomfort with small tips (of a dollar or so) that tenants give them just for "doing their job." In fact, most claim that they refuse to accept tips from their tenants. Donald, for example, says:

> We don't have many tenants. But they are very generous. And there are no tips during the year. Other buildings I worked for before there's tips during the year. Here, they don't tip. [If you are getting a taxi for someone, do they give you money?] You can't do that. I know them and I feel funny, you know, personally, because I'm not used to getting it. And when they offer, [I say,]"No, that's not necessary." I mean, what is it, a couple of dollars? Especially if, you know, the person is very generous to you at Christmas, how can you possibly accept it? A dollar?

Echoing these comments, Felix describes the situation is his building:

> Right, well this building, I mean, it's not really a good tip building, but you can tell the more genuine, because they'll talk more to you. They'll come down. If they order food, they might give you some.

The problem doormen experience is that it is awkward to accept tips from their tenants from a phenomenological point of view. The tip challenges two aspects of their lifeworld. First, it inscribes the social distance between tenants and doormen into the lobby, fixing more firmly the inequalities in the relationship. The tip happens in a moment, at a specific time in response to a specific act. By giving the tip, the tenant defines the service received as over. The tip is the neutralizer of relationality. Second, because doormen bridge this distance by making an unusual professional claim — that they provide as part of their professional life a particular personalized service — tips for such services, on the boundaries of the formal job description, undercut the legitimacy of the claim. Consequently, they erode one of the core bases for doormen's sense of self, of status. Thus, doormen would prefer to not have to confront the tip, even if they would prefer, at the end of the day, to have some more money in their pockets. There are ways to avoid such direct confrontation, which may also make tenants uneasy as well, for the constancy of the services doormen provide makes them too close to tip with impunity, as if the doorman were simply an anonymous porter at a hotel. As Chris says, this is one of the many things that pockets were made for.

> They'd put it in my pocket. You know what I'm saying? And I won't take it out of their hand, but when I'm closing the door, they'll just put it in my pocket, or I'll come back and I'll see it.

It is worth noting, in this context, that where social distance is greatest, tips are smallest, and the bonus at the end of the year more significant. Where social distance is least, tenants try to encode their social superiority more frequently through small tips for small services received. Doormen do not see this shift in behavior as social distance per se. Rather they use a richer currency, distinguishing between new and old money people. New money people, less secure than old, tip more often. But then they may need to in order to gain distinction, for their distance to the door is not as far as it seems. As Ian says:

> It all depends on the neighborhood. This neighborhood is one of the best neighborhoods in Manhattan. When I worked as a doorman at another building, the [xxx], there was a younger crowd so you get more tips. I used to make like eighty dollars on a Sunday, a hundred dollars on Sunday, and over here I don't get that kind of tips and stuff like that. This area is kind of old money, not compared to the Upper East Side, where it's new money, people just toss their money around. Over here, they hold on to money. I'm not saying they're hard up or anything, but they are kind of stingy, well, not stingy, but they're more like . . . It's not like where I worked at before, the [xxx]. People used to tip you all the time. It has a lot to do with the area; the area is the main thing. Gramercy, the people are ritzier, they still have the same money, they use it differently is all.

OVERVIEW

Since the bonus comprises a significant component of the doorman's wage packet, doormen think about it quite a bit. But because it comes once a year, they rarely consider it part of their annual salary and in this sense they do not work for it. Instead, they work for their salary and the overtime hours that accrue to them. The bonus is experienced phenomenologically as a bonus. This allows them to claim in all seriousness that they do not work for the bonus. At the same time, they do work for tenants, and they distinguish tenants in terms of their qualities. Some are assholes and some are nice. The assholes rarely give bonuses worth thinking about, and they receive services that are commensurate, that is, the doormen hold back on the "extras." These tenants perceive their doormen to be generally idle and of little use. But they interpret their role in the building as minor — mainly provision of security and announcing visitors. In contrast, most tenants are trained by doormen to develop and articulate preferences with respect to things that the doormen can do for them. Doormen justify this descent into particularism as the essential component of their job, and it provides the basis of their claim to professional status. Doormen walk a fine line between "being the slaves" of their tenants (that is, being subject to their whims) and delivering customized service. The bonus provides one mechanism for joint recognition of the professional nature of the job, ironically arriving as a gift, ostensibly therefore putting the doorman into the debt of the tenant. The doormen, though, turn the tables on the tenants. Refusing to allow the bonus to be interpreted as a down payment on the subsequent year, doormen enhance their service to everyone — bonus or not — immediately after Christmas. By doing so, they suggest that the pre-Christmas enhancement was in their tenants' imaginations.

Tenants experience more anxiety about the bonus than anything else in the building. They try to manage this anxiety by restricting the bonuses given by others, and by ending up on the top — or close to the top — of the bonus distribution sweepstakes. They provide bad information to their friends and neighbors to further their own ends. Even when they agree to share the burden collectively by creating a pool system, they cheat on each other. They do this because they want the doormen to like them. They want the doormen to like them so that the doormen will continue to treat them well. But also they are worried that the doormen know them too well. Psychologically the bonus re-creates the distance between the doormen and the tenants broken down by the "professional" closeness of particular service. Oddly, if doormen always worked to rule, they would not be close to their tenants, and so the latent function of the bonus, to re-create social distance, would be absent.

CHAPTER 7

The Union

CONCIERGE: *No, you cannot have your dry cleaning delivered during the strike.*

BUILDING RESIDENT: *Then how do I get my dry cleaning?*

CONCIERGE: *You go to the store where you left it, and you pick it up.*

BUILDING RESIDENT: *(Incredulously) I can do that?*

— RON ALEXANDER, "Metropolitan Diary," *New York Times*, April 30, 1977

Managers and doormen strike a hard line entering into wage and contract negotiations. The newspapers start to issue dire warnings of an impending strike. Negotiators take harder and harder positions, making a strike seem inevitable. As the strike approaches, doormen help their tenants prepare for the worst. They check and double-check the elevators to make sure they are working well. They spend extra time polishing the brass and cleaning on each floor. They show the tenants how to care for the plants in the lobby, process packages and mail, and change the videotape on the tape monitors. They order extra lightbulbs, cleaning supplies, and garbage bags. They work hard to make sure that the tenants — who they have trained to replace them — will not suffer any inconveniences. Tenants in turn make extra sure to tell the doormen that they are with them 100%. They set up committees to manage the building in the doormen's absence and to provide coffee and doughnuts to doormen on the picket line. They put together support packages for doormen with families and little children. Both doormen and tenants commiserate about how sad it is that they "have to go out." In what other world do workers help and support the scabs who take their jobs when they are on strike? In what other world do the scabs bring coffee and doughnuts to workers on the picket line? Why is there this strange tango between doormen and tenants and what makes it possible? That is the first puzzle. The second puzzle is related to this strange dance. Doormen wages and benefits are exceptional. How is it that they are so high, when doormen wield almost no structural power and when the strike threat — which one would think was effective because it threatens disruption — is almost completely undercut by their own efforts to minimize discomfort for their tenants? This chapter solves these problems. The solution takes us down a circuitous path through the history of the union that represents doormen.[1]

32 B - 32 J

The majority of doormen are members of Local 32B-32J (hereafter, 32BJ) of the Service Employees International Union (SEIU-AFL), the union that represents roughly seventy thousand workers in roughly three thousand Manhattan apartment and commercial buildings.[2] Many of the most important labor leaders in the SEIU and AFL were at one time associated with 32BJ, including John Sweeney, a former president of the AFL. For a small local union in a historically underrepresented sector of the labor movement (in contrast to manufacturing), 32BJ has thus had an unusual importance in the national labor movement. Local 32BJ has also earned a reputation as one of the most corrupt unions in the country. These two facts are not exactly unrelated.

This notwithstanding, as is true for most workers, doormen have historically benefited from unionization with respect to wages, conditions of

---

1. This chapter is concerned with these two problems. To understand how tenants and doormen align against management requires us to understand why (historically) doormen have been able to distance themselves from their union. The corruption of 32BJ served to drive members away from all but nominal membership. Consequently, the union seemed alien, and workers were alienated from it. Today, the doormen know less about their union than the union would prefer. At one level this indicates that the union does a remarkable job providing protection, wages, and benefits to its members — and more so now than in the past. But at another level, it means that the new leadership of 32BJ has a long battle ahead in terms of redefining the role of the union in the lives of its members. Part of the problem 32BJ faces is also, ironically, one of their historic strengths — long average tenure. For doormen in the union throughout the corrupt Bevona period, it may take a long time to relearn the benefits of labor. The scope conditions for this chapter are thus quite strong. While it would be interesting to understand how the union thinks of the doormen, here I am only concerned with how doormen think about the union — for it is their thoughts that shape their relations with tenants and make possible the specific arrangement I observe.

2. Not all of the workers are doormen. The union also represents cleaning service workers and elevator operators. The split between residential doormen (the B) and commercial janitors (the J) is considered subsequently.

employment, and benefits. Local 32 BJ, as with most unions, appears to the doormen to play only a small role in their daily work life. This sense provides one indicator of the success of the union in creating protections for workers with respect to hours and conditions of employment, although to make this claim involves one in a peculiar kind of counterfactual logic. Here, for example, one would have to think that if the union were not here, then workers would have to work so many more hours under such worse conditions for so much less pay and without so many protections from arbitrary exercise of authority. In this sense, the union, like parents, might consider that they do a good job if the workers (like kids) do not feel that they are treated poorly. The absence of thought about the union might then be read as a positive statement — that the union is providing for its members. And there is some truth to this idea, since 32 BJ has been able to secure quite remarkable contracts for its members, given their structural power in the labor movement.

In the history of labor organizing, workers in the extractive (for example, mining) and in the manufacturing sectors are more easily organized than those in the service sector. There are a number of reasons for this. The first is that extractive and manufacturing workers have significant structural power. When workers in an auto plant go on strike, they stop auto manufacturing, of course. But they also create substantial production problems in the downstream industrial sectors whose products are used to compose automobiles. Likewise, a strike at a major glass manufacturer creates major problems for upstream sectors, automobiles, new home construction, and so on. This upstream and downstream linkage provides substantial structural power to workers, since withdrawing labor power from one sector can have substantial impacts on the economic fortunes of other sectors. The integration of capital — in the form of joint ownership, joint investment, shared board membership, and so on — means that strikes in one industrial sector threaten interests individuals have in other sectors. Consequently, workers' strikes in one sector can percolate through the system, inducing a domino effect on outputs in sectors that seem on the surface quite far removed. In this sense, one can think of workers as having structural power in the system, by virtue of their centrality in down- and upstream commodity exchange networks. Because workers have potential structural power, unions are able to more effectively extract concessions from management by threatening (or actually going out on) a strike. Workers can thus see the benefits from unionization relatively quickly, relative to situations where their structural power is limited and the threat of a strike is met with disdain. Doormen lack such obvious structural power, a point I return to subsequently.

Second, workers in extractive and manufacturing sectors see themselves as workers — even in the United States, where class rarely structures discourse or self-identification. The conditions of work mean in large part that competing images of their activity — as professionals, as white-collar workers, and so on — are not easily sustained. Workers on assembly lines — where products arrive on fixed schedules, the pace of which is determined by management — are not able to make discretionary decisions about their work. Consequently, they confront their work as alien to them. In contrast, many service workers see their activities quite differently. Only the most jaded teachers confront their students as alien to them, as objects to be processed in a uniform manner. Likewise, administrative assistants in large firms are more likely to feel that they control the pace and intensity of their work, and that their control is the result of their own discretionary judgment. These workers in the service industry therefore tend to see themselves as professionals and to reject the worker label. In contrast, burger flippers in fast-food restaurants, typists in typing pools, and mail clerks in delivery rooms, whose work is routinized and stripped of discretion, are more likely to experience their labor as alien. When work is seen as not constitutive of the self but rather as something that one does in order to eat (and thus have a self outside of work), one can come to think of oneself as a worker. This self-conception provides an opening for unions to organize — for organization is easier when people see themselves as workers. Doormen have substantial discretion and often see themselves as professionals. Consequently, one would expect that the union would be weak, at least with respect to their ability to issue a credible strike threat. This, however, is not the case, for reasons I consider below.

Finally, although de-skilling in the extractive and manufacturing sector is quite pronounced — after all, management benefits when all labor is transposable, thus making it possible to replace any worker with anyone else — de-skilling in the some regions of the service sector has been even more profound. This is almost uniformly the case in the building trades. The skill demands for cleaning are not substantial nor, on the surface, are the skill demands for serving as a porter or even a doorman. In general, where others seeking work easily replace workers, unions are substantially weakened, since the strike threat can be easily countered by hiring scabs.

Against this background, it is puzzling that 32BJ has any importance at all. Organizing workers whose structural power seems limited, who appear to have easily replaceable skills, and who tend not to think of themselves as workers is generally both difficult and without substantial payoff for members. One is tempted to think that 32BJ is able to provide substantial benefits to workers because one of the most significant threats to labor in the manufacturing and extractive sectors — the threat of plant closure and overseas location — is missing. There is obviously some truth to this idea, since residential building managers cannot decide to move their doormen to apartments in Bolivia because labor costs are cheaper there. But there is more going on. The simplest way to see this is to note that other building workers represented by other local unions seem far less able to deliver substantial benefits to their workers who, like 32BJ workers, do not face job loss from overseas relocation. Why does 32BJ work for its members where other unions fail? There are many possible answers to this question. One is that corruption pays. A second is that doormen, in New York, wield unusual power. The third — and correct answer — is more complicated. To arrive at the correct answer, it helps to get some context. And the place to start is in a penthouse apartment, back in the past.

THE PENTHOUSE APARTMENT

As noted above, 32BJ represents most doormen. From 1983 to 1999, 32BJ was controlled by President Gus Bevona, a reclusive leader who lived in a luxurious 3,000-square-foot penthouse apartment on the Avenue of Americas, just north of Canal Street.[3] The penthouse, opened for public view after Bevona was forced out, was remarkable even by New York City standards. In the kitchen were seven stainless-steel refrigerators, a double oven, a separate stovetop, forty white cupboards, and the requisite island for food preparation. Bevona may have had separate interests in the marble business. The *New York Times* reported that there "was enough marble to empty a quarry"; almost every description (and one can find many) of the penthouse focuses on the marble fetish. The two bathrooms were marble-walled, countered,

---

3. Actually, Bevona always denied using the penthouse as his main residence. He also owned a 5,000-plus-square-foot waterfront home in Babylon, New York (assessed at only $860,000) replete with swimming pool, air-conditioned boathouse, and hot tub. But by comparison to the penthouse, this was modest living.

and floored (with marble shower stalls doubling as steam rooms), linked to two dressing rooms (one with a 20-by-6-foot mirror, the other with twenty-one built-in drawers, both with three cedar closets). In some other rooms, the floors were marble (in others, the floors and walls were rosewood, including an eight-foot built-in rosewood liquor cabinet that included two refrigerators, and the nine-foot rosewood home entertainment center with three VCRs and a thirty-two-inch television), the dressing-room counters were marble, and the tables in the four conference rooms were marble. Like Ross Perot, Bevona loved technology. He had gadgets for raising and lowering coffee tables, dropping panels (to cover the home entertainment center), and spying on his employees. In his 35-by-40-foot office, right next to the three paper shredders, Bevona had twelve television monitors, which allowed him to keep an eye on subordinates inside his building (also owned by the union, at a rental cost of $197 million over twenty years). One of those employees was his wife, Elaine, who labored as an administrative assistant for a paltry $41,000 per year. Bevona did better however, earning roughly $530,000 per year (roughly ten times what a doorman would earn). Bevona lived well, but few knew exactly how well. He was obsessive about privacy and only rarely appeared in public.[4] In one of his last public appearances before being deposed, five years earlier in 1996, Bevona claimed that his salary was justified because he provided members of the union with the highest salaries and best benefits of any building service worker in the country.

The penthouse was only finally revealed when Bevona was toppled following a series of legal challenges engineered by Carlos Guzman (with the help of leading dissident labor lawyer Arthur Schwartz). Guzman, a porter in the World Trade Center for twenty-eight years, spent the better part of the 1990s suing Bevona. The conflict started in 1990, when Bevona proposed a 25% raise for himself and a dues increase to support it. In response to Guzman's challenge, Bevona hired private detectives (often described as union goons) to get some dirt on Guzman (and presumably the other rank-and-file workers associated with the reform movement, Members for a Better Union). As Guzman relates, when the union hired thugs to stake out his apartment, he was forced to move to different friends' homes each night, never sleeping in the same place two nights in a row. But Guzman claims

---

4. Even those closest to Bevona saw little of him; the two executive secretaries that worked in his office suite, for example, had never been allowed into his private office.

to not have been fazed. Since he was from Ecuador, he was used to political repression: "The soldiers [there] had guns and bullets, we just had stones to throw at them."[5]

Fazed or not, Guzman successfully sued and won $100,000 in a settlement against the union leader for infringement of his rights. The story might have ended there, and Bevona could have kept his penthouse, except that Schwartz discovered that Bevona used union dues to pay for the fine, the $400,000 in attorney fees that Schwartz racked up, and over $1 million in legal fees that Bevona accumulated in his unsuccessful defense. This was compounded by a union investment of over $600,000 in a "history" book about the union. The book devoted unusual amounts of space to positive comments on Bevona and critical comments about the dissidents (the book was sent gratis to sixty thousand 32 BJ members) and led to another suit sponsored by Guzman and Schwartz. In this suit, they demanded repayment of the $2.4 million of union funds they claimed were misappropriated to pay for the court costs and the book. Ultimately, a series of court losses pushed Bevona out the door. But it took time and sustained court involvement. Bevona gave up the ghost only after the SEIU was forbidden from supporting his defense and union lawyers were forbidden to work on the case. The final straw was likely rejection of an AFL-CIO amicus brief filed with the court on Bevona's behalf, arguing that if the courts held union bosses personally liable, that "grave consequences to the internal affairs of other unions would follow."[6]

The brief was not really surprising, since John Sweeney, then-president of the AFL-CIO, had previously served as president of 32 BJ and had been taking substantial salary support (well over $200,000) from the local from 1986 to 1999, in exchange for unspecified services. Faced with certain defeat and massive court expenses, Bevona stepped gracefully into a $1.5 million retirement package, approved by Sweeney, leaving the penthouse, which one union representative confessed was indeed "an odd space — not quite office, not quite apartment. And a lot of people aren't crazy about having everything in marble."[7] What to do with the penthouse apartment was a puzzle. One Bevona critic wanted it opened for all members to see; another suggested

---

5. "Local Prez Gets the Porkchop Parachute."

6. National Legal and Policy Center, *Union Corruption Update*, September 21, 1998.

7. Quoted soon after the penthouse space was revealed to the public and before union officials decided to turn the space into an office for political action. Cf. www.pipeline.com/~rgibson/bogusjanitors.htm.

renting it to a millionaire; others proposed gutting it. But the first act was simply to seal it off, until the union decided what to do with it.

VOTE NO

The real problems were not exactly about the penthouse, though the penthouse signified the absence of democratic decision making in the union. The central problems focused on voice, and here Guzman, Dominick Bentivegna, and the other reformers in the dissident movement concentrated much of their efforts throughout the 1990s. In the last election before Bevona resigned, union members — led by the reformers — were able to consider support of Bevona's slate, challenges to his autocratic rule, and perhaps, hitting where it would hurt the most, an initiative that would have cut his salary to $125,000 and put all new contracts up for actual membership ratification, rather than simple executive fiat. With very limited hours to vote, extremely long lines in a small room jammed with Bevona agents wearing large stickers saying "VOTE NO," standing guard as members filled their ballots (in plain view) at the registration table, with each ballot (above the proposed reforms) stating that "the joint executive board has unanimously rejected them and recommends that you vote no" printed in English only (despite the predominantly foreign-born and Spanish-speaking membership), cronies of Bevona stuffing the boxes with four or five ballots at a time, and other high jinks, the initiatives failed. The election made events in the subsequent Florida election fiasco appear clean as a whistle.[8]

Consequently, the results were thrown out (following legal challenges by Guzman and Schwartz in support of which the presiding judge found evidence for an "enormous risk of abuse of power by the incumbent leadership"), and elections were held again.[9] When Bevona won that election as well, using many of the tricks displayed earlier, the federal courts intervened and ordered new elections to be held at work sites run by court-appointed election officers. This decision prompted mayoral candidate, Queens assemblyman, and then-director of the 500-union Central Labor Council to support an appeal of the decision, since the court "challenged the right of the unions to self-govern."[10] This was exactly what the court, on behalf of the

---

8. Hirsch, "Gunning for Gus."
9. Hirsch, "Union Boss Backs Bad Boy Bevona."
10. Hirsch, "Union Boss Backs Bad Boy Bevona."

dissident plaintiffs, was doing. Still, the influence of Bevona over the labor movement, despite a series of striking court losses and personal defeats, was remarkably strong. Since he presided over an essentially immigrant labor pool and made little or no effort to involve his members in politics, one has to wonder where his strength came from.

Two ideas immediately come to mind. Either he was extremely successful as a labor leader, garnering unusually high wages and benefits for his members and exploiting with efficiency their structural power, or he deployed his unilateral power over contract negotiation, settlement, and the strike to garner political power indirectly. Bevona, as noted above, claimed that he was successful because he was an effective leader for his members. I consider this first hypothesis below and, subsequently, the second.

MEASURING SUCCESS?

So, how well did the union do during the Bevona period? There is no question that over the long term, workers benefited a great deal from unionization. After more than twenty years of often-intense labor struggle, which until 1932 always resulted in the failure to organize workers due to significant employee opposition, 32BJ (riding on the coattails of the NIRA, which provided some fledgling legal protections for workers to form and join unions of their own choosing) was formally established. At the time, doorman wages were strikingly low. Workers in apartment buildings received wages from $55 to $70 per month, for what was typically a seventy-hour week for day workers and seventy-seven hours for night workers, seven days a week, without paid vacations or paid sick leave. Most workers received their jobs through employment service agencies, which claimed the first week's pay and often had kickback arrangements with supers, who would hire and terminate workers after extremely short tenures, thus adding additional wages to the agencies' coffers (and the supers' pockets). Doormen had to provide their own uniforms, typically charged at exorbitant rates by the building owners.[11] In

---

11. Today, buildings provide doormen with their uniforms if required. For doormen in buildings requiring unusual attire (tails, vests, white gloves, and top hats, for example), uniforms can be expensive to keep clean. The typical doorman is responsible for laundering, which for dry-clean-only materials cuts into the weekly wage. As an aside, in 1978, before Bevona, a 32BJ spokesman accounted for the disproportionate number of European immigrants serving as doormen by noting that "one thing that attracted many European immigrants to the job were the impressive uniforms." "For Doormen, Few Frills."

contrast, by the time of Bevona's eviction, doormen earned wages that put them in the top half of the U.S. income distribution, worked forty hours per week, and received remarkable free medical and dental care, substantial training opportunities, essentially free computers for all members, free legal support for problems arising both from work and personal life, guaranteed pensions of over $1,000 per month (now $1,175 maximum, but later to increase to $1,500 per month, in addition to social security earnings[12]), a liberal sick-day policy (ten days for longer-term employees), union representation in all disciplinary actions, one personal day off (not otherwise counted), and substantial (twenty to twenty-five days per year for employees working more than six years) paid vacation time. Clearly there had been significant change.

But at the same time, the vast majority of workers in the United States improved their working conditions between 1932 and 1999. Aside from agricultural laborers, most workers in the United States now work a forty-hour week. Most earn paid vacation time of at least two weeks, and most receive some support (though often inadequate) for dental and medical insurance. So, did Bevona and 32BJ simply ride out the times, garnering average wage increases for their members? In the housing trade, most of the substantial gains were made early on, but doormen still earned less than the national average for all workers well past the Second World War. By the mid-1950s, for example, doormen no longer worked seventy-seven-hour weeks. Instead, they worked only forty-six hours per week, and wages had increased fourfold, ranging from $53.25 per week to $59.71 per week. By comparison, in 1954 the average salary for production workers in the United States was $1.65 per hour (or $75.90 per week, for a forty-six-hour week), so doormen took home roughly 75% of the income of an average American worker. In 1971 the relative position of doormen had improved. Doorman wages were $132.77 per week, or $3.32 per hour, whereas the average service sector employee brought home $3.04 per hour, or $121.60 per forty-hour

---

12. The pension is roughly linearly, linked to years of service. A doorman with five continuous years of employment upon retirement in 2002 could expect to bring home only $160 per month, this doubles to $356 after ten years, but increases by more than 100% after twenty years, to $779. Maximum pension is obtained after twenty-five years of continuous service. Since the employee contributions to the pension do not appear to be made during vacation time, it takes a doorman longer than twenty-five years of work (as versus service), as far as I can ascertain from the most recent contract, to get a full pension. This structure rewards long-term employment.

week, and the average production worker brought home $3.45 per hour, or $138 per forty-hour week.[13]

The key baseline is 1983, when Bevona assumed control of the union from Sweeney. At that time, doormen earned $8.41 per hour, or $336.40 per week. By comparison, production workers earned $8.03 per hour, or $16,742 per year. Doorman wages were thus roughly 105% of the national working average. Five years later, in 1988, doorman wages had increased precipitously to $462.73 (or $11.56 per hour), whereas comparable workers in the service sector earned $8.88 per hour, or $355.20 per week, and production workers overall brought home $9.28 per hour, or $371.20 per week. Thus in the thirty-four years from 1954 to 1988, doormen moved from earning .75 of the average weekly wage to 1.30 times the average wage. While relative wages decreased slightly throughout the 1990s, despite the fact that the New York City housing sector experienced the most sustained growth in value ever recorded, doormen, who made $16.62 per hour, still earned more than a typical U.S. production worker, whose average hourly salary was just under $16 per hour ($15.94).[14] Bevona and 32BJ clearly had something they believed they could brag about, since doorman salaries exceeded those in the service sector by a factor of 1.25, although it is generally accepted that salaries in New York City ought to be roughly 25% higher than in other areas, to make up for the higher cost of living. Yet there was also evidence of non-trivial slippage in the position of doormen since 1988, when their salaries peaked in relation to comparable workers. One could conclude that the Bevona record is mixed. Even so, one might be surprised that doormen made much money at all, since their threat to withhold labor seems on the surface to be weak. Who would they really hurt, anyway, if they walked off the job is one reasonable question to ask.

By contrast, one might expect that the workers in commercial buildings would fare better in relative terms, since they appear to have more structural

---

13. United States Department of Labor, Bureau of Labor Statistics, www.bls.gov.

14. Under the contract agreement reached without a strike on April 20, 2001, doormen received over $17 per hour, with negotiated raises that will bring them modest increases each year for the following two years, not counting new provisions for COLA increases. These may, as the economic situation continues to show signs of minor inflationary pressures, be brought into play. While this agreement was less than the union set out to obtain — and while the bottom line is generally hourly salary for evaluating success — 32BJ was able to garner significant increases in employee contributions to pension, health, dental, and legal services. All in all, it seemed to be a strong contract for the members, and even those in the dissident wing did not articulate complaints about the outcome, just the process.

power, at least potentially; that is, the threat to withhold labor power appears on the surface to touch on a number of relatively critical interests. Minimally, of course, while one can imagine living without doorman service for a month or so — the majority of people in New York City in fact do just this — it is hard to imagine just how unhealthy a building would be if it were not cleaned for a month. But the main issue may best be thought of in terms of multiplier effects, that is, in thinking about group strength as best measured by the set of interests downstream that are impacted by withholding labor, and this we can define as structural power.

There is evidence that Bevona was aware of the structural power commercial cleaners had and deployed it when necessary. Throughout the early 1990s, Bevona was capable of flexing significant muscle if he wished. Evidence of his influence is provided by his intervention in the campaign of Janitors for Justice (JFJ), who had been engaged in a bitter struggle with the ISS Corporation in Century City, Los Angeles. After a series of unsuccessful direct actions, JFJ organized a march in Century City for June 15, 1990. Although the janitors had a legal permit, LAPD police refused to allow them to pass, and as the marchers pressed forward, police forces brutally attacked them with batons. Videotapes of the beatings, including the beating of a pregnant woman who subsequently lost her child, were repeatedly shown on local TV stations, prompting Mayor Tom Bradley to intervene. Nevertheless, while embarrassed, ISS withstood the storm over the police response to the march and held firm on rejection of a union contract for its cleaning staff, who were making less than $4.50 per hour. Gus Bevona is credited with shifting the ISS position; having been sent tapes of police action against the JFJ activists, Bevona reputedly called the president of ISS, made him wait on the phone for more than thirty minutes, and then told him that if ISS did not solve the Los Angeles problem, Bevona would pull the five thousand ISS New York City commercial building workers off the job in a sympathy strike. ISS signed a contract with JFJ two weeks later.[15]

Thus, perhaps not surprisingly, unionized commercial building workers in New York City achieved significant gains under Bevona's leadership, against the background of much more costly and aggressive labor action. By 1997, for example, 32BJ represented janitors in New York City earned $600 per week, easily double the industry average and in some locations —

---

15. Erickson et al., "Justice for Janitors in Los Angeles and Beyond."

for example, Los Angeles — tripling weekly take-home pay. At the same time, 32 BJ was forced to make a series of concessions with managers in the commercial sector. The most important was to initiate a two-tiered wage policy. Whereas long tenures for doormen made such a policy rational for the union, shorter tenures in the commercial sector led to significant wage slippage for many workers. In addition, 32 BJ faced serious hemorrhages of labor in the commercial sector, losing as many as fifteen thousand workers to side agreements allowing contractors to run non-union cleaning crews. Thus, the workers who appear to have the most structural power (cleaners in commercial buildings) failed to consistently exert the same effective pressures as doormen, whose threat to withdraw labor — while inconvenient for tenants — posed few challenges to employers as a whole. Bevona's inability to retain cleaning personnel in commercial buildings suggests that he pursued a two-tiered labor policy, one that sacrificed the interests of workers with structural power in favor of workers, in this case doormen, whose role was less critical. The clearest indication of this two-tiered policy is that even in the midst of active contract negotiations — and in some instances while commercial workers were on strike, Bevona, acting without membership approval, signed numerous one-shot contracts with managers and commercial property owners. This meant in practice that some employers could, with the help of corrupt union administrators, arrive at their own personal deals. Because Bevona had the authority to send workers back to work or to negotiate their contracts, employers quickly realized that there were substantial benefits to buttering up the Bevona machine. Needless to say, the possibility for side deals that would send workers back to work in some buildings while leaving others on the picket lines (in some instances, across the street from buildings where workers were sent back) had a demoralizing effect on the striking commercial workers and weakened their negotiating position considerably. The specific reasons for the failure of 32 BJ with respect to commercial cleaners are beyond the purview of this discussion, but, unquestionably, corruption in the leadership was the key reason for loss of workers, on the one hand, and side contracts, on the other.

Across the spectrum of workers 32 BJ represented, increases in basic wages and benefits, as in other sectors of the labor market, were not made easily, and doormen threatened to strike at almost every contract renegotiation between 1954 and 2001. In some instances — most recently in 1997, 2001, and 2003 — negotiations averted a strike at the last minute.

On the eve of the 1997 strike decision, Bevona faced significant challenges from dissidents in the union opposed to his dictatorial control over union finances and practices. Dissidents had hoped to block Bevona from unilaterally calling a strike, preferring instead to allow rank-and-file workers the opportunity to review management offers and vote on whether to strike or not. But Bevona, mocking the dissidents and insisting that the democratic reforms they were calling for would weaken the union, refused to open the meeting to remarks from the floor.[16] Union goons working for Bevona strong-armed dissidents lucky enough to enter the hall and courageous enough to try to speak, forcing them out of the room. It was surprising that they even got into the room, for Bevona was widely acknowledged to have packed the hall with sympathizers and thus prevented many known dissidents from within the union from attending. Not surprisingly, he prevailed among the more than one thousand delegates attending the meeting, thereby reaffirming his right to call a strike should negotiations falter.

Meanwhile, across the three thousand apartment buildings where doormen worked, building managers and doormen were making preparations for the strike. In 1997, and subsequently in 2001, managers were ready for a strike. Lessons learned in the 1991 strike stuck. Thus, as they had in 1991, some managers hired security guards and other scab workers to operate the manual elevators still in place in many of the prewar buildings on the Upper East Side. Cooperatives approached the strike with slightly different resources than standard rental buildings. Many cooperatives asked tenants to sit at the front desk, typically for no more than four hours per week; others set up systems for sorting the mail, taking the garbage out, and even mopping the lobby and hallway floors. In many buildings, tenants, nannies, and domestic helpers were issued special identification cards, and tenant volunteer doormen were instructed to not let anyone up without such cards, whether or not their names were on a list of visitors or they were already tenants in the building. Predictably, some tenants complained that their neighbors — whom they recognized by name and face from years of living in the same building — would not let them into their apartments, unless someone came down to escort them, should they have forgotten their

---

16. The irony is obvious. While Bevona was silencing opposition from within the union as counterproductive to union negotiating strength, he was breaking the will of strikers by sending coworkers back to work on contracts significantly below the union negotiating position.

identification card.[17] As might be expected from the Zimbardo experiments, some tenants pursued their newly won authority with great zeal, assuming the formal trappings of the doorman role, but without the doormen's professional sensibility and familiarity with substantive (as versus formal) commitment to rules.[18] Buildings stocked up on garbage bags and topped off the oil tanks, since fuel delivery drivers were unlikely to cross picket lines. In 1997, as it turned out, no strike was called, as the union signed what many consider to have been a relatively good contract. The final terms were below what they had asked in terms of wage increases, but closer on key elements they pursued regarding employer contributions to the pension, medical, dental, and legal funds.

AFTER THE REFORM

But Bevona was not around long enough to enjoy the benefits of the new contract. He was lucky to escape. With Gus Bevona out the door with his $1.5 million golden parachute in retirement at his Babylon, New York, retreat, now able to enjoy his private pier, motorboats, and hot tubs, 32BJ began the arduous process of transforming itself from a Bevona self-help organization into a workers union. The transition has been rapid. First, the union has experienced considerable growth and has managed to build membership closer to the pre-1995 levels, before the massive hemorrhage experienced in the final years of the Bevona regime. Likewise, despite continued challenges

---

17. The *New York Times* reported a probably apocryphal conversation overheard in the lobby:

"May I see your ID card," a friendly volunteer desk woman inquired of a formidable lady charging toward the elevators.

"I live here," resisted the formidable lady.

"But I don't know you," persisted the dutiful desk woman, ever on the lookout for potential robbers and friends.

"But I know you," said the formidable lady.

"What's my name?"

"Well, I actually don't know you, but I know your dog's name." A decisive retort — mutually recognized.

LESLEY H. GELB, "On Speaking Terms," *New York Times*, May 1, 1991

18. Zimbardo, "The Pathology of Imprisonment," reports that individuals randomly selected to act as prison guards in an experiment involving assumption of role behaviors tended to abuse their power and dominate "prisoners" with sadistic pleasure. Here, the impact seems subtle in comparison, but most tenants spent significantly less time as doormen than in the Zimbardo case, where stereotypical guard behavior emerged in interaction with prisoner docility.

from dissidents whose successful efforts to dethrone Bevona did not yield (for the most part) leadership roles in the union, the public face of the union has improved dramatically. The penthouse has been converted to office space, and the new union president — Michael Fishman, appointed by SEIU president Andy Stern — has made efforts to engage in the public debate over work in New York City, open union processes to members, and seek member support for union-related activities.

Some of the fruits of this new openness can be seen in the passage of major legislation limiting the rights of employers to fire workers without warning. Early in December 2002, 32BJ succeeded in sponsoring its first piece of legislation — the Displaced Building Service Worker Protection Act — which requires owners and contractors of newly acquired commercial or residential properties to retain both current union and non-union employees for a ninety-day period, ending the right of large building managers to summarily dismiss workers without warning upon acquisition of new property. For 32BJ, the largest non-municipal union in the city, the legislation (239A) represents a significant development. As John Hamill, spokesperson for 32BJ, said: "We've got 70,000 members, and they've never backed a piece of legislation before. They had a history of not being politically involved; now they are very involved. It establishes that we are a force to be reckoned with in city politics."[19]

Local 32BJ had only mixed success in flexing their political muscle directly. In the 2001 mayoral primaries, the union strongly supported Mark Green, whereas most other New York City unions supported Fernando Ferrer, an Hispanic candidate. The Green candidacy collapsed as a result of egregious strategic errors and misstatements, leaving 32BJ on the wrong side of the mayoral election. Support for the Green candidacy created problems within the union as well. Dissident union members charged the leadership of 32BJ with forcing members to volunteer for Green and illegally shuttling over $3 million of union funds (from dues) into the Green campaign. Tensions ran unusually high after Green made remarks during the campaign that Ferrer supporters construed as racist. Since many 32BJ members are Hispanic and the dissident group is strongly linked to the ethnic doormen, the absence of Ferrer support was especially rankling. While the union denied the charges and denied that racial issues motivated Green support,

---

19. Dasun Allah, "Purple-Shirt Politics," *Village Voice*, December 4–10, 2002.

32BJ did acknowledge contributing more than $700,000 to various campaigns in the tri-state area. These funds were thought to be critical in the reelection of twenty-seven members of the New York City Council, which passed 239A. Thus, union leaders could feel at the end of the day that they had influenced the outcome of city elections. In comparison to the millions of dollars that Mayor Michael Bloomberg contributed to his own campaign, union forays into local politics to support worker-friendly candidates were extremely modest, and it is unclear whether any set of organizations could ferret out from members, supporters, and fellow travelers the kind of cash contributions necessary to match the Bloomberg effort.

While Bevona drifted off the front pages of the local tabloids — this, after all, was the union leader who stated publicly that he would shoot President Clinton if he were in the room — Fishman was unable to remove all of Bevona's cronies, some of whom retained their influential union positions. So it was not completely surprising for New Yorkers to read that in May 2001 the slumlord Abe Weider, owner of the giant Vanderveer Estates project in east Flatbush (a small city with 59 six-story apartment buildings with over 2,500 units and 12,000 residents, not too much smaller than the city of Babylon, New York [population 13,000], where Bevona slipped into obscurity), was arrested for conspiring with Mafia figures in the Genovese crime family (with assistance from the Gambino and Bonanno families) to get the building service workers "off his back." In a massive sting operation that netted forty-five mobsters and their friends for a variety of crimes, from murder to extortion and stock-market manipulation, Weider and a 32BJ official from the Bevona era, Ismet Kukic, were charged with conspiracy and bribery. Weider was familiar to city officials. In the past year, the city had issued him over thirteen thousand housing code violations, instituted eleven court cases, and sued him eight times for failure to provide heating to his residents. Obviously, he was not the kind of company 32BJ would like to have in its reformed state.

In this case, prosecutors claimed that Weider contracted with Salvatore "Sammy Meatballs" Aparo, a capo in the Genovese family, to find a compliant 32BJ union official to help him get rid of union workers and replace them with lower-paid non-union workers. Aparo, Louis Vallario, and John "Johnny Green" Faraci found Kukic, and in meetings at a Wendy's restaurant (this is something one never sees on the *Sopranos*; Tony never goes to Wendy's!) arranged for Kukic to step in and do his magic. Kukic, immediately suspended without pay after his arrest on bribery charges, was not the best choice, perhaps: his area of responsibility was lower Manhattan, far away from Flatbush. But that did not bother Weider and his cronies, who had thought they found the right man.[20] The fact that Kukic was the best that could be found may be the clearest indicator that the Fishman reforms have penetrated deeply.

While Fishman was aggressive about cleaning the 32BJ house of Bevona supporters, stating publicly that he wanted to look toward the future and not back to the past, the new reform leadership was under constant attack from the internal dissident movement, who felt that the post-Bevona union should have been handed over to them. The old dissidents may have preferred the old days under Bevona. Under Fishman, Bentivegna clearly felt out of his element and appeared to be longing for the simpler days when Bevona ruled the union with an iron fist. In congressional testimony, Bentivegna stated that the current leadership was worse than Bevona because

> with Gus, you knew where you stood. These guys throw rallies and parties and smile, but while they're doing it they have their arm around you and their hand in your pocket. They are deceptive. . . . They give the illusion of democracy.[21]

Local 32BJ is hardly a perfect democracy, but the illusion is likely more real than phantom, and despite the criticism of Bentivegna, progress under Fishman with respect to core reforms in the union has been apparent.

So what, one might ask. If Fishman has succeeded in turning 32BJ around, why tell the story of corruption? The answer is as follows. Because the union was corrupt, doormen were encouraged to distance themselves from union affairs. Union decisions, rather than being the product of participatory democracy, were made by others. But member distance from the union had its benefits, for this distance allowed members to ally with tenants. In the event of a potential strike, doormen could present the demand to strike as something that was happening to them, as if they were simply the playthings of alien powers. Further, by distancing themselves from the union as workers, doormen were better able to make and sustain their claim to professional status. At the same time, tenants would distance themselves from management in contract negotiations, partly because tenants see landlords

---

20. Information about the Abe Weider case and Vanderveer estates is drawn mainly from Robbins, "One More Woe for Ailing Brooklyn Development."

21. National Legal and Policy Center, *Union Corruption Update*, April 15, 2002.

as avaricious, whatever their rent. This double alienation allowed doormen and tenants to engage in the strange dance I started this chapter with. The joint alliance, the indirect product of the Bevona corruption machine, made possible the great wage and benefit packages that Bevona was able to negotiate. How this took place is considered subsequently.

LOOKING UP

For most doormen, contact with the union means little more than paying the dues, which before the last contract was $30 per month, or slightly more than 1% of their official income. Even this minimal contact is passive, for the union ensures that doormen do not fall into arrears with respect to their dues payments. In each contract that 32 BJ negotiates with employers, it is specified that the employer deducts dues from each paycheck and remits the funds directly to the union. In exchange for their dues, most doormen are aware that the union provides access to health care and other benefits, including a variety of classes. The most popular benefit by far is the almost-free computer. For many doormen, the provision of computers at $200 was seen as an extra bonus — the union Christmas present. Not surprisingly, for these doormen, this was their first computer ever, and they approached its arrival with great enthusiasm, purchasing books on using Microsoft Word, the Internet, and so on.

Beyond the computer, members recognize that the union protects them in disputes with management. Members believe that while the union cannot prevent a member from termination, the contract employers sign carries with it relatively strict provisions governing the termination process. If employers have a grievance with a union member, they have to specify in writing to the member (copied to the union) the nature of the grievance and the improper action that the member took. The union has the right to dispute the grievance in a hearing with their union officer present. Termination can only be initiated after the official receipt of three grievance letters in a twelve-month span. After twelve months have passed, the initial "write-up" is discarded, and the series has to start afresh. Most members think that this process provides no specific guarantees for the employee. If an employer files three grievances in a twelve-month span, they have the right to terminate the employee, even if the union disputes the validity of the complaint(s). Doormen understandings are not quite accurate. The current arbitration system provides significant protections beyond these steps.

Doormen concentrate on union protection from purely arbitrary dismissal simply because that is important to them. As is often the case in the labor movement, the union faces a difficult task educating membership as to the benefits they offer. In this sense, member ignorance is not unusual and is found elsewhere in the labor movement. But for 32 BJ, the problem is more acute, because the estrangement of workers under the old corruption regime was quite intense. Since doormen have unusually long tenures, most men on the door today were around when Bevona was in charge, so their understandings and attitudes toward the union are deeply shaped by the past.

Even so, one thing that members know is that if they get fired, they have recourse. As Ernesto, who works on the East Side, says:

> Without the union, you cannot work. You cannot be a doorman. Now, there are some buildings that don't have unionized doormen. The only difference is that they cannot fire you when you are in the union. So here, if they fire me, we have to fight them in the court.

Echoing these comments, Mitch relates how a young doorman working in his building who was fired the night before could have avoided losing his job if he had joined the union. In this case, described in more detail in chapter 4, his "mistake" was to get hugged by a tenant just as the super's wife passed through the lobby.

> I kept telling the kid to join; it's like after three months it's mandatory by the union to join, to go down to the union and whatever, it's manda- tory that you have that option anyway. And this knuckle-head had been here for like eight or nine months, and I kept telling him, "Go down there, go down there," you know it's like $30 a month, but it's very in- expensive for what you get. You know, you get family coverage, if you're single you have your medical, your dental, and you have, like, you even get one pair of glasses like every two years. . . . Those are actually union benefits, if you're not [in the union], you don't get that. . . . There's so many different classes, you can even become a super, and they encour- age you. You know they have like standpipe licenses, classes for — they teach like, whatever it's called — superintendent I, superintendent II, whatever it's called, they've ridiculous classes like that. But basically what you need to do is to get your standpipe license and have a little bit of a background and you can go to being a super . . . but, I mean, once you're in the union, it's mandatory that, well, they just can't fire

you. If he [the supervisor] had a grievance with me, he'd have to send me a written letter and the same letter to the union. You get like three letters within a year and they can fire you. So you have like a twelve-month span, so I mean technically, if this was his first letter, he'd have two more letters to go, but because he wasn't in the union, the boss just said, "Hey, see you." So in a way the union benefits the individual greatly.

In addition to protection from arbitrary termination, many members are aware (like Mitch) that the union offers a variety of other benefits. Some have even taken the classes that they offer, although by far, most do not. The classes cover a range of topics. As Bruce notes:

The union has lots of courses, and it is available to anybody who is a member of the union. From building systems, heating, refrigeration, air-conditioning, whatever you have in the building. The boilers, the steam, whatever you have, all those, so it is a little bit complex system, the building, it's not like you go in and that's where you live, it's a lot of knowledge, a lot of experience, to create it and make it go. They have different classes, a couple of them are six hours a week, twice, three times, or one time you can take lessons. This is actually the sixth year I am going to those courses. I have a refrigeration course. I have a license for it. Then, in case of fire, fire — what is it called — fire safety, and then there is different types of courses, whatever, superintendent, superintendent I, superintendent II, electrician, small appliances if things go wrong in an apartment, from vacuum cleaners to a toaster, you can do it yourself, fix them. I think it is an excellent opportunity, people can distinguish themselves, so if I would be in the management of the building, I would make sure that people who put the effort into, including the knowledge of the building, and lessons, and going, and using their time instead of having fun playing Nintendo at home, but go to classes, I would be giving them the opportunity first, you know, to go, and give them a better job in a better building or a higher position, I would give them a chance to be before those who really do nothing, just come in and spend time until they retire.

Bruce may wish that there was a clearer pathway between acquisition of skill and promotion, but the doorman position, like the high school teacher, has few avenues for promotion. The only job above them is super, and in most buildings, the promotion possibilities are relatively low, since supers tend to have long tenures. Still, others take classes because they like to learn specific skills, some of which are helpful in their job as well. Bob, for example, reports that he is taking classes in mechanical engineering. While his father was a union delegate and he is considering moving in that direction, he is not sure whether he wants that kind of life.

> My father was a porter, and my uncle was a doorman. My father is also a delegate in the union, so that helps. He started as a porter and then moved up in the ranks. Went to college while he was working as a porter, doing what I'm doing now. I'm going to school now. He moved up in the ranks, became a delegate representing union members. I'm twenty-four years old. Right now I'm taking mechanical engineering. I told him, I said, "I like working with tools. Pops, I understand you like making phone calls; I like working with tools." So, he said, you know, "Do what you think is right." But I feel comfortable with it, and I said in a couple years I might decide — it's still an open issue. I could still sway in that direction. But right now I'm taking mechanical engineering, that's what I doing now. It's a trade. That's what I'm doing, and the union provides that for all doormen and porters and union members.

Timoto reflects one typical response to questions about the union — a general awareness of the opportunities, but little interest.

> They provide adult education programs for people that don't speak English, English programs, computer programs. Basically train people in fields that are related to industries. And they have scholarships for children of a member. They provide legal services. If you have a bankruptcy or divorce or if you want to buy a house, they help us with that.

Chaim echoes this sentiment: "The union? You just pay union dues. You get benefits and all sorts of other treatments. Whatever ailment or whatever you need."

More than a few members, though, talk about the union as if it was still corrupt. As noted above, this is especially true for older workers who started under the Bevona machine. And despite the passage of time, corruption is what members tend to start off with in describing the union, whether they are old or young. By itself, this suggests the distance 32BJ has to go. But in some ways, while doormen will talk about corruption, they don't really know what to make of it. The fact that 32 BJ was corrupt doesn't really strike most doormen as fundamentally wrong. In part, this is because like a lot of American workers they find most of the systems they encounter corrupt. Doormen, then, see little difference between their old union and city politics, or national politics in general. They share some of the rhetoric of "little people" who "get by" from honest work. A few examples help to provide focus:

> They are just like the rest of them. It's one pot or another pot. There's no difference but except what pot they got their hand in. [Abram, Upper West Side]

> If something is wrong here, for example, the elevators are dangerous to operate, you are supposed to go to the union and they are supposed to help you get that fixed. But the union is tight with the politicians, who are tight with the managers, who are tight with the OSHA safety inspectors, so they come out and see nothing. They look after themselves first. We get what's left. [Sam, Upper East Side]

> The old bosses were mobbed up. Now they have a new group. They say they are different. Who knows? [Parda, Chelsea]

Even if Fishman knows, he has a hard job getting past the distrust. One might think that doormen care about their union, but not too many doormen seem to care either, and lack of concern makes the problem of building a democratic union even more problematic. In the past, corruption cut both ways, and while the sense of alienation from a corrupt union playing a larger game is higher among those in the dissident (primarily Hispanic) group, most doormen are indifferent to their union. At the same time, many doormen see themselves as part of the group of people who know how to get things done. They know how to get people apartments, how to get into buildings, how to deal with the powerbrokers, and so on. This knowledge arises from experience. For most of them, this is how they got their job, after all. And some of the doormen have benefited from union corruption. As Bill says:

> My boss has been here since 1974. Another doorman has been here since 1982. Then a guy came in '83 and another in '86. I was the next one after that. And anyone who comes in is either known by the super or known by the office. There are no outside people walking in off

the streets into these buildings getting jobs. It's impossible. There are people paying for these jobs, a whole lot of money to get these jobs. They just shook the whole union up. The union was very corrupt. People were buying jobs from union reps. They are in tight with the managing agencies. If you know a union rep, you get a job. I knew a union rep; I got a job. Even with my father with eighteen years of service as a doorman couldn't get me in. Impeccable record. You got to know someone.

With many doormen thinking that they belong to things like the "Hungarian Mafia" or similar, corruption is seen as just normal business practice. And the fact that they may have benefited does not strike them as corrupt, since this is the way the system works. These doormen believe that people who don't figure out how to benefit from corruption are just naive. They see a connection between corruption and the ability to deliver a good contract. Since they subscribe to the idea that nothing in life is "free," it follows that grease on one wheel helps the whole system go around. Consequently, the older generation thinks that if Bevona got good deals from building owners, it is because he delivered good deals to them. At the macro-level, there is some truth to this idea. Bevona was effective because he could deliver contracts for workers and guarantee certainty for owners. Managers and owners have strong preferences for negotiating with union leaders who can deliver the contract without opposition, since the worst outcomes come from wildcat actions led by strong insurgent movements. Since there is substantial value in institutionalizing labor relations, forward-looking owners are more prepared to negotiate settlements that contribute to union stability. But Bevona may have been most successful because he facilitated the transition from worker to professional, albeit inadvertently.

At the micro-level, the benefits of corruption seem less clear. In some cases — helping others get a job, for example — a corrupt union can work for individual members, but perhaps not as often as they think. Still, many workers remember using the union for their own benefit. For others, the union seems foreign, an alien institution that plays little role in the direction of their activities and everyday life. Alienated from the leadership by virtue of its history of corruption, these doormen perceive the union to be irrelevant, except that it tells them whether to strike or not. To return to a point made at the start of this chapter, this perception of irrelevance is not something one can take lightly. If the union is successful, workers will not have reason to think about it. Their work setting and their work experiences are taken for granted. The tension for the union, then, is to remind workers that their gains come from membership. This friendly reminder has historically come every few years, when contracts get renegotiated, but needs to come more frequently if 32 BJ is to make substantial headway.

IN THE TRENCHES

Every three years with the union, we get together and say what we want in terms of more money and then they go to the owner and negotiate with them.

As noted above, many of the union gains were achieved in the context of threatened or actual labor conflicts. In the past decade, 32 BJ has avoided doorman strikes (this is not the case with the commercial building workers, who participated in more militant labor action), and the last major strike took place in 1991. This is remarkably still within the memory of most doormen (after all, mean tenure exceeds ten years) and tenants. While management approached the problem of the strike as if they were members of the War Industries Board mobilizing industrial resources for a prolonged overseas conflict, tenants and doormen had remarkably different orientations. First, in many buildings, the doormen's immediate supervisor — the super — is also unionized and expected to go on strike.[22] So doormen cannot personalize the strike in opposition to their direct supervisor. This dulls the sharp edge of potential anger, for typically in strikes, conflict is experienced most intensely at the "point of production." Second, for most doormen, even those working in cooperative buildings, management — rather than tenants with whom they have evolved relationships — is construed as the absent (and abstract) owner or ownership group. The tenants are not, in any case, theorized in terms of an oppositional management, and doormen have nothing against them in the strike. Third, tenants, even true for many in cooperative buildings whose policies confront them as alien and not of their own authorship, do not see themselves as management in their homes. If they do construe an oppositional relationship in the building, it is between them

---

22. This is the case in all buildings with five or fewer full-time staff. For buildings with more than five full-time staff, the supers are hired on another contract.

and the owners to whom they provide rent and who can always be castigated for shirking on the provision of services in exchange for rent. While the same dynamic is absent in cooperatives, those whose tenure in cooperative buildings is through a sublease may also develop the same orientation to their "landlords." And finally, tenants and doormen spend a lot of time together and through long-term interactions mutually adjust their rhythms to each other. This mutual adjustment, similar in form (though not in scale) to the subtle adjustments long-term friends make to the peculiarities of the other, invokes a specific form of closeness, an intimacy of timing and expectation that is in contrast to the norms of labor conflict. Thus, when the strike does occur or is threatened to occur, one observes a strange negative posturing.

This posturing is not all that different from what one observes when watching the sequence of events that constitute a small dinner engagement. Consider the dynamics. One invites friends for dinner. The guests try to counter the gift of the dinner by negating its value, asking what they can bring to the meal. The host insists that they bring nothing. Despite this, the proper guests arrive at the door with wine, dessert, or flowers. The host insists that they should not have brought anything. The guests insist that their gift is truly nothing. The hosts serve the dinner that they have prepared. The guests relate how much the dinner pleased them. The hosts insist that the preparation was nothing — even if it was evidently quite something. The guests prepare to leave and thank the hosts for the meal. The hosts insist on thanking the guests for coming. They say it was their pleasure. The guests insist that it was their pleasure. Both parties in this strange social dance give gifts and insist that they are worthless; both expend effort and deny that the effort was meaningful. Both desire to achieve the coveted role of the giver, yet the social script is written as if to deny that they are the givers.

This negative posturing in which the value of the gift given is denied at the moment given finds its counterpart in the similarly strange interactions that doormen have with their tenants on the eve of a strike or a potential strike. Doormen hope publicly that they will not strike, and they go out of their way to help tenants make the necessary adjustments to their routines so they will not experience hardship with the doormen's absence. They develop lists of tenants for the tenant volunteer doormen to use in the event of their absence; they hand out large trash bags and detailed instructions on how to manage the trash system for the building. They check and double-check the elevators to make sure that they will work for the duration of the strike. For buildings with plants in the foyer and/or lobby, they instruct tenants on the watering needs of the plants. And most of all, doormen try to reassure the tenants that everything will be fine if they have to strike and that they will do well without them. In short, they actively work to minimize the effects of the strike and discursively deny the importance of their role, insisting that tenants will not even miss them. Imagine, by comparison, workers on an assembly line working harder to make sure that their factory does not run out of finished goods for as long as possible, ensuring that the line operates smoothly in their absence by training their own replacements, carefully handing out collective supplies so that those most directly touched by the strike will hopefully not experience any real discomfort, and reassuring management that they will be fine![23]

There were other voices in the movement as well. But even the more aggressive supporters of the need for a better contract with management when discussing the possibility of a strike in 2001 were concerned about minimizing the potential discomforts that their absence might bring to tenants. For example, John, one of the more militant union members on the Upper West Side, notes that

> going out is something I don't want to do. I don't get paid and I need the money. But if we got to go, then we go. They don't leave us a choice sometimes. Now, we all need more money; it's as simple as that. It's hard on the people in the building to see us outside. And things can get messed up if we leave. They won't get their packages. All the deliveries get screwed up. The lobby is messy. It's just a big pain for everyone, even if we get everything ready, you know for the garbage, making sure that everything works.

On the other hand, Robert is less union-oriented. He is hoping not to strike and is concerned about the old people in the building who need extra help. Still, if he has to go out he will:

---

23. On the eve of the 1991 strike, doormen and tenants set up the systems that would ensure that the doormen were not really missed, including, for example, trash collection. As reported in the *New York Times*, one tenant complained to her doorman, "Peter I don't want to live with my garbage," as the doorman behind the front desk at 215 West Eighty-Fourth Street handed her five heavy-duty garbage bags and checked her name off his list. "Oh god, this is going to be a pain." *New York Times*, April 22, 1991, B2–3.

Nothing good is going to come of it. But if they don't want to settle, we have to go out, that's what people don't understand. We want to work, see, but they don't want us to. And they don't worry about the old people in the building who need us. So we have to tell them and get them help too.

If workers are helping tenants prepare for their absence, tenants engage in the same apparently weird dance. They publicly support the doormen in their efforts. They moan about the hardships that the doormen will have to endure while on strike, and they form committees to help care for the doormen should they be forced to walk out — providing them with coffee, cookies, doughnuts, and other refreshments as needed. They proudly agree to serve the building for free, to chip in for as long as the strike must be, in order to sort the mail, provide security, handle deliveries, watch the door, screen tenants, mop the halls, water the plants, and care for the appearance of the lobby. At the same time, they tell their doormen how much they will miss them and how hard it will be to get by without them. They reassure them that they are really wanted. Imagine by comparison managers at a factory about to be shut down gracefully volunteering to work the line for free so that the workers, when they do come back, find everything just as it was, reassuring the workers that they support them, and that they will be missed![24]

Here, like the hosts and their guests, engaged in a fierce battle to deny the reality of their efforts to define the value of the gift of dinner in their interests, doormen and tenants appear to be in a fierce battle to deny the fact that they have opposing interests. The tenants urge the doormen to strike if they need to, and the doormen urge the tenants to not need them, in much the same way that hosts deny the value of their dinner and the guests deny the value of their gift. Is anything at stake?

From the tenants' perspective, doorman raises are not cost-neutral, and building managers claim that they must fight excessive salary increases as their key justification for opposing doorman wage demands. One can always find some basis for manager's claims. Labor accounts for roughly 35% of operating expenses at most co-ops and somewhat less in rental

---

24. There are easily found a host of amusing conversations recorded during the 1991 strike by enterprising journalists. Here are some representative snippets. "'I just feel lucky to be living here and I want to do my share,' said Alma, a trim blond desk volunteer, as a company of teenagers swept the lobby floor." "Somebody yelled at my daughter for not sorting the mail alphabetically, and that's impossible because she has a genius IQ, about 180." Gelb, "On Speaking Terms."

properties under independent management. Assume for the sake of the example that all of the labor costs are covered under the 32BJ collective bargaining agreement, although this is not exactly the case. Looking first at the recent settlement, where management agreed on a 3.46% increase in wages and an additional 1.5% in benefits, the total cost of the first year is roughly 5%, which represents a 1.75% increase in the overall operating costs. Thus, a co-op owner facing $500 per month service fees before the settlement would face fees that increase to $508.75. By comparison, for $8.75 in New York City, one can purchase a six-pack of beer, a hamburger, or a falafel sandwich, pretzel, and a soda. In more expensive co-ops, where service fees can cross over (say) $10,000 per year, costs associated with doorman salary increases would creep closer to $200 per year.

This is objectively very little, yet strangely the same relatively small increase starts to feel like a lot if one is in a rental unit. In rental properties, by extension, if costs for labor are passed on completely, tenants paying $2,500 per month before the wage increase could be expected to pay $43.75 more per month. In New York City, that buys one a pretty good dinner out, even with some wine. So here, it would appear that tenants face some sacrifices. Three things mitigate the impact of wage increases. First, rent control sets limits on the rate of rent increases. While increased labor costs are factored into the equation for determining increases under rent control, the increases are experienced across all apartment units in the city. For psychological reasons, large rent increases that touch all people bother people less than a smaller increase that they would have to bear alone. Second, in rental apartments, labor costs do not generally reach 35% of building operating expenses, and so the pass-through is correspondingly less onerous. And finally, relative to the other factors that drive rents in the city, salary increases are relatively small-fry stuff. Those in rent-control apartments are happy enough paying what they know is below-market rents. Where rent control is not operative, increased labor costs are a drop in the bucket, and tenants can safely ignore them as key factors driving the rent they dole out. So even if tenants have real economic interest at stake, they tend to ignore it — which is an appropriate response, against a background of stronger inflationary drivers governing rental rates.

Tenants and cooperative owners thus have objectively little riding on the outcome of wage negotiations with doormen. Symbolically, they have strong incentive to argue for higher wage packets, for there is something awkward about driving a hard bargain with one's doorman. Those who want to drive such a bargain willingly turn over responsibility to management negotiating groups. By doing so, this enables a specific kind of negative posturing. In a mirror of the doormen, tenants can claim that these negotiating groups don't really represent them. Instead, the negotiations are — it would seem — conducted between shadow aliens whose relationship to those in the lobby is distant and mysterious. This is not the case, obviously, but tenant posturing, combined with the absence of real interest (in contrast to doormen), means that tenants have less of a stomach for a strike. They thus bring substantial pressure on management negotiators to settle. And when they do settle, doormen end up with relatively good benefit and wage packets.

In the event of a strike, at least considering the outcomes of the 1991 strike, building managers turn out not to lose too much of anything, and in this regard, the 1991 strike may have been instructive for all parties and one of the reasons everyone has managed to avert subsequent strikes. In 1991 doormen started by demanding wage increases of 5% per year. Managers countered with a 2% wage offer. After twelve days on the picket line, managers and doormen split the difference, settling on just under 3.5% per year. Doormen stood to gain $16 per week extra salary, or $832 in the first year. It looked like a good deal, except that by the time they settled, they had already lost twelve days' pay, or more than $1,000 in wages, not counting suspended benefit payments. Managers, relying on free labor provided by their tenants and the goodwill of doormen and supers in the days preceding the strike, rode out the settlement, making money on the first year, certainly knowing that after a week of doormen being off the job, they would break even.[25] Doormen, meanwhile, stood to gain in real terms not much more, over the course of the three-year agreement, than the 2% per annum initially proposed by the managers, if one only looked at the short term (i.e., the three-year window). Oddly, one source of doorman weakness with respect to generating an oppositional orientation to tenants (long tenures) turns out to be a source of strength in terms of the value of the negotiated settlements. Doormen may be one of the few working groups whose expected tenure in the job is greater than that of management. This

---

25. The union also negotiated several small increases in benefits such as a $50 per month raise in the maximum pension and additional college scholarships, partially supported by employers. Consequently, the twelve days was probably the true break-even point, although some of the employee concessions were associated with high-enough discount rates that their true value was hard to estimate.

shift in orientation toward the long term has been an unexpected bonus for 32 BJ and provides one of the reasons why the residential side of the union has achieved more success, as a ratio of potential influence, than the commercial side, with less contention.

The focus on the long term dulls the sharp edge of labor contention for doormen. Tenants, meanwhile, are largely insensitive to the small increases passed along by managers or their co-op in support of potential wage increases. The major issue in the 1997 contract negotiations was also centered on the long term. In the recently signed deal with the commercial building employers, Bevona had agreed to a two-tiered salary system that paid new recruits 20% less than those with long tenures. On the eve of the 1997 residential strike, Bevona insisted that he would not agree to a similar two-tiered wage policy for residential workers, but this turned out to be simple posturing. The final contract called for workers in their first thirty months to receive 20% less pay and released the employers from paying annuities to workers in their first two years. By also allowing temporary replacement workers to be paid 40% less than regular union workers, the contract was essentially free to employers, despite the 8.83% pay raise negotiated for regular doormen with tenure.[26] The contract, though, was a bet on the future, with 32 BJ assuming that their doormen would be in for the long term, and hence able to reap the benefits of the relatively large raise and employee contributions to the pension plan. Managers of buildings opted for short-term minimization of contract impact, presuming that they could subsequently renegotiate elements of the contract that protected labor once tenured. In fact, in many of the larger buildings, the critical issue that has emerged as a consequence of the two-tiered policy has been management efforts to terminate workers. This provides, in part, motivation for 32 BJ to engage more directly in legislation to prevent unjust termination, reflected in the recent passage of 239A, discussed above.

Still, all things considered, labor problems and thus a strike (or strike threat) itself appear to doormen and tenants be an alien — outside the

---

26. The actual cost to owners depended on the size and tenure distribution of their workforce. In one building with 148 units and five regular staff, for example, owners faced an increase of $5,869 in regular wages but stood to save $4,347 on temporary hires for vacation (they had nineteen weeks of vacation time at 60% salary). The net loss was then $1,522 for the year. When spread across the 148 units, this turns out to be less than $1 per month, not even worth passing on, in a budget of over $650,000 per annum.

specific powers and interests of each group, directed and executed by others.[27] Both groups prepare for the strike by taking the side of the other and denying their own role in the contestation. They are, in short, psychologically unprepared for conflict. The fact that tenants assume doorman jobs as a kind of play support for doormen has, in turn, some strange implications. These are considered below, but first I consider the role of the other active players in the "labor wars."

MANAGERS, POLICE, AND CITY OFFICIALS

If neither the doormen nor the tenants are psychologically prepared for a strike, management and city officials are. For city bureaucrats, a potential doorman strike causes headaches far less serious that those induced by threats of labor action by central service providers — for example, transit workers or sanitation personnel. Still, doorman strikes are problematic for the city with respect to a host of potential issues related to health, crime, and sanitation. Consequently, the city tends to respond strongly in the face of potential labor action. In 1991 police prepared an emergency operation to coordinate the services of city agencies for garbage removal, elevator repair, and rescue; deliveries to the disabled and elderly; and maintenance of heat and hot water supplies where necessary. The city set up a hotline for problems, managed by the police, and residents and building managers were asked to call to report problems of the most diverse sort. Similar emergency measures were set up in anticipation of a strike in 1997 and 2001. In 2001 city planners pursued even more aggressive strategies for countering the potential disruption of a doorman strike, with a proposal from the Giuliani administration to use workfare workers as security guards and trash handlers. Workfare, the Giuliani welfare reform innovation, is a system that places persons on welfare in unpaid public employment during the period that they collect subsidies from the city. Since the workers are not paid

27. Ironically, the fact the 32 BJ was corrupt and did not allow for member voice provided doormen with a useful script in response to conversations about striking — the decision was made by others, there is nothing I can do, and so on. Should 32 BJ decisions with regard to striking (and the settlement) actually become more democratic, this elegant rhetoric will slip away. It will also, and Bevona clearly had the right instinct, reduce the capacity of doormen to get good deals, since they will be more likely to settle, not sharing the classic worker opposition model. Since tenants are always represented by an abstract negotiating group, they will not experience this limitation.

wages, the system bears a close relationship to eighteenth- and nineteenth-century poor relief, except that rather than being assigned to work in private factories (thus providing sweatshop operators with a free source of labor), workfare participants are assigned to city service positions, such as street sweepers, park cleaners, and so on. The fact that the Giuliani administration considered using workfare workers as temporary doormen suggests, then, that they saw averting the potential negative outcomes from a strike as critical for the recovery of the city. Why is it, then, that building managers and city officials, but not tenants, seem so concerned about the potential of a strike? Does their concern suggest that doormen have significantly more structural power than they are aware of? What, in short, accounts for the asymmetry in views?

The problem could be as simple as a public relations problem. One idea is that tenants recognize that others think that doormen are a luxury item, and that their confessing to an inability to survive without luxury feels and sounds bad against a background where most New Yorkers live perfectly well without doorman services. This idea would also fit with their apparent disinterest in the scale of the economic penalty they should expect to incur should doormen win wage increases. Another idea is that many high-end tenants actually want to pay more for luxury. There are many buildings in New York where just getting past the board (for co-ops) requires being worth millions of dollars. In some Upper East Side buildings, rumor has it that one cannot even think about getting an apartment unless one is worth a billion dollars.[28] Even in modest condo buildings (ignoring the really upscale buildings where condos sell for $10 to $20 million) where average apartment prices break the $2 million barrier, tenants get value from buying status.

Less well-off tenants may not be disinterested, but they lack the capacity to articulate why they want to pay less for a luxury service against a background where people tend to assess the value of luxury goods quite differently than ordinary breadbasket items. So if some tenants care, they are unable to find a rhetoric that legitimizes their concerns. If this is the case, why do others appear to care so much? Why should they be concerned with the loss of luxury services, if those losing the service fail to articulate its significance? What makes it possible for them to speak for tenants?

---

28. Nadine Brozan, "The Price of 'Wow!' Keeps on Rising," *New York Times*, September 7, 2003.

First, consider building managers who are clearly in a different situation than their tenants. They manage, rent, and sell apartments in a competitive environment in which provision of services is one of the few features of the living situation that they can actively control, since key determinants of value — namely, location, views, and apartment design and size — are fixed. Managers are often split. In the high-end sector, where demand for apartments is intense, managers need not worry about too high a vacancy rate, but they do need to worry about prestige. Since addresses gain prestige by the tenants who reside there, tenant dissatisfaction points to increased probability of status loss. In this framework, managers explicitly recognize that they are in the luxury goods market. They may not care so much about keeping costs down, but they care enormously about capacity to deliver service. While these tenants may not say they cannot live without doormen, managers recognize that their buildings cannot survive without them. This dependence on doormen weakens managers' resistance to their wage demands and suggests that the strike threat might have teeth in it. At the very least, high-end managers feel they have something that they can lose. Managers of less prestigious buildings have to worry about costs. But their capacity to fight wage increases is severely limited. As the strike deadline looms, high-end owners are more likely to defect. The threat of defection challenges the collective posture adopted at the start of negotiations and creates opportunities for the union. This is why contract negotiations tend to go the whole nine yards. Early settlement is harmful to the union, since it fails to reveal cleavages among the managers.

City officials confront the possibility of a strike from another perspective. They are not concerned with manager competition, but they are concerned about retaining high-end apartments in the city, increased crime, and pressures on the public health infrastructure, which is already relatively shaky. But most critical for the city is perceived quality of life, and two of the three elements that most profoundly shape perceptions of quality of life — crime and garbage — are directly associated with doormen. The third element, traffic and transportation, is only marginally connected to the lobby. The scope of garbage collection in the city is so large that people cannot simply put their garbage out in cans or on the street every day. If they did, armies of rats would leave their river and subway abodes and stream onto the streets. So garbage has to go out on specified times, and in all buildings with doormen, they are responsible for getting it to the street in a timely manner — not too early and not too late. The city thus recognizes that doormen manage garbage and that the management of garbage is important for the functioning of the city. Crime is different. While doormen rarely actively stop crime, there is always the possibility that their presence prevents crimes that might have occurred in their absence. The police are sensitive to this possibility. While managers and the newspapers fear that criminals may read the doorman strike as a new opportunity and plot to enter unprotected buildings, the police don't believe this is likely.[29] Instead, police are concerned with the street, and here they have some good instincts, for they do think that doormen keep strangers off their ends of the street. By analogy, doormen, as the police see it, have been engaged in proactive, preventive crime work for the past fifty years.

Well before police got around to believing that they could control the streets by making it difficult for potential criminals to move around without being stopped, doormen have been operating in the space between the inside world of the building and the chaotic street. While doormen may not stop building crimes, they may — police believe — deter street crimes. So the city is concerned with the loss of important policing functions. Since both garbage and safety are crucial determinants of mayoral popularity, city hall tends to react strongly to the threat of a strike. So here, too, one senses that the doormen have more influence than previously thought. The key, though, may be that doormen are not easily replaced — that is, other workers cannot step into their shoes as easily as they could, for example, commercial building cleaners, whose jobs were frequently lost to subcontractors throughout the period. While doormen don't need formal skills, the skills they do have (as we saw earlier) are not replaceable. This is because their skill comes from knowledge of tenants, gained only from experience.

STRUCTURAL POWER

One idea proposed earlier is that doormen have more structural power than it seems. Defined in terms of upstream and downstream linkage, it is hard

---

29. The police do not believe that doormen keep undesirable people out of buildings, but they do believe that they keep them off the streets in front of their buildings. Thus, in order to ensure that quality-of-life crimes do not increase, the police in the event of a strike have to step up street patrols in the up-market neighborhoods. This is why the police, while not resistant to volunteer tenant desk persons handling the inside routines of the buildings, consider the protection offered by them as minimal, since they do not leave the lobby and fail to focus on the street. Here is why Giuliani could actually imagine that workfare participants could help. By working the door, they would work the street at the same time. Of course, the grotesque parody of unpaid welfare recipients holding doors for those who "control the economic fate" of the city was too much to bear by the tabloids, usually relatively quiescent on labor issues.

to see where this power could come from, though. But still, when Bevona threatened the president of ISS with a strike of the five thousand cleaners working for ISS in New York if he did not arrive at a fair settlement in the California case, 32BJ exercised structural power with remarkable results. Before considering Bevona's capacity to deploy power on behalf of janitors thousands of miles away from New York, it will help to consider the idea of structural power more carefully. Perhaps it is possible to define power in a more subtle way.

The idea of structural power arises from Marx but is given its fullest development in an important book by Michael Schwartz, *Radical Protest and Social Structure*, chronicling the collapse of the southern Farmers Alliance at the turn of the century. The book describes how, just before the turn of the twentieth century, southern farmers faced a desperate situation — seemingly no matter how good the harvests were, farmers were confronted with greater and greater debts each year, increasing their dependence on cotton and the grip of the debt peonage system they had fallen into. Against this background, they sought to reverse their slide into peonage by coordinated efforts over the marketing of their products. While the story is long and complicated, the essential elements are easily grasped. Farmers, organized into a Farmers Alliance, would scour the countryside and buy cotton at market rates, purchase seed and fertilizer in bulk, and sell it at market rates to alliance members at alliance stores (Granges). In this way, farmers could escape the slide into debt, landlords would be forced to sell products in their stores at reasonable rates without crushing interest, and farmers would regain their freedom.

Consequently, agents from the Farmers Alliance left for the country to buy cotton early on in the harvest season. They were beaten and lynched. Still they prevailed, managing to bring significant supplies to the Grange. Farmers traveled to the Grange to purchase seed and food for the year, on the value of their cotton crop, to be delivered in the subsequent year. It looked like relief had arrived. But life was not as simple as the alliance members thought. Downstream, a series of bad things started to happen. Landlords' stores went broke and owners began to default on bank loans. The banks, already shaky, appealed to the northern controllers of the railroads, asking them to block shipment of Farmers Alliance cotton to markets in Texas, Charleston, and New Orleans. The lines complied, forcing the alliance to develop alternative (and more expensive) transportation routes. This they succeeding in doing, but once their cotton arrived at the markets, they discovered that they could not sell their crops because the major cotton factors in England insisted that the cotton be wrapped in jute, which the alliance did not control and could not purchase. The Granges collapsed in debt, farmers were forced back into the hands of their landlords, and the process of debt peonage, delayed momentarily, continued unabated.

The story is about the location of structural power. Farmers controlled the production of cotton but were unable to market it. When they developed competing local markets, these markets threatened store owners and landlords. Their economic ruin threatened banks, which escalated the conflict and blocked alliance use of long-distance transportation networks. When the alliance countered the control of the railroads through development of competing transportation systems, the railroads lost control of their monopoly, consequently, English investors were faced with losses in their investment. In order to protect their interests in the railroads, they blocked the shipment of cotton to England unless wrapped in jute. And the jute market was theirs.

At the end of the day, the alliance discovered that real power in the system resided one step above where they carefully developed alternative marketing arrangements designed to give them control over agricultural production. Producers could not succeed in establishing alternative exchange systems, because their structural power rested not with exchange but with production. In order to be successful, they would have needed to directly withdraw their labor from cotton production — or participate in the emergent racial state. In the South, the latter alternative was pursued, thereby breaking down the possibility of collective action across the race line and condemning black and white tenant farmers to generations of poverty.[30]

Back to New York, California, and Gus Bevona. Bevona was able to influence the ISS labor negotiations for the simple reason that ISS had stronger interests in New York City than Century City, L.A. Faced with the possibility of debilitating labor action in the city, in support of a distant strike involving a significantly smaller labor force in a significantly less critical market sector, ISS appeared to crumble and accede to the wage demands of the Century City janitors. That such demands were modest no doubt helped achieve resolution with remarkable speed, but the key element in this case was the

---

30. Cf. Schwartz, *Radical Protest and Social Structure*; and Redding, *Making Race and Power*.

intervention of 32BJ. In contrast to the Farmers Alliance, Bevona, on behalf of 32BJ, was able to escalate the struggle to impact core ISS interests in New York City. In turn, ISS, at least over the short term, could do little to block such escalation as firms up- and downstream in the New York context were not likely to be sympathetic to ISS problems in a small California market where wage demands were so meager.

What is striking, then, is the inability of 32BJ to ratchet up, beyond the levels achieved, more significant wage gains for their members in the commercial sector. Why could they exercise structural power on behalf of workers thousands of miles away but fail to have the muscle to prevent erosion of commercial wage gains locally? Historically, the answer was corruption, expressed in the union's willingness to settle contracts on the fly and to allow substantial sectors of the commercial labor force to slip out of union contracts.[31] Since its renewal under Fishman, 32BJ has been able to garner better contracts for its commercial workers while reversing the membership hemorrhage.

Residential doormen, though, were more protected than commercial doormen were, and one has to be surprised that doormen, who evidently have less structural power, could negotiate for and achieve such high salaries. There are three possible accounts. One idea is that doormen really do have structural power, even if the direct beneficiaries of their labor — the tenants — deny that they are dependent on them. If tenants are not dependent on doormen, management may be, for as noted above, in the high-stakes luxury market, managers cannot afford even temporary loss of service. The second idea is that the doormen rode on the coattails of the commercial workers, at least as far as they could, even benefiting from the 1996 commercial workers contract, signed after a bitter strike that impoverished its members.[32] The third idea is that tenants provide substantial support for doormen.

---

31. The fact that organized crime interests believed that they could wrangle concessions from the union in the residential sector suggests that corrupt union leaders participated in the member hemorrhage of the 1990s, thereby weakening their base. The wage decline that commercial workers experienced in the 1990s, relative to other workers in the production and service sector, was likely a consequence of corruption.

32. There is a another version as well, which is that subsequent to the ISS strike and 32BJ support for the Century City workers in the early 1990s, ISS and other large corporations set out to cripple the capacity of 32BJ to influence labor agreements outside of New York. While taking substantially harder positions on the negotiating table, reflected in worse contracts to commercial workers, the

Riding the coattails of the commercial workers' structural power through the mid-1990s would be a likely account, but it fails to make sense of a deep irony. When the union threatens to strike, doormen will do better by not striking if they announce they do not want to strike and help "defeat" the strike in advance by preparing tenants so that they will do fine without them. If the strike threat is believable, doormen earn tremendous goodwill from their tenants whom they strive to serve, so long as the threat does not come from them, but from some disembodied union officials. Under Bevona, such self-alienation from the union was easier — in part because it was encouraged by union leaders arrayed against any sign of participatory democracy. Doormen could always talk about the union and management as "them," both arrayed against an "us" that includes the tenants. The negative posturing allows those tenants who care to join their side, against their building management. In rental properties, conflict can be escalated up to mysterious landlords or management groups, and tenants can array their interests with doormen. In condos, tenants can plead that the case is being argued on behalf of tenants in rental properties, whose class status is lower than theirs. In such a context, even elite tenants can gain status from expression of "solidarity" with workers. Either way, an unusual alliance can develop — one that strengthens the relationship between doormen and tenants in the long run. While doormen deny they are needed, no one really believes their denial. After all, it sounds too much like one's mother who says, "Don't worry about coming over for the holiday, I can eat chicken soup by myself." And in any case, tenants — even if they cannot or will not say so publicly — need doormen, not mainly for the services that they provide, but for their social status. One cannot say that one needs doormen for status, for such a statement is paramount to admitting that one does not actually have any.

When doormen prepare tenants to take over their jobs in the event of the strike, tenants can enter into the play world of the imaginary. This world

---

main attack focused on exploiting the weaknesses of the corruption machine, by making it attractive for Bevona and his group to sacrifice membership for personal benefit. In this model, the capacity to escalate the conflict to another level, the hallmark of structural power in complex systems, shifted away from workers and back to employers. This shift left workers in the residential sector largely alone, for major employers had little interest in the residential contracts that workers signed with the typically small employer groups representing landlords and building managers. Left to their own devices, and with the gift of a corrupt union that allowed doormen and tenants to rhetorically align their interests together, doormen reaped contract benefits in the absence of labor action.

allows them to vicariously feel like they are chipping in, not to defeat the strike, which is the last thing they would want, but to help the doormen for their return. The potential strike provides both the doormen and the tenants with a wonderful chance to express solidarity. Even in this "solidaristic" context, the deep asymmetries involved are not noticed. No one would think that doormen should play at being tenants every few years and take over their apartments and lifestyle. But for tenants playing at being doormen, and for doormen facilitating their travels to the familiar world of the lobby with foreign eyes, the experience (in thought) is, as one tenant said, "Something I will always remember."

OVERVIEW

Local 32 BJ represents most doormen in the city and used to be a notoriously corrupt union. Under normal circumstances, leadership corruption weakens the bargaining position of workers as they seek to improve their wage and benefit claims. This, in the end, was certainly the case with the commercial workers represented by 32 BJ. But for residential doormen, the historical corruption of the union allowed doormen to align themselves with tenants on the eve of a strike and to secure tenant support for their threatened labor action. Doormen trained tenants to do their jobs and helped tenants make the best of what would be a messy situation in the event of a labor action. Tenants, in turn, assured doormen that they had their support. Faced with city officials who confronted the risk of a doorman strike in crisis mode, tenants whose support for the doormen was palpable, and management's sense that tenants were indifferent to the costs of labor action, the capacity to hold the line in labor negotiations was seriously weakened. In this regard, corruption indirectly served members' interests, allowing doormen to not see themselves as industrial workers but rather as professionals in the business of providing highly differentiated service to clientele whose preferences they have helped shape, thereby inducing greater distance between them and the union.

An irony is that under routinized union management, where workers' interests are aligned practically and symbolically with union goals, threats of labor action will induce the possibility of greater tenant-doorman strife and, hence, poorer wage settlements. Here could be a remarkable puzzle. In the short term, one might suspect that the better, in a normative sense, the union is, the worse it will perform. Cleaning up 32 BJ risks killing the goose that lays the golden egg. The egg is the claim to professionalism and the goose is the luxury market. Those who see themselves as workers cannot effectively staff such markets. Ironically, if 32BJ succeeds in turning doormen into workers, it may remove the foundation for its success. At least historically, only insofar as doormen could distance themselves from the union could they join in the otherwise weird tango that brought together tenants and doormen against distant enemies (management and the union) and ultimately broke the back of managers seeking to hold labor costs down.

But there are models for successful unionization of professional workers — whose unionization does not strip them of the autonomy necessary to make substantive decisions and act with discretion. Local 32BJ could succeed in organizing workers along these lines. Should they do so, it will mark an amazing transformation. For one need not think too far in the past when doormen, recent immigrants to the city, slaved away for seventy hours or more per week for little compensation, no security, and certainly without the sense that those who followed in their footsteps could legitimately make the kinds of social and wage claims that they now do.

CHAPTER 8

Conclusion

Acustomary conceit in field studies is to conclude with a brief note on how the subjects of the study have fared in the shorter or longer time that has elapsed between leaving the field and wrapping up the book. We could call this the *revisiting* idea.[1] Revisiting as defined above has a number of attractive features. First, it satisfies what I think is a crucial test for any good sociological study — which is that any result arrived at is interesting. I call this the two-tailed test, though it bears no relationship to the statistical test of the same name. The general idea is that projects are worth pursuing when either of the competing hypotheses that guide the researcher can turn out to be true and that both outcomes are interesting.[2] In "revisiting" studies, this is guaranteed to be the case, for one could find that the subjects and contexts have changed, stayed the same, or changed in some ways and stayed the same in others. Then, any of the possible changes make for an interesting story, which can be cast in any number of tropes.[3]

In this instance, in the time between research and writing, it is possible that many things did change for doormen and their tenants. Most of the research was conducted immediately before and after September 11, 2001.

---

1. This strategy is facilitated by another ethnographic conceit — detailed profiling of a few main subjects. Such profiling is often used in ethnographic accounts as it allows readers to follow the course of a complex narrative through the unfolding experiences of a few individuals. If you have gotten this far, you know that I have not followed this path.

2. The first part of the test requires that a theory be falsifiable; multiple outcomes have to be possible. The second is more stringent, namely, that all outcomes need to be interesting. By interesting, I mean not obviously tautological (though tautology is often extremely useful) and not obviously expected for the situation. This is not to say that one should only do sociology if results are interesting only if unexpected. The expected can be interesting in many situations.

3. At the risk of being pedantic, I note that all subjects change, even those who continue to rely on the same behavior routines and have the same thoughts. Since they are older, they use these routines and have these thoughts for longer. Consequently, they are likely more deeply entrenched, for good or for ill. The examples of this genre are truly endless.

One would suspect that in some fundamental way, the events of September 11 and its aftermath would have restructured the nature of the doorman's job and his relationship with tenants. Certainly, the extent to which Americans are subject to enhanced supervision under the guise of security has markedly increased. And just as certainly, Americans are becoming more used to such supervision. Video cameras that used to provide a source of unique amusement for kids are now ubiquitous in public settings. Security routines that would have just a few years ago been met with hostility are now blithely accepted as the price of living in the international age. And government intrusion into the lives of ordinary citizens that would have been met with marked hostility by a cluster of interests, on both the left and the right, are now just another part of the reality in which we live.

This heightened concern with and acceptance of security issues has also had an effect on the psyche of ordinary Americans, who seem from casual observation to be cowed into a sheepish acquiescence to demands governing their comportment in public spaces. Some of these changes seem almost for the better. Certainly one observes fewer "scenes" in public places than one did before September 11. If attempts to govern comportment on the basis of claims to civility were unsuccessful, security has won the day. Now, in settings where authorities have the capacity to monitor individual behavior — in bus terminals, train stations, malls and stores, gas station lines, schools, and parks — scenes are regarded with suspicion and are often handled with excess force, as if to make an example for others. Just thinking about airports, one can find countless incidents in which planes have been delayed because of idle jokes of flight passengers, gates have been cleared because of disruptions over boarding routines, and individuals have been arrested for complaining too vociferously about this or that.

One also senses a loss of openness, one of the more attractive features of America before September 11 and its aftermath. Isaac (who got his job through the Hungarian Mafia) told us that that America was distinct because of her openness to others.

> Americans in general are much more polite than people in Europe. I tell everyone, in Europe, when you go to another country, they say, "Why are you there?" People are still suspicious of each other. Americans are much more accepting; the whole spirit of the country, everyone at some point were immigrants, some generations down.

And so this openness has been one of the clearest casualties of the events of September 11 and its aftermath. The aforementioned security guards and other guardians of the public domain no longer seem so friendly and chatty. Instead, one more often than not encounters the sort of pettiness that one can only expect from the small tyrant. Lines marked in public waiting rooms become virtual walls, as petty officials project their authority onto waiting crowds. This projection of authority, always a goal of the minor functionary, is now legitimized under the guise of security and safety. And because these guardians of the public are more often than not unable to make substantive decisions, they tend to adhere more strongly to formal rule systems, even in the face of self-evident absurdity.

None of this is exactly new. For the past thirty years or so, academic and non-academic pundits of all stripes have complained that substantive judgment is being chased out of the world, replaced by a hollow formalism. Likewise, for both the United States and elsewhere, numerous observers have noticed how those with little power strive to project authority within their narrow domains. And finally, for some time now, many have been concerned with the privatization of everyday life, for it is this privatization that constitutes the greatest risk for despotism, whether benevolent (that is, for our security) or not.[4]

One form this privatization takes is increased paranoia and suspicion of persons not known or unfamiliar in appearance. Or put somewhat differently, trust has taken a hit. But if not exactly new, these tendencies (toward privatization of everyday life, increased government monitoring, and enhanced projection of authority by ever-increasing cadres of small functionaries) are perhaps qualitatively different by virtue of their quantitative expansion. Whatever the cluster of changes can be called, and whatever their extent, they all come to shape the ways in which individuals negotiate the transition into the public sphere, their encounters with authorities within this sphere, and their relationship to others both near and far, known and unknown. And it is this changed context in which doormen and tenants now work together to construct their joint world. How the events of September 11 and its aftermath have shaped this construction is one concern of this conclusion, where I first revisit the settings and problems encountered in

---

4. Slater, *Pursuit of Loneliness*; Bellah et al., *Habits of the Heart*; Putnam, *Bowling Alone*.

earlier chapters; now with an eye toward assessing whether anything of note has changed. Here, the evidence I can marshal is from simple observation, limited to just a few snapshots of scenes observed here and there.

SMALL CHANGE

Such an approach may miss change, but it seems, perhaps oddly, that very little has changed. Understanding why is instructive; I believe that there are a number of reasons for stability. First, security in doorman buildings was always pretty good, and most buildings did not need to change their security systems in the aftermath of September 11. While many commercial buildings made significant shifts in their access policies, most commonly requiring photo identification, residential buildings had already in place similar systems. If doormen did not exactly take photographs of visitors, their "photo bank" allowed them to recognize most people who came in, to associate them with tenants, and to know what to do in response to their arrival. Second, doormen have always had formal security systems and routines in residential buildings. They have not followed these systems, because if they did, they would create all sorts of substantive irrationalities, lose their claim to professional status, and fail to deliver service. Nonetheless, they have had the rules. And they have always worked with the rules to discipline tenants into becoming clients. In the immediate aftermath of September 11, while many buildings issued new security rules and posted new signs informing tenants that doormen must abide by these rules, the particularistic nature of the doorman-tenant relationship has remained unchanged. But today, doormen still train tenants to have preferences, still follow their lead in establishing contact routines, and still bend rules to achieve substantive rationality. If they did not, they could not hold on to their claim to professional status. At the same time, tenants could not hold on to and shape their status claims, for it is a meaningless status that forces everyone to be treated in the same way, however well. The demands of the lobby entail discretion, in order to induce distinction, and, in this sense, security remains as tight, or as lax, as it has always been.

In contrast, before September 11, commercial and public spaces that did not have security systems tended to install systems that could be operated without the exercise of substantive judgment. Speed of setup played some role in this, but most of all, commercial systems are designed so that anyone with a modicum of training and intelligence can operate them.[5] In public spaces where security was already present but seemingly not fail-proof, the only direction that one could move in was toward the exercise of blind formalism, that is, a system in which the formal rules already in place were ruthlessly adhered to. If such systems are now followed in public and commercial spaces, they cannot be, and are not, followed in the residential buildings where doormen work.

In the country at large, there is an increased attentiveness to the rhetoric of security. One need think of only the welter of new monitoring and supervising systems now justified ex post facto as security systems. Likewise, new systems for processing persons more efficiently — designed as labor-saving devices — are frequently described as necessary security protections, with the result that inconvenience is blanketed in a rhetorical structure that cannot be easily challenged. Finally, security has provided owners of private spaces used by the public — such as malls and plazas — new tools for removing those "elements" that appear to be bad for business. While this development has shaped the structure of interactions in a whole array of settings, from banks to department stores, a characteristic feature of the lobby setting is that the rhetoric of security — before September 11 — was already hegemonic, even if it lacked tangible reality. On the one hand, this meant that neither doormen nor tenants needed to make a psychic adjustment to a new security regime. Before September 11, tenants who were uncomfortable with conspicuous consumption of luxury were always able to account for their doormen in terms of security. Now the rhetoric has even greater "transportability"; for the invocation of "security" provides an immediately recognizable justification for service.[6] September 11 and its aftermath have simply solidified this rhetorical trick. Ironically,

---

5. This, of course, is what is most frustrating. Neither the functionaries nor the systems are capable of making substantive decisions; and because the small security operators tend to have few skills for negotiating the gray zones where judgment and diplomacy are called for, they tend to react poorly to challenges. Because they tend to react poorly, the system is organized to come to each individual's defense in rapid deployment of force, whether justified or not. Thus, for example, the suspension of a flight for making a bad joke about a shoe bomb.

6. Much the same transition occurred in the airline industry many years earlier, when stewardesses, whose main function was to service passengers, were transformed into flight attendants, whose principal job is to ensure the safety of the clients and crew in the event of an airline crash. That the frequency of airline crashes hardly justified such a shift is unimportant; doormen who do not stop crime because crime rarely occurs made the same transition as well.

the increased national focus on security has provided those who do care about conspicuous consumption of luxury goods more latitude in describing the services in their building as *services*. While building managers stress that their buildings are safe, safety is now a taken-for-granted attribute of doorman buildings. Since this is no longer market worthy, service specialization is. In this context, many doorman buildings since September 11 have jumped on the concierge bandwagon, hiring individuals to provide specialized services for their tenants — ranging from provision of roses for romantic evenings, tickets for special occasions, and even monogrammed pillowcases for visitors.

While psychic adjustment to the security regime has been unproblematic, the new social structure of security writ large has provided doormen with a better bag of tricks. Prior to September 11, doormen would use the formal rules to their advantage when necessary. Thus, tenants who treated them as workers were often handled as if they were employers — that is, in strict accordance with the "doorman rule book." If doormen were required to log in packages, they would do so. But they might not notify the tenant that a package had arrived. Likewise, if food arrived in the lobby and doormen were not allowed to send deliverymen to the upper floors without supervision, they could and would call the tenants downstairs to retrieve their order. Under such a regime, tenants savvy enough to recognize that others were getting different treatment would learn to work with doormen. Others might stew, but since the doormen were working to rule, tenants could find few bases for complaint. The formal changes in the "doorman rule book" after September 11 provide doormen with a few more weapons in their disciplinary armor. Since security is always on the tip of everyone's tongue, claiming that they could not do something because it risks security has been generally sufficient to soak up tenant dissatisfaction. While the portability of the security rhetoric seems greater, the bag of tricks is the same, and there is no reason to think that the old bag was insufficient.

Likewise, it is hard to find evidence that interaction dynamics in the lobby have changed since September 11. In part this is due to the nature of the doorman's job, which is to insulate the lobby from the uncertainty and disorder of the street. When doormen greet their tenants coming in or going out of the building, even something as subtle as the quick hello or slight nod of recognition serves to symbolically demarcate the inside from the outside. This symbolic demarcation makes it possible for old routines to flourish even in new contexts. Since doormen insulate the lobby from the disorder of the exterior world, it is no surprise that changes in the exterior world penetrate the small world of the building unevenly if at all.

Some changes in the exterior world have made work more difficult for doormen in some respects and easier in others. In the aftermath of September 11, the city entered a difficult period of financial retrenchment and economic decline. Despite a soft economic recovery, one easily senses the impact of harder times. In the elite neighborhoods on the Upper and Lower West Sides, the streets are now dirtier than they were before September 11. They are also less well policed and increasingly occupied by the burgeoning homeless population, whose objective situation has declined precipitously in the past two years. Considering only those elite areas where doormen work, other signs of urban decay are apparent as well, for example, sightings of large numbers of rats in and around garbage areas, broken benches in public areas, and less well-tended public spaces for sitting and playing. In other areas of Manhattan, those where tourists rarely venture, decay is more visible, and the full impact of the economic impact of September 11 is correspondingly much more obvious. On the negative side, erratic police presence has provided doormen with fewer opportunities to help their tenants by watching their cars so as to ensure that they do not get a ticket. This means that they have "less to do," but also fewer services to provide. Likewise, subtle declines in tourism have made cabs easier to hail. And this means that tenants seem to need doormen less than they did before. Likewise, management of the garbage in the context of feared rodent invasions has become much more pressing. Equally problematic have been the flip-flops by the Bloomberg administration over recycling programs that created widespread confusion among New Yorkers as to what is and is not recyclable. This confusion has played havoc with the garbage routine in most buildings. On the positive side, subtle changes in the structure of everyday life have increased opportunities for doormen, though also of course the pace of work. Doormen report that tenants are much more likely now than previously to order take-out foods, watch movies at home, and receive deliveries from major Internet retailers. All of these changes in some sense reflect the increasing privatization of everyday life, and while none are directly attributable to September 11, they reflect a deepening of the boundaries between the private and the public spheres. As this boundary continues to deepen, one suspects that the role of the doorman will become more important for tenants, since they stand between the exterior world of the street and market and the interior world of the apartment and heart (or stomach).

WINDOW-SHOPPING

A few days ago I was having a beer with a colleague who, having discovered that I was near to finishing this book, asked me to say what, in a *single* sentence, it was about. This is a fair question, and just a bit later I provide such a sentence. For social scientists, this is often a difficult question, especially for those whose work, like this, is neither narrative nor theory driven, but rather strives for description of social context in order to reveal patterns of interaction and understanding that may be relevant for observation of other diverse settings. There are a number of small answers to this question. And in this book, I have proposed some answers to some puzzles relevant for the experiences of doormen and other workers, tenants and other clients. One set of puzzles concerns social closure and the experience of discrimination, another set of puzzles concerns the problems of managing priority queues in server systems, and yet another concerns the bases for claims to professionalism, among others. I have tried to show that focusing on interaction mechanisms in tangible social structures solves these substantive puzzles. This is a book about the dualities that structure interaction, managed uncertainty, impurity absorption, matching proclivities in markets, trust networks, weak ties, the norm to serve as strategy and tactic, induced preferences in the significant other, small numbers exigencies, at the same time that it is a study of the new professional working class. This kind of answer is a bit like window-shopping. You see a lot of interesting things but sometimes not buying anything is frustrating.

Puzzle solving is not an end in itself, or at least I want to suggest that we can do more than solve puzzles. To show this, I return to three statements that can be made from the particular window I have explored in the book, focusing on three questions that I started with.

Why are doormen not racist yet act in ways that appear discriminatory? It is a simple point, but behavior and attitudes are often discrepant when attitudes are decoupled for the contexts in which behavior occurs. When doormen treat black visitors differently than white visitors, it is not because they dislike or distrust blacks; it is because their behavior with respect to visitors is based on a homophily theory that is extremely effective. Because social class (and race) segregates friendship, doormen who work in predominantly white buildings express their tenants' preferences for white visitors by checking on blacks. In this case, the doormen's behavior becomes a window, not only into their own mind, but also into the mind of their tenants.

Why do supers who are not racist engage in hiring practices that are, in aggregate, discriminatory? Supers hire small numbers of doormen. In making hiring decisions, they rely on recommendations from friends, doormen, and the union. The closer their friends are to them, the more they can resonate with and understand the foundation from which the recommendation is based. Consequently, they prefer to hire within relatively close weak-ties networks. Because such networks are ethnically based, supers get information about co-ethnics. Each decision is rational at the micro-level, yet leads to uneven hiring practices. In this case as well, the supers' behavior is a window, not only into their mind, but also into the structure of the friendship networks in which they are embedded.

What can doormen do to overcome the fact that when tenants need them, they are most often busy, even though when tenants see them, they are most often idle? Doormen manufacture preferences for services that induce distinction among tenants in order to provide personalized services to tenants. This allows them to project a willingness to serve, even if they cannot serve when they are needed. And in this case, the preferences that tenants have thus not only provide a window into the tenants' minds, but also to the tricks of the trade that the doormen have to manage tenant perceptions.

One could go through the entire list of questions providing answers already found elsewhere in this book. But that would be redundant. What seems self-evident from this short list is that observation and interviews may bring one closer to the mind of the subject, in all cases, but can also bring one closer to the contexts that express themselves through those minds.

MANUFACTURING INTENT

On factory floors where piece rates determine compensation, workers often work to balance two contradictory demands, the demand of the shop floor, which exerts strong norms against rate busting, and the demand of self-interest, which exerts a strong claim for making just a little bit more money.[7] When workers work, they also reproduce the conditions for the reproduction of capitalism; they do not intend this, but the structure of the piece rate and the norms of the shop floor produce, as a by-product of their labor, their consent to the manufacturing process. Workers in such settings are locally rational and deploy local knowledge to make the best deal that they can, individually and collectively, under the conditions of employment they find themselves. That under other conditions they would prefer other deals is unquestionable, but largely irrelevant for our understanding of the ways in which the structure of the shop floor speaks through individuals. Here as well, not so far from the shop floor, in the lobby, the structures that confront doormen (and tenants and supers and guests and delivery people) shape problem orientations, solutions, knowledge, and aspirations, which are best understood by focusing on the ways in which inchoate local understandings of the terms of trade give rise to behavioral routines that may be globally irrational but locally rational. To make sense of this tension, one searches for the local logics that determine definitions of situations. These logics are not likely to be transparent to actors, but their trace is revealed in their practical activities, their management of time, people, and their flows in and out of the lobby.

Like workers on the shop floor managing the contradictory demands of collective interest and self-interest, doormen respond to constraints of their job to pursue individual and collective ends that if not always contradictory are often in tension. Thus, for example, doormen respond to the contradictions of the server systems in which they are embedded by manufacturing distinction (across tenants) in order to provide service. This construction of distinction bears an affinity with tenant desires to feel special, either as a vehicle for them to express their own status, or just to counter the alienation of life in the "big city." If tenants were uninterested in relationships with doormen and if doormen were uninterested in delivering professional, personalized service, we would not expect that practical routines capable of inducing distinction among tenants would arise. At the same time, there is no reason for doormen or tenants to articulate that their interactive goal is to induce such distinctions. In fact, it is not their goal, which is both more modest and more ambitious. Modestly, doormen and tenants want to

---

7. Burawoy, *Manufacturing Consent*; Mitchell, *Social Networks in Urban Situations*.

get through their day with some joy and perhaps even some grace. More ambitiously, doormen and tenants want to solve the problem of order. The induction of distinction turns out to make contributions to both.

At the start of this book, I noted that sociologists tend not to be interested in the ordinary social mechanics of ordinary occupations. Avoidance of the routine is unfortunate, if only because most people spend most of their time in such settings and it seems sociology as a discipline ought to have something to say about such orthodox worlds. One reason for this disinterest rests on the salience of the two-tailed test described above. If one studies a "weird" population, one is guaranteed an interesting result, for either the expected is found (therefore making the weird group just like us after all) or is not found (thereby making them weird and worthy of study). In contrast, studies of orthodox populations run the risk of revealing orthodox underpinnings for their social behavior, thoughts, and understandings. A second reason for this disinterest is practical: everyday mechanisms are harder to see in everyday settings than they are in unusual settings. Sociologists intuitively know this, since (contrary to many methodological arguments) distance between the sociologist and the field facilitates rather than hinders capacity for new insight.[8] Hence, they search out distant subjects as an aid to insight. But ironically, if the windows of observation reveal not the mind of the observed but instead the theories, tricks, minds, and processes of other(s), study of the distant may provide a much more limited view than typically thought — namely, a view of the distant through the mind of the other.

Here, through the window of observed behavior, we observe that the real springs for social action rest in a nest of workable theories, bags of tricks, and larger network processes. These theories, tricks, and processes appear to be social facts, that is, things that are not changeable by the will of a single individual — either the researcher or the research subject. It is the underlying social facts of the lobby and interaction dynamics — invoked for solving problems large and small, from how much to give as a bonus to whom to hire for a vacant position — that I have striven to identify in this book. I believe these can provide a partial framework for other comparative studies

---

8. An odd irony against this background is that sociologists who imagine that they are not like others tend to study themselves, as if knowledge of the self somehow provided useful benchmarks for analysis of others. There are supporting views for the general idea that distance assists understanding. This argument and others like it take the general form that the last thing to discover water will be a fish.

of ordinary people in ordinary occupations. In this regard, readers ought to finish reading this book with a better understanding of the dynamics of race discrimination in hiring and access to apartments, switching dynamics in conversation, and the irrational generation of status arrays from Christmas bonuses. For those with an intrinsic interest in doormen and the life they lead at work, and tenants and the life they lead in the public domain of the lobby, these understandings may provide fodder for new thoughts. But these understandings are not designed to be limited to doormen and their tenants. The dynamics of job acquisition described here work also in numerous other arenas, from searches for managers of high-tech firms to waiters and waitresses in corner diners. Likewise, the seemingly irrational dynamics underlying the search for the perfect bonus can be found in diverse contexts, whenever individuals strive to signal status in a context of interdependency. And finally, doormen can be seen as the leading edge of the new professional working class. Joining them in service will be both those of the traditional working class claiming new status and those in sales and service whose objective position in the class structure, destabilized by increasing inequality, strive to redefine their relationships to clients, managers, and themselves through adoption of professional rhetoric and, perhaps, routine.

OPENING DOORS

At the same time, there is more that one can extract from a descriptive book of this kind, and it is toward this goal that I devote the next few paragraphs. The first idea is simple, which is that description is enhanced by limited consideration of more formal models for describing processes and dynamics. Here, I have experimented with informal presentation of models for switching dynamics in conversation, network dynamics for job acquisition, collective action dynamics for giving the right bonus, and queuing dynamics for organizing server systems. The fact that bodies of work arising from different substantive research areas in the social sciences lie behind these models provides us with a natural comparison to the specific (and necessarily limited) setting that we consider here. The implicit idea is that such models can help to shed light on dynamics that would otherwise appear to be idiosyncratic. That they do or do not is for the reader to decide. Obviously, I believe that they do and, consequently, believe that future descriptive work should strive for a more or less formal consideration of more or less formal models. One way to gain leverage over context is to wrest observation to models. If such were to be the case, formal modelers would benefit as well, for while the beauty of a formal model lies in its parsimony, there is little value for models that fail to relate to context. Abstraction alone is not the goal of sociology; abstraction that is faithful to context is. Modelers would benefit from studies that strive to assess the fit between the formal model and the dynamics actually revealed.

The second idea is less simple and concerns one of the core elements of a doorman's everyday experience. A central aspect of the doormen's world is that they are simultaneously close to and distant from tenants. As noted earlier, there are other occupations whose members are close to their clients. Lawyers, doctors, psychiatrists, teachers, social workers, and personal advisers are all close to their clients, and all come to learn much about their clients through the services that they provide. This closeness is buffered by the fact that most close professionals have the same or higher status than those they serve and by the fact that their knowledge is discrete and limited. These buffers allow those in contact with those in the close professions to segregate domains if they wish, thereby limiting access to just that which they agree is professionally accessible.

In contrast, there are occupational positions where the principal buffer against closeness lies neither in segregated domains nor established professional boundaries, but in social distance. As noted earlier, protection from closeness has been handled differently in different times, but in all previous historical cases, such protection has come from culturally engineered social death. This is not an option today. Thus, for those who do live in such buildings, doormen may be uncomfortably close. In contrast to the kinds of limited information that professionals collect on their clients as a necessary foundation for providing professional service, doormen collect a wide range of surface information, which tends to be highly personal because it arises from the home. As noted earlier, the information that doormen receive about their tenants is substantial. Doormen know what kinds of movies their tenants watch. They know what kinds of foods they like to eat. They know how often they go out (if at all). They know what and how often they drink, what kinds of people come to visit them, when people come to visit them, and members of their household. They know what kind of job their tenants have and their tenants' travel and work schedules.

This essentially useless information is not useless to doormen because it provides a foundation for their delivery of personal service to tenants. As noted earlier, if doormen were content to be automatons who just held doors and followed rules, they would not need this knowledge. But neither tenants nor doormen want this. Tenants want to feel that they are distinct, and doormen want to act professionally. For tenants to be distinct and doormen to be professionals, doormen have to become "closer" to tenants.

Doormen pay attention to the flow, in order to draft a model of each tenant. This model is then used to develop a relationship that allows the doorman to provide tailor-made service. Tenants who see that the door is open to their world agree to the terms of exchange, because it allows them to establish a relationship, thus containing the information that the doorman has within a social envelope. Doormen see their knowledge as the vehicle for doing their job well, for acting substantively in pursuit of particular-ized — that is, professional — service. Tenants see in the relationship a way to simultaneously control knowledge and achieve distinction.

When doormen and tenants are in sync, they jointly establish, legitimize, and buttress their status aims. Tenants strive for distinction and doormen strive to be professionals. As noted earlier, for doormen to be professionals, they must have distinct tenants. For tenants to have distinction, they must have professional doormen. For the system to work, then, both sides have to bridge the extraordinary gap between too much closeness and too much distance, acknowledging both but connecting each side through the patina of professional service. This connection once made sets bounds on the kinds of knowledge doormen need to have about their tenants. In this regard, one can say that the relationship is normalized by the capacity to make legitimate claims to professional status. There are many possible ways to organize social routines and relations. Professionalism is but a single trope among many. It happens to be what is used here. Whatever the mechanism, it is an enduring aspect of human activity to smooth tensions by commitment to rhetoric.

In a single sentence, this book is about the capacity of humans to jointly construct a workable social world and provides one such description of the micro-mechanics involved in such construction.

If through joint construction, tenants and doormen can achieve their ends — ends requiring that both be elevated in status — it seems reasonable to assume that other interacting groups in other settings can achieve the same thing, given sufficient latitude to do so. The latitude that is required is the latitude that makes possible discretionary decision making in the pursuit of substantively rational ends.

For that goal, the door to the future is open. In the meantime, on the way out:

Have a good day. Be careful out there. Be prepared for rain. Watch out for traffic. Keep busy.

See you later, alligator.

APPENDIX: STUDY DESIGN (AND SOME NOTES ON TEACHING FIELD-BASED CLASSES)

In chapter 1, I noted that doormen create a special kind of sample bias by blocking survey researchers from access to wealthy people. This is important because if the sample one works with is biased, then one cannot make inference to the whole population. Arriving at an unbiased sample is the first major problem I address in this appendix. One thing about doormen is that in Manhattan it is extremely easy to see them around. Visitors to the city often comment on the number of doormen that they see; doormen appear to be ubiquitous. While doormen are easy to find, it is not easy to design a study that ensures that the respondents are a representative sample of the men who work as doormen. The problem is simple enough: the visible doormen are those working in areas we tend to go at the times we tend to be out. Equally obvious, they look like doormen or, more precisely, what we imagine doormen ought to look like. And the visible doormen tend to be outside, or at least visible from the street. Consequently, the doormen we see are those with uniforms, whose jobs involve standing outside or leaving the building and hailing cabs, who work in the neighborhoods we are most likely to be in during the hours that we are awake. In short, they are doormen who look like we think doormen ought to look and who are engaged in activities that we think doormen are engaged in. What if our ideas about doormen were not accurate or only captured a segment (large or small) of the occupation?

The problem is that the visible doormen, while the majority, are different from the less visible. First, they are likely to be unionized, they are likely to work in the fancier and larger buildings, and they are likely to be working in contexts that give them access to the public. Thus, casual observation misses the doormen who are in the back, operating the elevators, taking out the garbage, not wearing uniforms, and who are in areas where one simply does not expect to find them. Even in the limited areas that one observes, one cannot see all the doormen, either because they do not all look like doormen or because they are inside their buildings, away from view. And the doormen missed are different from those seen. As a consequence, convenience samples of doormen, selected from those who are easily visible, provide a non-representative sample of the population. Any inferences one makes from such a sample to the larger population are therefore likely to be biased.

In order to draw a representative sample, researchers would have to select at random some doormen from the larger population. The problem that is immediately obvious is that without knowing anything about the distribution of the population, it is impossible to select a sample. One simple strategy, often used in sociological research, would be to work through a gatekeeping organization. In this case, one could have approached the local union(s) that represent doormen in New York City and asked them for a list of their members.[1] From such list(s), one could select (using a random number generator or some other system) every nth doorman from the list, until a desired sample size was reached (in this case three hundred or so). There were three problems with this strategy. The first problem is always present when one decides to work through gatekeeping institutions, whether schools, factories, or firms. By contacting the union, researchers place themselves at risk to a refusal. In this case, if the union refused to endorse the research — and provision of a membership list would require endorsement — I was concerned that they would then inform their members that they should not talk with us.

The second problem with using institutional gatekeepers is a consequence of human subjects' protection. The fact that respondents have the right to know how they were selected meant that if the class had used union lists, we would be required by human subjects protection norms to tell them that this is how we got their name. One can immediately see that doormen disengaged from the union would be less likely to participate in the study for fear that their responses would not be confidential. Consequently, I was worried that knowledge that the union was implicitly endorsing the study would bias answers to our questions — especially the questions that we had about union membership. These two problems are generic to research designs that rest on the use of intermediaries to provide a sample frame. Because these problems may be overcome with care, many research designs take advantage of the easy access that such organizations provide. We might have worked around them as well, except that the third problem was the most significant, and for this research could not be overcome.

Not all doormen are in the local union. Consequently, reliance on union lists would have meant that the sample that we drew from a roster would be nonrepresentative. If the bias in a sample is independent of any of the outcomes that one is interested in explaining, there is no problem with using a biased sample. But in this instance, the class was easily able to come up with a number of good reasons to expect that the experience of being a doorman, the understandings that doormen had about their world, and the relationship between doormen and tenants — the precise aspects we were most interested in exploring — would be related to union membership. In order to assess this idea, we would have to have the possibility of recruiting non-union doormen into the sample.

Not being able to use union membership lists meant that the class had to develop another strategy; one the depended first on enumerating the population of doormen in the city, and then selecting some of them at random to be interviewed. Because

---

1. Most unionized doormen belong to the local union 32BJ. The union's website claims 70,000 active members: http://www.seiu32bj.org/index.asp?.

we knew that the doormen we saw would not be representative, we had to think about sampling buildings (where doormen we could not see might work), and then select doormen from the buildings we selected. As there are thousands of buildings in Manhattan and twenty-four hours in each day, walking across the city, mile after mile, hour after hour, to enumerate doorman was out of the question. Instead, the class devised a sampling scheme that allowed us to select a small number of small neighborhoods (technically, cells) and exhaustively investigate all the buildings in each cell, with the aim of establishing whether they contained any doormen. As long as the cells were representative and selected at random, and as long as enumerators hit each building, the doormen located in each cell would also be representative. As noted in the preface, a benefit is that at the same time, the buildings we selected would be representative of buildings with doormen. This means that the tenants from those buildings are also representative of buildings with doormen.

SELECTION OF DOORMEN IN NEW YORK CITY

The first step was to define the area from which to draw the sample. I knew in advance that the class should focus on New York City. The city, though, extends well beyond Manhattan Island and includes the four major boroughs (Queens, the Bronx, Staten Island, Brooklyn), and sprawls well beyond even these administrative boundaries, into New Jersey, Long Island, and the close suburbs just north of the Bronx. While some residential doormen work in the outer boroughs, it was too inefficient to try to systematically sample these areas. Consequently, I focused our attention on Manhattan.

Even in Manhattan, it made little sense to arbitrarily partition the island into discrete cells and sample intensively within them. Residential doormen are not found working in Central Park, Lincoln Center, Grand Central Station, the Empire State Building, Madison Square Garden, Macy's, or any of the other large commercial stores in the city. Along the Hudson River, below Fifty-ninth Street almost all the way to Battery Park City, lie the major working ports of the city, and just below and to the west of Lincoln Center lies one of the city sanitation depots. On the East River, the United Nations takes up a whole stretch of the Midtown coastline. Doormen don't work in any of these places. Consequently, it makes little sense to look for them there. In the same way, residential doormen are not found, for the most part, in the sprawling slums above 125th Street in Manhattan, the Bronx, or in the middle-class suburbs of Queens, Riverdale (a part of the Bronx), or most parts of Brooklyn.[2]

---

2. This is a general rule. Actually, in the densely settled parts of Riverdale, around Washington Heights (at 168th Street and Broadway), and in some of the newer complexes in Brooklyn and Queens, a few residential doormen can be found. But their number is few relative to the geographic area, and sampling them would have been extremely difficult.

I excluded the region above 125th Street for two practical reasons. First, I did not expect it to include a significant number of residential buildings with doormen. It would have been inefficient to look for doormen. Equally important in the context of this study, I was concerned about the safety of our student enumerators. As the enumeration process required walking up to all building entrances and looking inside for signs of doormen, I wanted to make sure that the students, many without much street savvy, were not placed at undue risk. This eliminated the poorer neighborhoods.

Since the greater part of Manhattan consists of a grid of horizontal streets and vertical avenues, we imposed a simple two-by-two spatial grid upon a map of Manhattan. Removing areas where doormen could not be found (Central Park, Penn Station, the United Nations, etc.) and limiting our frame to below 125th Street, the superimposed grid over eligible areas yielded 648 cells. These cells define the first sampling stage. Each of the 648 cells was assigned an identifying number. We selected fifty cells for building-by-building enumeration using a random number generator with replacement. To assess whether the sampled cells were representative, we considered a broad set of demographic and socioeconomic indicator variables for all 648 cells and compared the sample of cells we selected on these characteristics to the characteristics of the city as a whole. The general idea was that the sampled cells ought to be comparable across a wide range of characteristics to all of the neighborhoods in the city, and if they were, then the sample of neighborhoods could be considered representative. If the sample of neighborhoods could be representative, then the buildings in them would be representative, and the doormen in those buildings would also be representative of all doormen in the city. Some details about the sample design are reported here. Panel A reports the distribution of cells across Manhattan neighborhoods. Panel B reports the proportion of cells for each neighborhood that were in our sample. Within the sample, panel C reports the distribution of cells; and panel D reports the location of the doormen interviewed by neighborhood.

Aggregate data at the census tract level were available for the 1990 U.S. Census, with projected values for 1997. For all cells in our sample, we identified the appropriate census tract in which they were located. In cases where a cell was intersected by more than one census tract, we selected the tract that contained the centroid of the cell. We selected 50 variables that describe neighborhoods and the people within them in order to compare descriptive statistics for the sample and the population. We tested the equality of estimates for the mean and standard deviation of each indicator. Out of the 50 indicators we selected, we found statistically significant differences in means for only 4 variables. This is what one ought to expect to observe, since on average one should expect that out of 50 comparisons 2 to 3 would be significantly different at the .05 level (out of 100, we should expect about

TABLE A.1. Sample Design

Neighborhood	Panel A: Total population of cells	Panel B: Cells in sample (% of total in neighborhood)	Panel C: Distribution of cells across neighborhoods within sample	Panel D: Doormen interviewed* (% across neighborhoods)
Downtown	268 (41.4%)	20 (7.5%)	20 (30.3%)	17 (8.0%)
Midtown West	125 (19.3%)	9 (7.2%)	9 (13.6%)	11 (5.2%)
Midtown East	68 (10.5%)	10 (14.7%)	10 (15.2%)	39 (18.4%)
Upper East Side	72 (11.1%)	11 (15.3%)	11 (16.7%)	84 (39.6%)
Upper West Side	115 (17.7%)	16 (13.9%)	16 (24.2%)	61 (28.8%)
Totals	648 (100%)	66 (10.2%)	66 (100%)	212 (100%)

*Response rate: 212 completed interviews out of 336 contacts = 63.1%.

5 to be different). These observed differences are substantively without meaning. Table A.1 reports sample and population means and standard deviations for the 50 indicator variables. It is evident that the sample is representative of the city as a whole. Consequently, we can have some confidence in our inferences with respect to neighborhood characteristics. For our purposes, this meant that the enumeration conducted in the sampled neighborhoods would allow us to have confidence in our inference to the city as a whole.

ENUMERATING BUILDINGS AND DOORMEN

The next step was to visit the sampled cells and to enumerate residential buildings where doormen work. This involved walking up to each building, recording how many units it had, and determining whether or not a doorman might work there. In some buildings, it was obvious — doormen were working there. In others, signs indicated the hours for doorman service; desks or podiums in the front lobby suggested that a doorman worked there some of the time. In other buildings, interviewers had to ask tenants or neighbors if doormen were around. Whenever we found a building with a doorman, we obtained an estimate of the number of men who worked there. In those cases where a doorman was present, this was easily achieved by asking him. In other instances, we asked tenants. Across the 50 cells, we found 287 residential buildings with doormen. Roughly 1,200 doormen worked in them, so on average, for the buildings we observed, there were roughly 4 doormen for each building.

For those familiar with Manhattan, there are no real surprises; residential buildings with doormen are not evenly distributed across the city. Doormen tend to be concentrated in some areas, while there are significantly fewer in others. Doormen

TABLE A.2. Estimated Means of Selected Indicator Variables for Zip Code Neighborhoods[*]

Indicators	Downtown	Midtown West	Midtown East	Upper East Side	Upper West Side
Total population	26,468	15,606	31,713	67,258	74,185
Population white	17,070	11,531	27,192	62,098	55,662
	(0.64)	(0.74)	(0.86)	(0.92)	(0.75)
Population black	2,130	1,790	1,538	1,725	9,795
	(0.08)	(0.11)	(0.05)	(0.03)	(0.13)
Population Native American	77	51	43	41	188
	(0.002)	(0.003)	(0.001)	(0.00)	(0.00)
Population Asian, Pacific Islander	4,939	1,032	2,409	2,643	3,154
	(0.19)	(0.07)	(0.08)	(0.04)	(0.04)
Population other race	2,251	1,200	529	749	5,385
	(0.09)	(0.08)	(0.02)	(0.01)	(0.07)
Population Hispanic	4,820	3,356	2,345	3,381	13,279
	(0.18)	(0.22)	(0.07)	(0.05)	(0.18)
Foreign-born population	6,990	3,982	7,305	12,894	16,096
	(0.26)	(0.26)	(0.23)	(0.19)	(0.22)
Speak language other than English at home	10,589	5,521	8,075	13,271	21,592
	(0.40)	(0.35)	(0.25)	(0.20)	(0.29)
In labor force	15,892	9,979	22,364	45,642	48,366
	(0.60)	(0.64)	(0.71)	(0.68)	(0.65)
Total number of households	13,028	8,635	20,141	39,383	40,054
Median household income (in US$)	38,102	29,534	46,517	52,166	42,281
Per capita income (in US$)	28,426	22,672	52,120	58,980	39,144
Total number of housing units	13,897	10,246	23,354	44,175	43,493
Median mortgage for owner-occupied units (in US$)	805	820	1,986	2,001	1,725
Median rent for renter-occupied units (in US$)	635	620	824	802	616
Estimated number of doormen (% of total)[**]	141 (11.8%)	34 (2.8%)	189 (15.8%)	537 (45.0%)	292 (24.5%)
Estimated number of residential buildings with doormen (% of total)[**]	35 (12.2%)	14 (4.9%)	39 (13.6%)	113 (39.4%)	86 (30.0%)

[*]Proportion of total population in parentheses.

[**]Total estimated number of doormen N = 1,193; total estimated number of buildings with doormen N = 287.

become especially rare the closer one gets to the southern tip of the island. It is obvious that the variation in the density of doormen across neighborhoods is related to other significant differences in those areas. For ease of comparison, I identify five main neighborhoods as shown on the map. The borders of these neighborhoods follow the postal zip codes for Manhattan: Downtown (10002 through 10007, 10009 through 10014, 10038, 10048), Midtown West (10001, 10018 through 10020, 10036), Midtown East (10016, 10017, 10022), the Upper East Side (10021, 10028, 10128), and the Upper West Side (10023–10027). These boundaries correspond roughly to the major divisions of the city, in local spatial organization.

The 1990 census also provides aggregate data on spatial areas at the zip code level. These data permit us to use the same indicator variables identified above to compare neighborhoods. A quick glance at the quantitative data reveals few surprises. The neighborhoods that contain the most doormen are disproportionately affluent. The majority of doormen tend to work in predominantly white neighborhoods and serve tenants who are economically affluent enough to be able to pay the high housing prices in these neighborhoods. These areas happen to be Midtown East, the Upper East Side, and to a lesser extent the Upper West Side.

Based on our count of residential buildings and our estimate of the number of doormen working within them, we developed a simple sample frame for each building, in order to try to recruit 300 doormen into the study. In all cases, we tried to interview the first doormen we met and to conduct the interview immediately upon contact. In most instances, we were able to accomplish this goal. Of 336 contacts that interviewers made with doormen, 212 agreed to participate in the study and filled out the questionnaire. This yielded a response rate of 63.1%.[3]

SAMPLE SELECTIVITY

Strategies for handling sampling selectivity in social science surveys assume that something is known about the individuals who refuse to participate in a study. If one knows something about them, it is possible to estimate the effect that their participation would have on the pattern of associations between variables that one does observe for the sampled population. For example, if we knew that a study was less likely to interview extremely affluent individuals, and we were interested in the relationship between wealth and attitudes, we would have to consider how the additional wealthy (whom we did not interview) would have weakened or strengthened the association we observed. In this case, all we have access to is data on

---

3. Some students were not "natural-born interviewers," to say the least. For example, one student lost twenty-three interviews to hard refusal. Without his contribution, our response rate would have been above 70%. On the other hand, some were natural interviewers, who never generated a refusal.

the neighborhood from which the refusal arose. Ignoring the roughly 7% of the interviews that were lost from a single cell (see note 4), since this was an interviewer rather than a cell effect, there are no neighborhood effects on the response rate. That is, doormen were equally likely to participate in the study from all the neighborhoods we worked in.

Many doormen did not want to participate in the study because they reported that they didn't have free time, could not talk to people while they were on duty, or did not speak English well enough to answer the questions we asked. But these reasons for refusal were not associated with neighborhood. While we had a group of interviewers who spoke Spanish and while we conducted interviews in Spanish where necessary, numerous doormen from Eastern Europe, recently arrived in the country, were simply inaccessible to our interviewers. Other doormen seemed concerned about their supers and worried about talking while on the job. The bias in the sample is therefore for doormen who were English speaking, under less immediate supervisory control, and who perceived that they had free time.[4] These conditions may have also led us to interview doormen with slightly longer tenures, for it is reasonable to assume that English competency as well as extent of supervision are both associated with tenure. These potential biases suggest that the dynamics I describe with respect to doorman-super relationships — and, to a lesser extent — doorman-tenant interactions, may be too positive. If the sample selection is slightly tilted toward doormen with longer tenures, then it is reasonable to assume that those doormen are happier with the jobs, do a better job, and have more positive relationships with their supervisor and their tenants. Thus, one can imagine that the "real values" might be more negatively charged than they appear, though I believe that this slight bias is largely inconsequential.

One other bias is worth mentioning, for it provides one of the scope conditions for this study. In general, neither I nor the students were successful in getting a sufficient number of in-depth interviews from doormen or tenants working or living in extremely elite co-op buildings, where average apartment value exceeds $5 million. These buildings are few and far between, yet they play an important role in the culture of the city and the relative attribution of status to neighborhoods. Thus, while we interviewed some tenants whose lifestyle could be easily described as elite — and whose net wealth was substantial — we did not make contact with tenants who have their own substantial staff. Inference, then, to tenant-doorman relations does not extend to the super wealthy.

---

4. The issue of free time was a bit complicated. Interviewers reported doormen with obviously nothing to do claiming that they were too busy, often observing them for twenty minutes or longer reading the paper. Busyness is often deployed as polite refusal, and more experienced (and perhaps aggressive) interviewers would have been able to work through such simple soft-refusal strategies.

QUESTIONNAIRES AND INTERVIEWS

Questionnaire data from the 212 interviews provide detailed information on current and past work experiences, tenure in the job and the current building, relationships with tenants and coworkers, attitudes toward work, job satisfaction, and aspirations. The questionnaire also collected data on how they got their job, what kind of duties their position entails, their average monthly income including tips and bonuses, whether family members have worked or are currently working as doormen, and the location of both workplace and their home. In addition, doormen were asked questions that allowed measurement of an array of standard socio-demographic items, family structure, and educational attainment, hobbies, and leisure time activities. Of 212 doormen, 201 provided the zip code for their home address. For these home zip codes, it was possible to obtain 1990 census data on race, household type, marital status, age, educational attainment, employment status, annual household and per capita income, poverty ratios, and home ownership. These census data permit one to compare the demographic and socioeconomic profiles of workplace and place of residence. The interview was designed to take twenty minutes. In practice, mean interview time was closer to an hour, and in some instances extended to almost two hours.

As part of the interview procedure, all doormen were also asked to participate in a follow-up in-depth interview. Ninety-three (44%) of the doormen who filled out the questionnaire agreed to participate in this second phase of the study. We solicited interviews with 43 of these. Our response rate for this second stage was 100%. All but one of the in-depth interviews was tape-recorded. In-depth interviews lasted from one to three hours. The vast majority of interviews were conducted on the job, either during breaks or while the doorman was working the lobby or door. A few doormen asked to be interviewed elsewhere. When students conducted the interviews, all such interviews were conducted in a public space, such as a café. Although they naturally vary in length and content depending on the interviewer and the respondent, the in-depth interviews add significant narrative detail on the life and career histories of doormen to the more structured questionnaire data. Subsequently, I interviewed additional doormen and spent many hours observing doormen across a number of settings. Tenant interviews were conducted in the spring and fall of 2001. Since there was no way to yield a representative sample of tenants, we interviewed individuals who were referred to us through a snowball procedure. Specifically, we asked individuals we knew to identify individuals that they knew (whom we did not) that might be interested in participating in a short study on doormen. Roughly 30 usable tenant interviews were completed. These ranged in duration from twenty minutes to two hours. The qualitative component of this project thus consists of hundreds of hours of formal and informal interviews.

SOME NOTES ON ORGANIZING COLLECTIVE
FIELDWORK-BASED PROJECT CLASSES

Collective class-based projects are significantly more complicated to orchestrate than I had imagined at the start. For those contemplating a similar structure, start thinking about it early on. My first time — resulting in this book — was probably sub-optimal because I didn't make especially good estimates of the work involved. I also didn't start thinking about it "practically" until just two or three weeks before the semester began, even though I had been thinking "theoretically" about using a collective study as a vehicle for teaching students how to evaluate evidence for a number of years. That did not help. I had planned initially — as I had for many years — to have each student design a small independent field study and report on the findings. Probably close to a thousand students in previous classes of mine conducted such studies, and no doubt many hundreds of thousands more in other classes taught by others have done so as well. Of those field projects — mainly composed of studies of behavior in elevators, counts of groups of different sizes, counts of groups of different sizes and their relationship to jaywalking, racial segregation in dining halls, the number of beers consumed in bars on Thursday nights, tests of church-sect theory, social network analyses of fraternities and athletic teams, surveys of college students attitudes toward this and that — only a few really stand out in my memory. Of these thousands, some stand out because they were unbelievably stupid,[5] and a few stand out because they were really innovative. It was always clear that learning something substantive was not the goal for these assignments, and, in fact, one worried if findings were new (or too linear) — but it was frustrating to see so much individual effort yield little cumulative knowledge that the students could share. The idea of a collective project arose from this frustration — and was dumped on the students in the doorman class quite without warning. In retrospect, I think it would be better to advertise the class as a field-based class, even though this would result in a different group of students, that is, a group of students selected for their interest in such classes.

---

5. My favorite stupid project — even better than the kid who wanted to see what would happen if he refused to ever let anyone pass him on Interstate 40 (the research question was "Do muscle cars go faster than others?" and the answer is that indeed some of these cars get close to a hundred miles an hour) — was the woman who went home and acted like a guest. This, as anyone who has taken a sociology class knows, is a time-tested winner. When students could not think of anything they were interested in or could study, I always gave a few examples of projects, one of which was "go home and act like a guest until you drive your parent(s) totally insane." The particular woman who took this project on started her paper by saying, "To start this experiment I called my mother and told her that I was going to come home that weekend and act like a guest for my sociology class, and that she should treat me like a guest." *And she did.*

But the doorman class was not so advertised, and, consequently, on the first day of class, students heard for the first time what was going to happen. It was worrisome to many. I could not promise success, nor could I promise that they would learn anything. From prior survey work, I was extremely concerned that we would get "blown out of the field" from negative publicity. We might put in a lot of work for nothing. Many were worried about their grades. If we got blown out of the field, on what basis would they be evaluated? I had absolutely no idea.

More vexing than what grade to give was coordinating effort to produce a collective good. I was not sure that we could organize the efforts of all the students so that everything got done on time. One thing should have been clearer to me even then. Research projects are fundamentally antithetical to the student lifestyle. First, things have to get done on time and in order. As noted just above, to interview doormen, we had to find doormen. To find doormen we had to enumerate buildings. To enumerate buildings, we had to survey the city. In research, everything has to proceed in a specific order, much like the old nursery rhyme "There was an old woman that swallowed a fly . . ." Left to their own devices, many students prefer to leave things for the last minute. So we spent a lot of time and effort making sure that each day's task was completed before continuing onto the next. The discipline necessary was often arduous. Second, most students are way too busy to add hours of fieldwork into their schedule, especially for uncertain return. And many students, paradoxically for Columbia perhaps, don't like to leave the small campus world. So getting students into the field absorbed a lot of our energy. The temporal demands of the project meant that when students did not do their assignment, someone else had to. In the end, this is why I ended up hiring research assistants. Classes like this need more support than the typical single TA can (or should) provide.

The goal of the class was to expose all students to all phases of the research — enumeration, questionnaire-based interviews, extraction of census data, observation of settings, and in-depth interviews. The hardest component to prepare for was the in-depth interview. Some students are shy. This project involved talking to people. We spent countless hours working with the shy students so that they could all manage an interview of some sort. We practiced scripts for introducing oneself, strategies for dealing with soft refusals, and strategies for communicating confidence. For all students, but especially those who were not shy, we practiced the most important thing about interviews: how to listen. In open-ended interviews, the first most difficult thing to learn is how to shut up and listen. For Columbia students, whose previous successes were based, in part, on not shutting up, this was especially hard.

There are actually two separate problems and I should be clearer. I think that students don't have trouble "listening" in the sense of entering into passive mode in response to aural material coming their way. Thus, with a list of questions in hand, students have no trouble asking question 1, "listening" to the answer, and then proceeding to question 2. But of course this is exactly what kills interviews, because there is nothing more deadly (as a respondent) than discovering that the interviewer is not listening to you, but is instead listening for conversational silences in order to proceed to the next item on the list. The problem is that many students (and people) have relatively poor active listening skills — that is, skills that enable them to listen to conversation and follow. Teaching students how to follow is difficult. It takes a lot of practice. As an aside, I do not have any sense that following skills — or active listening skills — are particularly gendered. At elite schools, this skill appears to be as absent among men as it is among women.

Students are also shy of collaborative projects. Partly this is because at a school like Columbia, many are used to being the best in their class. Some of these students don't like working in groups because they do not want to share credit for their achievements or be "dragged down by free riding." But their most pressing concern is often what grade they will get. In a class with a collective product, engaged in research that might collapse, there was a lot of uncertainty about the grade and about how the grade would be objectively assigned. Uncertainty does not quite convey the prevailing mood — perhaps obsessive anxiety is closer. Actually, in all classes, whatever their style and content, there is an obsession about grades.

Many of my colleagues are concerned about and complain that their students are grade-grubbers. They find it distasteful. We should be fair. Students who end up at places like the University of North Carolina or Columbia are selected by those institutions on the basis of characteristics that expressed themselves as capacity to get good grades in high school — for example, caring about grades, parental social class, orderliness in turning homework in, skills in handwriting, orientation to adults, parents who are obsessed by grades, middle-class manners and patterns of speech. The same could be said more or less of having good SAT scores — having parents who invest in Kaplan helps — or also the intangibles: life experiences, interests and hobbies, and so on. Grade-grubbing students may be annoying — but then when one goes to the well, one gets water not lemonade.

Sixty students showed up for the first class. At the end of the term, roughly half remained. It would be an exaggeration to say that all worked equally hard or that each was equally successful. Some never really got into the swing, and others devoted countless extra hours to the project. Still, the group that remained was in many ways remarkable. Those who dove into the work saw themselves as the "doorman group." They shared notes. They wrote (with guidance) all the questions for the questionnaire. They collected almost all the census data and entered almost all of the survey data into a spreadsheet. They completed a large number of the in-depth interviews. They learned to negotiate the human subject protocol. They gathered consent forms, kept data confidential, took many photographs, and kept all of our spirits alive when the fieldwork appeared to flounder. In small groups they took the lead in shaping new research questions, in short, they became researchers. When I passed them on campus, they said they could not now see a doorman without having an urge to interview him.

Finally, it should be noted that the doorman class was never intended to result in a book. It was designed as a pedagogical exercise. As such, although the class worked on designing a project that had the elements of a scientific sample, one could not, nor is it intended that one should, draw inference to doormen as a population.

A final word, before I list the students. One student, a pretty big guy, scared many of the doormen he tried to interview. He may have seemed scary to doormen, but they were mistaken. He was an exceptionally nice, polite, and easygoing; and, sadly, he was one of the many victims of the attack on the World Trade Center. Throughout the writing process, it was hard to not recall his presence in class, and after the fieldwork was completed, at a time when projects of mine often find themselves heading for the file cabinets to live out a dusty existence, his work on this project provided a substantial motivation to complete it.

Here, in alphabetical order, are the students whose work on all phases of this project made it possible, and whose enthusiasm for understanding a small slice of social life made teaching an enormously enjoyable experience for me: Candida Aguilar, Alexander Baker, Adam Braun, Joseph Case, Treg Duerksen, Mayara Fagundes, Peter Gerken, Ramin Hedayati, Bradford Johnson, Emma Katznelson, Jill Krizelman, Kerry Lear, Eric Levy, Logan Manning, Jordanna Matlon, Malte Mau, Rachel Polansky, Snehal Raisoni, Ian Rapoport, David Rothman, Michael Rotjan, Tiffany Rounsville, Laura Schlapkohl, Erika Smith, Tyler Ugolyn, Emily Voigt.

LITERATURE CITED

Abbott, Andrew. "Status and Status Strain in the Professions." *American Journal of Sociology* 86, no. 4 (1981): 819–35.

Ackerman, Andy, dir. "The Doorman." Written by Tom Gammill and Max Pross. *Seinfeld*. February 23, 1995.

Allah, Dasun. "Purple-Shirt Politics." *Village Voice*. December 4–10, 2002.

Anderson, Elijah. *Streetwise: Race, Class, and Change in an Urban Community*. Chicago: University of Chicago Press, 1992.

Andrea, Dree, director. *All Visitors Must Be Announced: The Lives and Loves of Doormen in New York City*. Amsterdam: Cinemien, 1997.

Bearman, Peter S. "Generalized Exchange." *American Journal of Sociology* 102, no. 5 (1997): 1383–415.

Bearman, Peter S., and Paolo Parigi. "Cloning Headless Frogs and Other Important Matters: The Structure of Discussion Networks in the United States." *Social Forces* (forthcoming).

Bellah, Robert H., et al. *Habits of the Heart: Individualism and Commitment in American Life*. New York: Harper and Row, 1996.

Bigus, Otis T. "The Milkman and His Customer: A Cultivated Relationship." *Urban Life and Culture* 1, no. 1 (1972): 131–65.

Brozan, Nadine. "The Price of 'Wow!' Keeps on Rising." *New York Times*. September 7, 2003.

Burawoy, Michael. *Manufacturing Consent: Changes in the Labor Process Under Monopoly Capitalism*. Chicago: University of Chicago Press, 1982.

Cohen, Michael D., James G. March, and Johan P. Olsen. "A Garbage Can Model of Organizational Choice." *Administrative Science Quarterly* 17, no. 1 (1972): 1–25.

Cohn, Werner. "Social Status and the Ambivalence Hypothesis: Some Critical Notes and a Suggestion." *American Sociological Review* 25, no. 4 (1960): 508–13.

Cole, Jonathan R., and Steven Cole. *Social Stratification in Science*. Chicago: University of Chicago Press, 1973.

"Costello Doorman Sticks to His Story." *New York Times*. May 17, 1958, 40.

Cox, D. R., Walter L. Smith et al. *Queues*. London: Methuen, 1961.

Douglas, Mary. *Purity and Danger: An Analysis of Concepts of Pollution and Taboo*. London: Routledge, 1984.

Dumont, Louis. *Homo Hierarchicus: The Caste System and Its Implications*. Chicago: University of Chicago Press, 1981.

Duneier, Mitchell. *Sidewalk*. New York: Farrar, Straus & Giroux, 2001.

————. *Slim's Table: Race, Respectability, and Masculinity*. Chicago: University of Chicago Press, 1994.

Erickson, Christopher, Catherine Fisk, Ruth Milkman, Daniel Mitchell, and Kent Wong. "Justice for Janitors in Los Angeles and Beyond: A New Form of Unionism in the 21st Century?" Paper presented at the 23rd Annual Middlebury Economics Conference: "The Changing Role of Unions." Middlebury, VT. May 2001.

Farnham, Brian. "Tipping Points: If It's True that Money Talks, What Are Your Tips Saying about You?" *New York Magazine*, August 21, 2000.

Faulkner, Robert. *Music on Demand: Composers and Careers in the Hollywood Film Industry*. New Brunswick, NJ: Transaction, 1983.

Fine, Gary Alan. *Kitchens: The Culture of Restaurant Work*. Berkeley: University of California Press, 1996.

"For Doormen, Few Frills." *New York Times*. June 25, 1978.

Gelb, Lesley H. "On Speaking Terms." *New York Times*. May 1, 1991.

Goffman, Erving. *Encounters*. New York: Bobbs-Merrill, 1961.

————. *The Presentation of Self in Everyday Life*. New York: Anchor Doubleday, 1959.

Gould, Roger V. *Collision of Wills*. Chicago: University of Chicago Press, 2003.

Granovetter, Mark. *Getting a Job: A Study of Contacts and Careers*. Cambridge, MA: Harvard University Press, 1974.

————. "The Strength of Weak Ties." *American Journal of Sociology* 78, no. 6 (1973): 1360–80.

Hirsch, Michael. "Gunning for Gus." *City Limits*. September/October 1998.

————. "Union Boss Backs Bad Boy Bevona." *City Limits*. February 1998.

Hirschman, Albert. *Exit, Voice, Loyalty: Responses to Declines in Firms, Organizations, and States*. Cambridge, MA: Harvard University Press, 1972.

Hochschild, Arlie. *The Managed Heart: The Commercialization of Human Feeling*. Berkeley: University of California Press, 1985.

Hodge, Robert W., Paul M. Siegel, and Peter H. Rossi. "Occupational Prestige in the United States, 1925–1963." *American Journal of Sociology* 70, no. 3 (1964): 286–302.

Homans, George, and David Schneider. *Marriage, Authority, and Final Causes: A Study of Unilateral Cross-Cousin Marriage*. Glencoe, IL: Free Press, 1955.

Humphreys, Laud. *Tearoom Trade: Impersonal Sex in Public Places*. Chicago: Aldine, 1974.

Kang, Miliann. "The Managed Hand: The Commercialization of Bodies and Emotions in Korean Immigrant-Owned Nail Salons." *Gender & Society* 17, no. 6 (2003): 820–39.

Kerr, Peter. "Holiday Tipping: Some Guidelines about Amounts." "Holiday Tipping: Guidelines about How Much to Give Who." *New York Times*. December 16, 1982, C1, C2.

Kleinman, Sheryl. *Equals Before God: Seminarians as Human Professionals*. Chicago: University of Chicago Press, 1984.

Kleinrock, Leonard, and Richard Gail. *Queueing Systems: Problems and Solutions*. New York: Wiley, 1996.

Kleinrock, Leonard, and Karreman Mathematics Research Collection. *Communication Nets: Stochastic Message Flow and Delay*. New York: McGraw-Hill, 1964.

———. *Queueing Systems*. New York: Wiley, 1975.

Latour, Bruno, and Steven Woolgar. *Laboratory Life: The Construction of Scientific Facts*. Princeton, NJ: Princeton University Press, 1994.

Laumann, Edward O., and R. T. Michael. *Sex, Love, and Health in America: Private Choices and Public Policies*. Chicago: University of Chicago Press, 2000.

Lee, Felicia. "For Racist Slights, the Meter Is Still Running." *New York Times*. November 28, 1999.

Lee, Nancy Howell. *The Search for an Abortionist*. Chicago: University of Chicago Press, 1969.

Lévi-Strauss, Claude. *Elementary Structures of Kinship*. Boston: Beacon Press, 1971.

Liebow, Elliott. *Tally's Corner: A Study of Negro Streetcorner Men*. Boston: Little Brown, 1968.

"Local Prez Gets the Porkchop Parachute." *Industrial Worker* 96, nos. 2–3 (February–March 1999).

Lynd, Robert S., and Helen M. Lynd. *Middletown: A Study in Contemporary American Culture*. New York: Harcourt Brace, 1926.

Lynn, Michael. "Seven Ways to Increase Your Servers' Tips." *Cornell Hotel and Restaurant Administration Quarterly* 37 (June 1996): 24–29.

Mariott, McKim. *India through Hindu Categories*. Thousand Oaks, CA: Sage Publications, 1990.

Mars, Gerald, and Michael Nicod. *The World of Waiters*. London: G. Allen & Unwin, 1984.

Merton, Robert K. "The Matthew Effect in Science." *Science* 159(1968): 56–63.

Mills, C. Wright. *The Sociological Imagination*. New York: Oxford University Press, 2000.

Mische, Ann, and Harrison White. "Between Conversation and Situation: Public Switching Dynamics across Network Domains." *Social Research* 65, no. 3 (1998): 695–724.

Mitchell, J. Clyde. *Social Networks in Urban Situations: Analyses of Personal Relationships in Central African Towns*. Manchester: Institute for Social Research, University of Zambia, Manchester University Press, 1969.

Moreland, John. *Millways of Kent*. New York: New College Press, 1958.

National Legal and Policy Center — Organized Labor Accountability Project. *Union Corruption Update* 1, no. 8 (September 21, 1998).

————. *Union Corruption Update* 5, no. 8 (April 15, 2002).

"New Yorkers Who Idle for Their Living." *New York Times*. March 6, 1927.

Peterson, Trond, Isjak Saporta, and Marc-David Seidel. "Offering a Job: Meritocracy and Social Networks." *American Journal of Sociology* 106, no. 3 (2000): 763–816.

Propp, Vladimir. *The Morphology of Fairy Tales*. Austin: University of Texas Press, 1986.

Putnam, Robert D. *Bowling Alone: The Collapse and Revival of American Community*. New York: Simon & Schuster, 2000.

Redding, Kent. *Making Race and Power: North Carolina's Road to Disfranchisement*. Urbana: University of Illinois, 2003.

Reisman, David, and Nathan Glazer. "The Meaning of an Opinion." *Public Opinion Quarterly* 12, no. 4 (1949): 633–48.

Rejnes, Ruth. "The Art of the Christmas Tip." *New York Times*. December 12, 1975, 6R.

————. "It's Time to Pass the Bucks." *New York Times*. December 10, 1972, Real Estate, 1, 8.

Robbins, Tom. "One More Woe for Ailing Brooklyn Development: Landlord Meets the Mob." *Village Voice*, May 9–15, 2001.

Roberts, Sam. "In Manhattan, Black Doormen Are Rare Breed." *New York Times*. May 6, 1991, B1.

Rosenthal, Robert, and Lenore Jacobson. *Pygmalion in the Classroom: Teacher Expectation and Pupils' Intellectual Development*. New York: Rinehart and Winston, 1968.

Schwartz, Michael. *Radical Protest and Social Structure: The Southern Farmer Alliance and Cotton Tenancy*. Chicago: University of Chicago Press, 1988.

"Servants on Spree Wreck Lihme Home, Ruin Art Treasures." *New York Times*. June 28, 1927, 1.

Simmel, Georg. *The Sociology of Georg Simmel*. Glencoe, IL: Free Press, 1950.

Slater, Phillip. *Pursuit of Loneliness: American Culture at the Breaking Point*. Boston: Beacon Press, 1970.

Smith, Tom W. "The Hidden 25 Percent: An Analysis of Nonresponse on the 1980 General Social Survey." *Public Opinion Quarterly* 47, no. 3 (1983): 386–404.

"Stolen Glemby Gems Are Officially Listed." *New York Times*. January 27, 1932.

"A Strange Case of Vandalism." Op-ed. *New York Times*. June 29, 1927.

Strauss, Anselem. *Negotiations: Varieties, Contexts, Processes, and Social Order*. San Francisco: Jossey-Bass, 1978.

Thomas, Robert. "The Doorman Who Is a She." *New York Times*. July 2, 1972.

"Tips on Tipping in Apartments: Christmas Varies for Employees." *New York Times*. December 19, 1965, VIII:1–2.

Upstairs, Downstairs. Sagitta Productions Ltd., in association with Eileen Atkins and Jean Marsh. London Weekend Television Production.

Waldinger, Roger. *Still the Promised City? African-Americans and New Immigrants in Postindustrial New York*. Cambridge, MA: Harvard University Press, 1996.

Waller, Willard. *On the Family, Education, and War*. Chicago: University of Chicago Press, 1970.

Warner, W. Lloyd, and Paul S. Lunt. *The Social Life of a Modern Community*. New Haven, CT: Yale University Press, 1941.

Weber, Max. *Economy and Society: An Outline of Interpretive Sociology*. Berkeley: University of California Press, 1979.

"Well-Dressed Doorman Trades Epaulets for Ivy League Look." *New York Times*. July 21, 1963, 187.

Whyte, William Foote. "The Social Structure of the Restaurant." *American Journal of Sociology* 54, no. 4 (1949): 302–10.

Whyte, William H. *The Organization Man*. New York: Simon & Schuster, 1956.

Wilgoren, Jodi. "Tips Grease for the Gears of City Life." *New York Times*. December 20, 1998, BU9.

Woodward, Julian L. "Public Opinion Research 1951–1970: A Not Too Reverent History." *Public Opinion Quarterly* 15, no. 3 (1951): 405–20.

Zelizer, Viviana. *The Social Meaning of Money*. New York: Basic Books, 1994.

Zerubavel, Eviatar. *Patterns of Time in Hospital Life: A Sociological Perspective*. Chicago: University of Chicago Press, 1979.

Zimbardo, P. "The Pathology of Imprisonment." *Society* 4, no. 6 (1972): 4–8.

Zuckerman, Harriet A., and Robert K. Merton. "Patterns of Evaluation in Science: Institutionalization Structure and Functions of the Referee System." *Minerva* 9, no. 1 (January 1971): 66–100.

Made in the USA
San Bernardino, CA
18 May 2020